ROYAL
BASTARDS

About the Authors

Peter Beauclerk-Dewar is a direct decendent of the bastard offspring of Charles II and Nell Gwyn. He is a heraldic consultant to Christies, has previously been an editor for *Burke's Peerage & Gentry*, and is a fellow of the Scottish Society of Antiquaries. He also a JP and a trustee of the Institute of Heraldic & Genealogical Studies at the University of Kent. He lives in London.

Roger Powell has been a professional genealogist for over 40 years. He was until his recent retirement a senior editor at *Burke's Peerage and Gentry* and Director of Debretts Ancestory Research. He was also a research assistant at the Royal College of Heralds. He is also related to the Duke of Monmouth, another bastard son of Charles II. He lives in Northamptonshire.

ROYAL
BASTARDS

Illegitimate Children of the British Royal Family

PETER BEAUCLERK-DEWAR
& ROGER POWELL

This edition first published 2008

The History Press Limited
The Mill, Brinscombe Port
Stroud, Gloucestershire, GL5 2QG
www.thehistorypress.co.uk

British Library Cataloguing in Publication Data.
A catalogue record for this book is available from the British Library.

ISBN 978 0 7524 4668 4

Typesetting and origination by The History Press Limited
Printed and bound by Ashford Colour Press Ltd, Gosport, Hampshire

Contents

Foreword

By HRH The Duke of Gloucester, KG, GCVO

Monarchy is by definition a family affair. The principle of heredity prevents conflict in the selection process. Illegitimacy confuses this event and causes uncertainty as occurred in the case of Edward V disqualified by his uncle Richard III.

Monarchs and their families are governed by the same laws of physics and biology as everyone else, but what sets them apart is the notice taken of what they do and what they might do next.

This intense and prolonged scrutiny can be clouded by the human desire to be 'in the know' and not to be thought unaware of what is happening. For this reason royal gossip and speculation has always been magnified compared to other gossip. In the distant past bastard children were acknowledged and promoted as an extension of royal power. Queen Victoria, influenced by Prince Albert was determined to change this attitude, leading, some would say, to a more hypocritical age.

It is easy to disapprove of the reckless way that Charles II shamed his barren wife by producing so many illegitimate children by so many different mothers. However it is difficult to regret it if you discover, as I did, that you are descended from several of them!

It was George III, who against all advice, insisted on the passing of the Royal Marriage Act, to give him greater control of his dynasty, and its potential for marriages of foreign policy advantage. He created the successions crisis of 1817, when Princess Charlotte died and in spite of having 14 children there was no eligible grand child to take the throne, for all his male children had chosen brides for themselves and married morganatically. The Duke of Kent rose to the challenge and produced Queen Victoria in time to solve the problem.

Bastard has come to be a term of abuse, as if anyone, who suffered the uncertainties of illegitimacy, was bound to have warped their morals and behaviour.

Peter Beauclerk-Dewar and Roger S. Powell have covered five centuries of alleged bastards, including those acknowledged by the father, as well as those merely speculated, and tried to examine the claims and counter claims dispassionately. Some were ignored by their putative fathers, others supported openly or discretely. If all of them were touched by a sense of importance and destiny, I would like to believe it would encourage them to feel that they should contribute to the nation's good rather than claim its benefits for themselves.

Introduction To First Edition

The word *bastard*, described by the *Oxford Dictionary* as *'one begotten and born out of wedlock'*, is no longer fashionable, now that nearly fifty per cent of all children in this country are born outside marriage. Moreover, it is claimed that the true fathers of many supposedly legitimate children are not in fact so, even though it has always probably been thus, for it is said that it is indeed a wise man who knows his own father. However, the advent of DNA has certainly injected rather more certainty into identifying paternity with all the embarrassments that this might cause.

As part of the research for this book, we have been able to identify the genetic 'y' chromosome of the Stuart Kings which is, of course, unique to the male line.

We have been able to do this by identifying the same 'y' chromosome in the DNA samples provided by four quite separate lines of male descendants of Stuart kings. This will now provide a benchmark against which other claimants can be measured, for all male line descendants of Stuart kings should all have this unique 'y' chromosome. But what it does do is to scotch, once and for all, the assertion that Colonel Robert Sidney was the father of the Duke of Monmouth, rather than King Charles II, as some had claimed.

Until recently, *Burke's Peerage & Baronetage* and *Burke's Landed Gentry* always drew a veil over illegitimacy and it is only in recent years that natural children have been included, other than, of course, those Royal Bastards who were ennobled and thus qualified for inclusion on those grounds.

Nevertheless the stigma attached to bastardy has always seemed rather unfair whereby the child is blamed for the sins of its parents. Yet in previous generations the stigma was all too real and the accident of birth could have far reaching effects upon the child as the laws of inheritance and succession to titles, names, estates and arms often precluded bastards. Yet conversely in the case of Royal Bastards, they were often given special titles, privileges and positions and the possibility of really lucrative marriage contracts, as we shall see.

It is amusing to find that, even today, the Royal Archives Security scanning system rejected our e-mail attachment of this text 'because it violates our acceptable use policy on profanity' following inclusion of the word 'bastard' in the title of the book.

Cecil Humphery Smith, the Principal and Founder of the Institute of Heraldic and Genealogical Studies in Canterbury, considers attitudes towards bastards in his thought-provoking article (*see* page 259). In 1979 he published a number of articles in *The Coat of Arms* entitled '*The armorial bearings of the illegitimate issue of the Kings of England*' and he has now consolidated and expanded these thoughts into an article (*see* page 270). Indeed, we acknowledge his contribution towards the heraldry contained in this volume.

Moreover, in keeping with changing public attitudes, the law relating to illegitimacy has also changed over the years, and from 1926 in England, those parents who subsequently marry, thereby legitimate any children they may have had beforehand, provided that they had been free to marry at the time of their child's birth. Under the *European Human Rights Convention*, bastards now enjoy most of the same rights as those children born in wedlock, except in the cases of succession to titles and arms. Indeed the present government has recently enacted leglisation whereby live-in couples and same sex couples will receive most of the same rights as their married counterparts and any illegitimate children involved will be treated the same as their legitimate counterparts. However, this will not affect the laws of arms and titles.

Whilst most of the royal bastards mentioned in this book may well have been conceived in love or lust, the king who was most prolific in fathering bastards was King Henry I, known as King Henry Beauclerk (1070–1135). He realised that by utilising a bevy of mistresses, he would be able to produce twenty or more royal bastards, as he did, who could then be married off to the leading families in Europe, thus promoting and strengthening his foreign policy. So because his wife could only provide one baby per nine months at best, he néeded to resort to outsourcing!

We start this volume with Arthur Plantagenet, Viscount Lisle (1462/4–1542), (*see* page 18), the son of King Edward IV, but we have not attempted to include earlier Royal Bastards because these have already been covered in *The Royal Bastards of Medieval England* 1066–1486 by Chris Given Wilson & Alice Curteis and elsewhere.

For many years, Roger Powell, a Deputy Editor of *Burke's Peerage* and of *Burke's Landed Gentry of Scotland,* has undertaken new research into the various Stuart bastards and as a result has cast new light upon conventional wisdom by disposing of a number of myths. He has also assisted in identifying and assembling many of the illustrations in this book, which has helped to bring this motley collection to life. It is intriguing to see how many of the subjects share that distinct Stuart resemblance. As we have both had many years involvement with Burke's publications, we are delighted that Burke's Peerage & Gentry are the publishers of this work and we thank Dr. Gordon Prestoungrange, Baron of Prestoungrange, for having made it possible and John Unwin for its design.

Of these definite Royal Bastards under review over five centuries, a total of forty-four in number, fifteen were sired by Charles II (by seven mothers) and six were by his brother James II (from two mothers), both of whose DNA 'y' chromosome has now been established. Moreover William IV (as Duke of Clarence) also had eleven bastards, ten being out of Mrs Jordan. The sheer variety of these forty-four official Royal Bastards, about whose origins there would seem to be little doubt, is impressive. Twenty-three of them are men whereas twenty-one are women. Many of them served in the army, some with much distinction, and a few served in the Royal Navy, whereas others joined the Church as clerics or nuns. In terms of age, the eldest died at the age of 89, whereas the youngest died at a few months, and the average lifespan was forty-five years. Of these many families, there would now seem to be only the four ducal families of Buccleuch, Grafton, St Albans and Richmond that are still represented today in the male line.

Of these forty-four Royal Bastards, ten became Dukes, two became Earls, one a viscount, several became Barons, nine were given the precedence of children of a Marquess and eight were appointed Knights of the Garter. Ten daughters made prestigious marriages with peers, but ten received little or nothing at all. Most were married and together they produced hoards of children which will ensure that there continues to be many thousands of descendants of Royal Bastards. In the St Albans family alone (*see* page 75), it is claimed that there are some two thousand living descendants of King Charles II and Nell Gwyn which range from dukes to dustmen (and of which both Samantha Cameron, (wife of David, the leader of the Conservative Party) and I are two) and this is probably true of many other families of Royal Bastards too.

Over the centuries, most kings have had one or more mistresses (*see* page 254) and many begat children by them, most of whom, at least until Queen Victoria's accession in 1837, were officially recognised. This has extended up to and including the twentieth century, although the details of any illegitimate progeny that Kings Edward VII and VIII are alleged to have had, are still largely shrouded in secrecy and gossip, never having been officially recognised. However, in the final section *Royal Loose Ends* (*see* page 167) we examine some of the fables about the alleged progeny of more recent monarchs, numbering twenty-two. But here we have also been able to lay to rest, once and for all, a number of tantalising ghosts and 'might-have-beens'.

Of course, it has long been suggested that a number of the children born to those Royal mistresses had had Royal fathers, even though officially their fathers were recorded as the husbands of the mistresses concerned, and certainly there have been many precedents for this over the centuries. All the Royal Bastards included in this book in Sections 1 to 3 have either been officially recognised by their Royal fathers or were incontrovertibly theirs. This work draws from much new research and is therefore the most comprehensive book upon the subject ever written.

Although we have also drawn heavily on a number of published reference works such as the *Dictionary of National Biography* and *The Complete Peerage,* we have also consulted many biographies and unpublished papers, including the surviving papers of the Benedictine Congregation in France and the Royal Archives at Windsor Castle, all of which are listed in the comprehensive Bibliography.

In the aftermath of the Queen's Golden Jubilee, we are taking a sympathetic look at these forty-four Royal Bastards, all of whom are the illegitimate offspring of English monarchs or their heirs apparent. Some have distinguished themselves whereas others have contributed little. Among their descendants are their Royal Highnesses Princes William and Harry who have five illegitimate Stuart descents through their mother, Diana, Princess of Wales, – three from Charles II (two through the Richmonds (*see* page 88), one through the Graftons (*see* page 60) and one from James II by Arabella Churchill. Moreover, through the late HRH Princess Alice, her son the Duke of Gloucester and his children all descend from Charles II through Lucy Walter and the Buccleuchs (*see* page 36), as does Sarah Duchess of York and her two daughters, TRH Princesses Beatrice and Eugenie of York, who have five quite separate illegitimate Stuart descents. Camilla Parker Bowles, now HRH The Duchess of Cornwall, also boasts a Stuart descent from Louise de Keroualle and Charles II. Thus much Stuart blood has already been introduced into the House of Windsor.

Of course, it is worth considering that had Lucy Walter married King Charles II, as many claimed she did, then the course of British history would have been very different, and the present King would be the present Duke of Buccleuch. However, we do not believe that this is regarded as a live issue by any of those involved, and in any case whatever proof there is alleged to have been is said to have been destroyed several generations ago. But at least we do now know for certain that the Dukes of Buccleuch do descend paternally from King Charles II, as most of us had always thought.

Even in a short work such as this, there are many people to thank. Firstly we are deeply grateful to Her Majesty The Queen for her gracious permission to carry out researches in the Royal Archives at Windsor Castle and for the use of both written and visual material relating largely to the FitzClarences. We also thank Miss Pamela Clark, the Registrar and Miss Allison Derrett, Assistant Registrar, for all their help and we are also most grateful to HRH The Duke of Gloucester for agreeing to write the Foreword (*see* page 7).

As with many things, good ideas often grow from very small beginnings and I am also grateful to Peter Pininski for his contribution about Charlotte Stuart, Duchess of Albany; to Thomas Woodcock, Norroy & Ulster King of Arms; Elizabeth Roads, Carrick Pursuivant of Arms and Lyon Clerk at the Court of the Lord Lyon, King of Arms; and to all our correspondants, including The Duke of Richmond and Gordon (with four dukedoms to his name), The Duke of St Albans and his heir Charles Beauclerk (Earl of Burford), Earl of Dalkeith (now Duke of Buccleuch with two dukedoms to his name), Earl of Euston (heir to the Duke of Grafton), Lord Montagu of Beaulieu, the late Stephen Dobson, Gordon Fergusson, Robert Innes-Smith, Mrs. Carol Mitchell, Tim Seely, Major Bruce Shand and Mrs. Michael Worthington and many others besides. We thank them all for their help and encouragement in turning this idea into reality, for it is certainly a colourful footnote to mainstream history.

We also acknowledge with thanks permission to reproduce pages 80-82 from *The King of Fools* (1988) by John Parker, relating to Tim Seely *(see page 247)*, as well as the many brief extracts from so many books listed in the bibliography; and to *The Sunday Times* relating to Clarence Guy Gordon Haddon *(see page 233)*. We also acknowledge with thanks permission to reproduce the various illustrations from the owners concerned, all as listed below *(see page 287)*, as well as to *Burke's Peerage* and *Burke's Landed Gentry, Burke's General Armory* and *Collins' Peerage* for permission to reproduce various armorial bearings.

PB-D March 2006

Introduction To Second Edition

The response to our first edition has been truly heartening and we thank our readers for their interest and our publishers, *Burke's Peerage & Gentry* for their help.

However, this second edition is being published in paperback by Tempus Publishing, who will be promoting the book rather more at home and overseas. This follows the success of the book, which has been used recently as a basis for two recent television programmes *'So You Think You're Royal'*, by Sky TV and Shine Ltd and *'In Search Of Lost Royals'* by Granada Television and ITV. Sadly, both companies took fright at the prospect of using our title *'Royal Bastards'* for fear of causing offence! We are also grateful to the BBC for inclusion in several of their Local Radio stations and for the many kind reviews and interviews we have had. Moreover, a lecture tour of South Africa generated much interest and we have now had bookings for some fifty lectures upon the subject. So it does seem to have provoked some interest

Happily, we have been informed of very few mistakes, but the opportunity of a second edition has enabled us to make a few minor corrections and additions. We have also been informed of a number of other possible candidates for inclusion, but the evidence is not strong enough to include them in this edition.

Meanwhile our energies are being directed towards our next book in the series *'Royal Affairs – Mistresses & Lovers of the English Monarchy'* which should be out next year.

PB-D, March 2008

SECTION I

TUDOR BASTARDS

1485–1603

Chapter I
The Bastards of Edward IV
(1442-83)

Arthur Plantagenet, KG, Viscount Lisle
(1462/4–1542)

King Edward IV reigned from 1461–83 and Arthur was his illegitimate son by Elizabeth Lucie, a widow. She was named by one source (Anstis) as having been the daughter of Thomas Wayte, of Hampshire, but Arthur's date of birth is still a matter of some conjecture; one source stating it was 1462/64 and another 1480.

The first would seem to be based on the chronicles of Hall and Holinshed who claimed that when Edward IV wanted to marry Elizabeth Woodville, his mother declared that he was already pre-contracted to marry Elizabeth Lucy, on whom he had begot a child before. However, the official version recorded in the *Rolls of Parliament*, stated that he was pre-contracted to Lady Eleanor Butler, the daughter of John (Talbot), Earl of Shrewsbury and his wife Margaret Beauchamp. Although not a contemporary source, Hall and Holinshed based their version on an earlier manuscript viz: *Chronicle of England* (Harl. 2408).

Unfortunately we know nothing about the beautiful widow who captured Edward's heart, but of Edward we are on much safer ground. According to the chronicler Hall, he was

> *'a man of goodly personage, of Stature high and exceeding all other in countenance, well-favoured, and comely, of eye quick and pleasant, broad-breasted and well-set; all other members down to his feet kept just proportion with the bulk of his body'.*

Sir Thomas More's description of him was no less flattering: *'of visage lovely, of body mighty, strong and clean made'* and he stood six feet three inches tall. The similarities between Edward and his grandson Henry VIII were striking not only in build but also in character – for both had close members of their own family executed. We cannot tell if Edward's bastard son resembled his father in looks but he certainly did not in character.

Although the sex of Elizabeth Lucie's child is not mentioned, it has been assumed that it was in fact Arthur. However, it is claimed that Elizabeth and Edward also had a daughter and namesake, who married Thomas Lumley, who died 1486/7, son of George Lord Lumley (*see* page 170). It is possible, therefore, that it is she who is referred to above.

The second date of 1480 is taken from the *Dictionary of National Biography* (DNB) and is entirely unsupported by any evidence. *The Oxford Dictionary of National Biography* concludes that he was born before 1470. However if it were true, Arthur would have been born towards the end of his father's reign, thus perhaps explaining why his father never acknowledged him. However, in support of a possible birth date of 1462/4 is an entry in the *Exchequer Records* of Edward IV's reign for a list of garments to be made for '*My Lord the Bastard*' in 1472, but the identificiation with Arthur is far from certain given that Edward IV might have had other bastards. Nevertheless the reference to Elizabeth Lucie being Edward's mistress before his marriage to Elizabeth Woodville in 1464, would seem to support 1462/4 as Arthur's birthdate.

What is known for certain of Arthur's early life is that he was originally known as Arthur Waite and that he appears for the first time in the pages of history in 1502 as a member of the household of Queen Elizabeth, wife of Henry VII, probably as an esquire of the body; prior to that he may have served in the household of Henry's mother the Lady Margaret Beaufort. The Wayte family owned the manors of Lee Marks and Segenworth in Titchfield, Hampshire from the fourteenth century but it is unclear when the young Arthur emerged from the shadows and took his place in the world.

Arthur was rescued from obscurity by his half sister Queen Elizabeth and after her death in 1503 he was transferred to the King's household where he again served as an esquire of the body. His duties demanded that he be '*attendant upon the King's person, to array and unray him, and to watch day and night'* and among his fellow squires were Charles Brandon, Richard Weston (born *c* 1465/6), Edward Guilford and Henry Wyat (born *ca* 1460). The royal favour continued under Henry VIII.

The years 1509–13 were the honeymoon period of Henry VIII's love for his first wife Katherine of Aragon and despite the birth and deaths of two infant Princes of Wales, he remained optimistic that she would eventually bear him healthy sons. During this period the King was generous and gracious to his kinsman and on Arthur's first marriage in 1511 to Elizabeth, subsequently Lady Lisle in her own right, widow of the notorious Edmund Dudley (the well known minister of Henry VII) he received a large grant of lands to sustain him and his wife as landed gentle folk. He also settled into a pattern of service as a Justice of the Peace for Hampshire and Sussex and this was followed in 1513 with a knighthood, just days after the death of the King's second son. The King also made him Sheriff of Hampshire in which county he had apparently some standing, the Earl of Surrey declaring that '*the country regards him best of any man hereabouts, and also he is sheriff of the shire, and dwelling within three mile of Portsmouth*'.

However, despite his royal blood, it would be another ten years before Henry VIII deemed him fit to be created a peer of the realm. In 1523 the King finally raised him to the peerage by creating him Viscount Lisle and in the next year he appointed him a Knight of the Garter. Further honours followed in 1525 when Lisle was appointed Vice-Admiral of England and acted as deputy for the King's illegitimate son Henry FitzRoy (*see* page 60), who was made Lord High Admiral as well as Duke of Richmond and Somerset. Henry's elevation of two royal bastards, one his own and the other his uncle, was interesting. His subsequent paranoia and suspicion of all his Plantagenet relatives, especially the Pole family, had clearly not yet manifested itself. It would only come with Reginald Pole's exhortation to Henry VIII not to ruin his own soul over his passion for Anne Boleyn. Lisle retained the position until 1533 when he was succeeded by the Duke of Norfolk, Richmond's father-in-law.

After the Pilgrimage of Grace and the birth of Prince Edward in 1537, Henry's thoughts turned increasingly towards securing his only son's unhindered succession to his kingdoms. The focus of his fears was the Pole and Courtenay families but his particular hatred was reserved for his near kinsman Cardinal Pole, on whom he had originally bestowed many royal favours including the offer of the archbishopric of York. When Henry sought his kinsman's support in his plan to divorce his wife and marry Anne Boleyn, Pole refused and condemned him for his actions. The king replied '*I will consider what you have said and you shall have my answer*'. The measured tones of his answer hid the anger that Henry felt at such an insult, but as he later confessed '*There was so much simplicity in his manner that it cheated my indignation, and I could not think he meaned me any ill*'. However, the resulting rift between the two was permanent and the discovery of '*a coat of arms found in the Duchess of Salisbury's coffer*' which impaled the royal arms of England with those of the Pole family all surrounded by pansies (for Pole) and marigolds (for Princess Mary) only confirmed Henry's suspicions. According to one contemporary John Worth, it was as if '*Pole intended to have married my Lady Mary and betwixt them both should again arise the old doctrine of Christ*'. When Henry struck it was swiftly and ruthlessly. Within a short period of time both the Marquess of Exeter, Henry's first cousin, and Lord Montague, Reginald Pole's brother, were executed. They were followed by Pole's mother the Countess of Salisbury in 1541.

Despite the past favour shown to him by Henry VIII, Lisle did not escape the dreadful reign of terror that the King launched against his relatives. The reason for Lisle's sudden arrest was his alleged part in the so called *Botolf Plot*. According to Holinshed the chronicler:

> '*The occasion of his trouble for which he was committed to the Tower rose upon suspicion that he should be privy to a practice which some of his men (as Philpot and Bryndeholme executed the last year as before ye have heard) had consented unto for the betraying of Calais to the French, whilst he was the King's Lieutenant there.*'

The instigator of the plot was Sir Gregory Botolf, one of Lisle's three domestic chaplains, who entered Lisle's service in 1538 and within a short time had earned himself the description of '*Gregory Sweet Lips*'. Sir Oliver Browne, another of Lisle's chaplains thought him '*the most*

mischievous knave that ever was born' and so it proved to be. By his own
subsequent declaration Botolf stated that:

> '*And know ye for a truth what my enterprise is, with the aid of God and such
> ways as I shall devise. I shall get the town of Calais into the hands of the Pope
> and Cardinal Pole. This is the matter that I went to Rome for.*'

The author of Lisle's arrest was none other than the King's minister,
Thomas Cromwell, who was concerned that Lisle's request for a
commission to be set up to implement the King's religious policy in
Calais, would expose his own reluctance to do the job. In doing so
Lisle effectively became an opponent of Cromwell, and the latter used
the alleged plot to frighten Henry into having his uncle arrested.

Ensconced in Calais, Lisle grew increasingly uneasy, and as his
position at Court became more difficult, he became a figure of suspicion. For seven years he had been Governor of Calais and from across
the Channel had watched as Henry struck down his relatives one by
one. When Lisle was finally arrested, in 1540, he was already a man
broken in health and spirit. As he mounted the steps to his prison, he
should have remembered the words of his friend Sir Francis Bryan
'*Keep all things secreter than you have been used, there is nothing done or
spoken but it is with speed knowen in the Court*'. His arrival was noted
by the French ambassador:

> '*Two days ago, at 10 o'clock at night, lord lisle, deputy of Calais, uncle to
> this King, was led prisoner to the Tower …It is commonly said he is accused
> of secret intelligence with Cardinal Pole, who was his near relation, and of
> certain practices to deliver the town of Calais to Pole*'.

For two years the King kept him confined in the Tower but was
eventually convinced of his innocence remarking to the French
Ambassador that '*he could not think the Deputy erred through malice,
but rather through simplicity and ignorance.*' Lisle was overjoyed when
Henry ordered his release and when the King, as proof of his regard,
sent him a diamond ring and a '*most gracious message*' it made such an
impression upon the poor man that he died from joy the following
night in 1541/2.

Although he had escaped the headsman's axe, Lisle had become another victim of Henry's reign of terror on all his surviving male relatives. During his lifetime he had witnessed many momentous events including Henry's breach with Rome, the Dissolution of the Monasteries, the Pilgrimage of Grace, the executions of Anne Boleyn, Sir Thomas More, Bishop Fisher and, his cousins, Henry Marquess of Exeter and Henry Lord Montague. A stronger man might have survived his confinement in the Tower but this scion of the blood royal '*The gentlest heart living*', Henry's description of him, possessed none of the steely character of his cousin the Countess of Salisbury who '*withstood days of relentless interrogation with the steadfastness of a strong man, and survived the rigours of three years imprisonment in the Tower before she was executed at the age of sixty seven*'. Indeed he was lucky to survive the debacle surrounding the trial and execution of Anne Boleyn for two of his more prominent friends Henry Norris and Sir Francis Bryan were accused of committing adultery with that unfortunate woman. The transformation of the King's character during these years earned him the contempt and disgust of many of his contemporaries including the French Ambassador who described him in 1539 as '*the most dangerous and cruel man in the world.*'

Unlike their kinsfolk none of Lord Lisle's children married into the higher eschelons of the nobility, but that did not stop them from being proud of their royal blood. Indeed when there seemed to be propects for a disputed succession to the Crown on the death of Elizabeth I, Lord Lisle's great-grandson Sir Robert Basset made known his pretensions:

> '*but not being able to make them good, he was forced to fly into France to save his head. To compound for which, together with his high and generous way of Living, Sir Robert Basset greatly Exhausted his Estate; Selling off etc, no less than thirty Mannors of Land*'.

Sir Robert remained in exile from 1603–11 and was but one of fourteen persons who had pretended titles to the crown in 1603. History, however, would be much kinder to George Monck, later 1st Duke of Albemarle, Lord Lisle's great-great-grandson, who was instrumental in the restoration of Charles II in 1660.

Chapter II
The Bastards of Richard III
(1452–85)

John De Gloucester, called De Pomfret, (1468?–99)

John of Gloucester, originally known as John of Pomfret, is the only known illegitimate son of King Richard III. He is a shadowy figure about whom very little is known, but during his short life, he posed a very substantial threat to the security of the early Tudor monarchy.

Despite the paucity of information about him, it is possible to piece together some information about his early life and career. Firstly he was almost certainly born no earlier than 1468, when Richard III was only sixteen years old. This would have made John about seventeen years old when his father appointed him to the office of Captain of Calais in 1485. However, it is possible that he was born in the early 1470s thus making him only about twelve years old in 1485. Either way he appears to have been born in Pomfret (Pontefract), Yorkshire or alternatively grew up there until he took up his post in Calais at the end of 1484. As his father was living at Pontefract under the tutelage of the Earl of Warwick from *circa* 1465–68, the former possibility seems the more likely.

In support of his birth between 1468–72 is a rather obscure reference in the records of the *Great Wardrobe of the King* in 1472 to a lord bastard. However, it must be said that this could equally have referred to Arthur Plantagenet, later Viscount Lisle, the illegitimate son of King Edward IV (*see* page 18). But as John was described as *'the lord bastard'* on two further occasions in 1484 and 1485, the 1472 reference could also have applied to him. Unfortunately his mother's name is unknown, although at least one historian has speculated that she could have been Katherine Haute, wife of James Haute, son of William Haute and Joan Woodville, cousin to Elizabeth Woodville, wife of King Edward IV.

In addition to his appointment as Captain of Calais, John was made Captain of the fortresses of Rysbank, Guisnes, Hammes and Lieutenant of the Marches of Picardy for life. He was actually out of the country when his father King Richard was defeated and slain at the Battle of Bosworth in 1485, but somewhat generously, Henry Tudor then proceeded to grant him an annual rent of twenty pounds, for life, from the revenues of the lordship of Kingston Lacy in Dorset. If John was born about 1468 he would have reached the age of twenty-one in 1489 or thereabouts, but following the grant of 1486, nothing further is heard of him until his death in prison in 1499.

George Buck, in his book '*The History of King Richard the Third*' published in 1619, alleges that John had been in prison a number of years before his death and he was referred to in the confession of Perkin Warbeck, another pretender to Henry Tudor's crown. The date given is 1491, the year in which Perkin Warbeck arrived in Ireland and the future Henry VIII was born. Why Henry decided to imprison John is unknown but it would seem to have a direct link with Warbeck's appearance in Ireland and later the following year in France at the express invitation of King Charles VIII. Nor is it known if John shared the same prison as the young Earl of Warwick, the only remaining legitimate male Plantagenet.

Henry's reaction to the threat of Warbeck was to invade France and besiege Boulogne. The French King quickly treated for terms and the resulting Treaty of Etaples stipulated that he pay the English an annual subsidy and banish Warbeck from the realm. Warbeck then appeared at the court of Margaret of Burgundy, sister of Edward IV and then paid a visit to the Holy Roman Emperor, who acknowledged him as Richard, younger son of Edward IV. Whilst Warbeck played out his semi-tragic role as the Yorkist heir to Henry's crown, John of Gloucester languished in prison. It is not known if he had married but prior to his imprisonment he could have taken a wife. If he did, her fate is unknown. Unlike his cousin Arthur, Edward IV's bastard, John, did not serve in the King's or Queen's household. In view of his age and his parentage he was clearly regarded as a threat to Henry Tudor and is reputed to have been disposed of because some unspecified Irishmen wanted to make him their ruler. The contrast in his fate to that of his cousin Arthur is quite striking and in the author's mind can only be explained by the character of the two men. John may have been of a more independent and outspoken in his views and unwilling to accept the change in his circumstances, whilst Arthur was the complete opposite. Whilst Arthur flourished under the patronage of the first two Tudors, John paid the ultimate price.

Katherine Plantagenet, Countess of Huntingdon (1468/70–87)

Katherine was the illegitimate daughter of King Richard III but very little indeed is known about her. Even her date of birth and her mother's name are unknown. All that can be stated with confidence is that she cannot have been born earlier than 1468 as her brother Richard was just 16 years old at the time. Nor is there any evidence to suggest a much later date of birth.

The earliest reference to Katherine is her marriage covenant, dated 29 February 1484, when William Herbert, Earl of Huntingdon agreed '*to take to wife Dame Katherine Plantagenet, daughter of the King before Michaelmas of that year*'. The Earl agreed to make her a jointure in lands of two hundred pounds whilst King Richard undertook to bear the whole cost of the marriage and settle lands and lordships on them to the value of one thousand marks per annum. Lands and lordships to the value of six hundred marks came from the King on the day of their marriage and a reversion of four hundred marks after the death of Lord Stanley. However, during the lifetime of the latter, they would have four hundred marks per annum from the revenues of the lordships of Newport, Brecknock and Hay. Lord Stanley's involvement was due to his wife's support of the Duke of Buckingham's rebellion. Lady Stanley being none other than Margaret Beaufort, mother of Henry Tudor, subsequently Henry VII.

The marriage appears to have taken place between March and May 1484, the former date being when King Richard granted the said annuity and the latter when '*William Erle of Huntingdon and Kateryn his wif*' received a grant of the proceeds of various manors in Devon, Cornwall and Somerset. The last reference to Katherine was in March 1485 when she and her husband received a further annuity of one hundred and fifty-two pounds ten shillings and ten pence from the King's possessions in the counties of Carmarthen and Cardigan and his lordship of Haverfordwest

When Katherine died is again unknown, but one contemporary source, a list of the nobility present at the Coronation of Henry VII on 25 November 1487, stated that her husband was then a widower. If this can be supported by additional evidence, Katherine was clearly dead by that date. The cause may have been childbirth, the infant not surviving. Thus she passes from the pages of history.

Chapter III
The Bastards of Henry VIII
(1491–1547)

Henry FitzRoy, KG, Duke of Richmond & Somerset (1519–36)

This young sprig of the House of Tudor was the illegitimate son of King Henry VIII and Elizabeth Blount, a lady of singular beauty, a maid of honour to his wife Catherine of Aragon.who '… *in syngyng, daunsyng, and in all goodly pastimes exceded all other, by whiche … she wan the kynges harte*'. Indeed her musical skills, physical charms and captivating personality made an indeliable impression on the young king whose own passion for music is well known. In his youth he had been taught to play the organ, lute and harpsichord and he even composed the words to several Court lyrics as well as several Masses.

The King's interest in Mistress Blount occurred as his belief in Queen Catherine's ability to produce a living son waned. Her last child, a daughter, was born in November 1518, only to die within a few hours. That he should look for a suitable distraction whilst his wife was with child, might be understandable. However, neither Mistress Blount nor her family seemed to benefit from the association and indeed it is quite possible that they may have disapproved. Nevertheless the possible opportunities that might arise from such an association would not have been lost on this worldly daughter of John Blount, of Knevet, in Shropshire. Indeed she made a very good marriage after the birth of her son to Gilbert, Lord Tailbois of Kyme, the son of Sir George Talboys, of Goltho, Lincolnshire.

Henry FitzRoy, for that is the surname the King gave him, was reputedly born in the summer of 1519 at Blackmore, Essex, an occasional retreat used by the King for his amorous escapades. Prior to the birth, his mother's last appearance at court was in October 1518 when she participated in the celebrations at York Place, organised by Cardinal Wolsey, to mark the betrothal of the two year old Princess Mary to the Dauphin of France. If her son Henry was created Duke of Richmond and Somerset on his sixth birthday, this suggests that he was conceived at the beginning of September 1518.

Three to four months after Henry's birth, his mother appears to have conceived again. This next child, a daughter named Elizabeth, was twenty-two years old in June 1542, and therefore was born *circa* June 1520. Within that three to four month gap, Elizabeth is believed to have married Gilbert Talbois, although no record of the marriage has survived. Why such great haste? Had Henry taken another mistress? Mary Boleyn, perhaps?

All we know for certain, is that there is no record of Henry VIII bestowing on his ex-mistress or her husband any honours worthy of the name in 1519–21 in celebration of their marriage. Indeed what honours Gilbert did receive, were all post-1521 and the earliest date at which she is described as Gilbert's wife is 1522. Elizabeth's third child, a son George, was sixteen years old in March 1539, therefore born pre-March 1523, and the earliest reference to his mother being married is in June 1522 when she and her husband were granted the manor of Rokeby/Rugby, co Warwick. Was this in celebration of their recent marriage? If so it raises the possibility of Mistress Blount bearing the King not just one child but two!

The reason for the break-up of this Royal relationship may have been due to the King's interest in Mary Boleyn, now the wife of William Carey. They had been married in 1520 and Mary bore two children, a daughter Catherine (born 1524) and son Henry (born 1525/6), whose paternity gossip attributed to the King. Although it was often said that Henry named one of his ships after Mary, it now seems that the ship in question originally belonged to her father and was subsequently bought by the king for his navy.

But what of the young Henry FitzRoy? He was according to contemporary accounts, '*a goodly man child in beauty like to the father and the mother*' and '*well brought up, like a Prince's child*' and was given his own establishment at Durham Place, Cardinal Wolsey's mansion in London. As the Cardinal was his godfather, this seemed a suitable solution. In his sixth year he was created Earl of Nottingham and Duke of Richmond and Somerset, with precedence over all other dukes, save for the King's lawful issue, (the ceremony being described in an heraldic manuscript quoted in the *Calendar of State Papers of Henry VIII*). He was placed by the King in the care of Master John Palsgrave, Master Parre and Master Page with the words

> *'I deliver unto you three my worldly jewel; you twain to have the guiding of his body, and thou Palsgrave, to bring him up in virtue and learning'.*

The following month Henry was created Lord High Admiral of England and Warden General of the Marches of Scotland, a clear indication of his intention to promote him to only the highest of offices. He was also made a Knight of the Garter and installed 25 June 1525. Eight years later in 1533 he was promoted to the Lieutenancy of the same Order.

Unfortunately the King's acknowledgement of his bastard son and his elevation to the peerage was not welcomed by all. Queen Catherine, in particular, resented the honour shown to her husband's bastard, a fact that was noted by a Venetian observer at the English court:

> *'It seems that the Queen resents the Earldom and Dukedom conferred on the King's natural son and remains dissatisfied, at the instigation it is said of three of her Spanish ladies her chief counsellors, so the King has dismissed them the court, a strong measure, but the Queen was obliged to submit and have patience'.*

Her fears were not unreasonable and were fuelled by her own inability to produce a healthy son of her own. Moreover, she feared that the King might make his bastard son and not their daughter, heir to his kingdoms as evidenced by the many other appointments that followed, including that of King's Lieutenant-General north of the Trent, Lord High Admiral of England, Wales, Ireland, Normandy, Gascony and Aquitaine, Warden-General of the Marches of Scotland, Chamberlain of Chester and North Wales, Receiver of Middleham and Sheriff Hutton, Yorkshire, Lord Lieutenant of Ireland, Constable of Dover Castle and finally Lord Warden of the Cinque Ports. It was often said that the King had in mind to make Henry the King of Ireland, for which all these appointments were a preparation. Indeed the King instructed his Ambassadors to describe the young Duke as one '*who is near of his blood and of excellent qualities, and is already furnished to keep the state of a great prince, and yet may be easily by the King's means exalted to higher things*'.

Indeed Henry's impact on his contemporaries was considerable and can best be summed up in the words of William Franklyn, Archdeacon of Durham who thought he was:

'a child of excellent wisdom and towardness; and, for his good and quick capacity, retentative memory, virtuous inclination to all honour, humanity and goodness, I think hard it would be to find any creature living twice his age, able or worthy to be compared with him'.

His tutor, Richard Croke, agreed declaring that '*although he is only eight years old, he can translate any passage of Caesar*'.

Until the birth of the Prince of Wales in 1537, young Henry was therefore the only son of King Henry to survive childhood. It is only natural, therefore, to expect some degree of speculation at Court on whether the King intended to legitimise him and place him in the direct line of the succession. Indeed in 1536 no less a person than the Earl of Sussex raised this very issue at a meeting of the Privy Council declaring:

'in the King's presence, that considering that the Princess (Mary) was a bastard, as well the Duke of Richmond, it was advisable to prefer the male to the female, for the succession to the Crown.'

Certainly, it was believed by many that: '*In case of there being no sons at all of this last marriage* (to Jane Seymour), *it is believed the King's determination was, that the succession should go to his bastard son the Duke of Richmont (sic).* His position at Court and in the King's affections was therefore unique, especially since the 1536 Act of Succession had confirmed Mary and Elizabeth's bastard status in law and gave Henry the right to choose his own successor. He was also assigned his father's Royal Arms, although *'within a bordure and debruised by a silver baton sinister and with a small shield in pretence'*.

Despite a certain amount of gossip linking Henry's name with a niece of Pope Clement VII, a Danish princess, a French princess and a daughter of Eleanor, Dowager Queen of Portugal, the young Duke of Richmond eventually married, in 1533, Mary, daughter of Thomas (Howard), 3rd Duke of Norfolk, but the marriage was never consummated. The match was arranged by the King, and the Duke of Norfolk had to break off a match he had arranged for Mary with Lord Bulbeck, son and heir of the Earl of Oxford. The choice was an interesting one, given that Queen Anne Boleyn was a cousin of the bride, and it is not stretching the imagination too far to suggest that she might have had some hand in the proceedings.

The Howard family's rise to prominence under the Tudors was quite extraordinary, but the price they had to pay was in many cases tragic. It began with the marriage of Edward IV's daughter Anne to Thomas Duke of Norfolk, a union that carried with it innate perils for any possible descendants. Fortunately all save one of their children died as infants, although a son Thomas survived until his early youth. When Henry VIII took Anne Boleyn as his wife, her uncle Thomas, Duke of Norfolk expected to benefit enormously from the relationship. However, unfortunately it never happened and the situation did not improve when it was discovered another relative, his nephew Thomas, had secretly proposed marriage to the King's neice Margaret Douglas, whom the King looked upon as a daughter. Thomas subsequently died in the Tower for his folly. That Norfolk survived all of these mishaps speaks volumes for his skill as a courtier, especially when it was discovered that Henry's fifth queen, Catherine Howard, another of Norfolk's neices, was found guilty of adultery. Not surprisingly Norfolk eventually found himself incarcerated in the Tower, and it was only the king's fortuitous death that saved him from the headsman's axe. The poor man had lost not only two neices to the executioner, but also his eldest son, the Earl of Surrey, and in 1572 his grandson was beheaded for conspiring with Mary, Queen of Scots. Clearly a most unfortunate family.

At the beginning of that momentous year of 1536, therefore, the young Duke of Richmond entered his seventeenth year and seemed poised to step out of his father's shadow and enter the pages of history in his own right. What happened next was completely unexpected, for within a month of the Earl of Sussex's impromptu speech to the King and members of his Privy Council on the possibilty of Richmond taking his place in the succession, he was struck down with what was then diagnosed as a rapid consumption.

He died in *'the kinges place in St James'*, on 23 July 1536, gossip attributing his demise to poison by the late queen (Anne Boleyn, whose execution he had attended two months earlier) and her brother Lord Rochford. As a result his widow, who never remarried, but later became a Lady in Waiting to Anne of Cleves, had some difficulty in establishing her right to her dowry, because the marriage had been unconsummated.

SECTION II

STUART BASTARDS

1603–1714

Chapter IV
The Bastards of Charles II
(1630–85)

Sir James FitzRoy, or Crofts, later Scott, KG, 1st Duke of Monmouth & 1st Duke of Buccleuch (1649-85)

Of all King Charles II's bastards, the Duke of Monmouth was undoubtedly his favourite. '*He was the King's greatest delight …His face and the exterior graces of his person such, that nature has perhaps never formed anything more accomplished*', enthused a contemporary. He had also '*A wonderful disposition for all sorts of exercise, an attractive address, an air of greatness, in fine all the personal advantages spoke in his favour; but his mind said not one word for him*'.

Born in Rotterdam, the child of Lucy Walter and the eldest of Charles II's fifteen 'officially' recognised bastards (by seven mothers), speculation still surrounds his birth. James II believed that he was the son of Colonel Robert Sidney and not King Charles, but James clearly had political reasons for making this claim; the evidence supporting the Sidney parentage is not convincing, quite apart from the obvious resemblance that Monmouth had to Charles II. In any case, this claim has now been refuted once and for all by the DNA results obtained. These show conclusively that the Dukes of Buccleuch descend in the male line from the same stock as do the Dukes of Grafton, St Albans and Richmond, which of course is from King Charles II.

Some believed that Charles had married Lucy, which if true, would have meant that the present Duke of Buccleuch would now be King of England. In support of this claim are statements made by Lucy's mother, who, when admonished about the life her daughter led, retorted that her daughter was married to King Charles. Then there was a conversation which took place several centuries later between the Dukes of Abercorn and Buccleuch to the effect that the latter had discovered a marriage certificate between King Charles II and Lucy in the muniment room at Dalkeith. After considering the matter for some time, they decided to destroy it.

At the age of eight, James was taken away from his mother and placed in the care of Father Stephen Goffe, chaplain to Henrietta Maria, a service he also performed for the illegitimate sons of King James II. It was a curious choice given that Father Goffe's brother, William, was one of the signatories to the death warrant of Charles I. The King appointed Thomas Ross as his tutor, in retrospect a very bad choice because Ross proceeded to fill the boy's head with stories of him being the King's legitimate son. Ross even approached Doctor Cosin asking him to sign a certificate of marriage between Charles and Lucy, which he promised to conceal during the Doctor's lifetime. However the doctor indignantly rejected the proposal and immediately informed the King. Was this perhaps the certificate found by the Duke of Buccleuch in the early part of the twentieth century?

Shortly before his return to England, young Jamie was placed in the care of William, Lord Crofts who passed him off as a relative. Again it was a very odd choice for the King to make, as Crofts was known to be '*a quarrelsome, pleasure-loving man, constantly engaged in duels and fond of dancing*'.

In retrospect it can be seen that the lack of any real formal education forced Monmouth to rely on other qualities in order to make his mark in the world. His physical beauty was quite remarkable and when presented at Court in 1662 Grammont described him as '*a dazzling astonishing beauty with his mother's sensuous seductiveness and his father's sweetness of nature*'. Court gossip even suggested that his father's new mistress, Barbara Villiers, of whom more anon (*see* page 50), took more than a passing interest in him and Charles is said to have expedited James's marriage so as to save him from her attentions.

In 1663, aged fourteen, he was betrothed and married Anne, Countess of Buccleuch, who was described as '*the greatest heiress and finest woman of her time*' with an annual income of ten thousand pounds. In consequence, he was created Duke of Monmouth and given precedence over all other dukes not of royal blood. After his marriage he and his wife were also created Duke and Duchess of Buccleuch.

Of all the royal bastards that appear in this book, Monmouth is the only one who sought to claim the Crown. In this he was unique and in spite of all the so called legal impediments preventing Monmouth from succeeding to his father's crown, there was widespread belief that he would make a better candidate than his Roman Catholic uncle, the Duke of York. Indeed his very illegitimacy was seen by at least one contemporary, Charles Blount, as a positive advantage viz:

> 'And remember, the old rule is, He who hath the worst title, ever makes the best King; as being constrain'd by a gracious government, to supply what he wants in Title; that instead of God and my Right, his Motto may be, God and my People'.

However, unlike his predecessor, Henry VIII, Charles II was not prepared to settle the succession question by statute. Indeed in many respects he was the architect of the whole succession problem. Had he simply divorced his wife and married again, there would almost certainly not have been a succession crisis. As the Earl of Shaftesbury pointed out:

> 'Can anyone doubt, if he looks at the King's face, as to his being capable of making children? He is only fifty. I know people of upwards of sixty who have no difficulty in making children.'

By refusing to agree to the exclusion of his brother James from the succession, Charles set the scene for Monmouth's subsequent invasion. In retrospect it could be argued therefore that Monmouth's attempt to take the Crown by force, despite his illegitimacy, was not the unprecedented act of a madman.

William of Normandy had done exactly the same thing in 1066, despite there being a legitimate heir male to the Crown with a superior title to his own. Charles had four options, to declare

Monmouth's legitimacy as a fact; to declare his legitimacy by an Act of Parliament; to decree that bastardy was not a bar to inheriting the crown; or to assert that *'unlawful marriage of parents ought not to illegitimate the children'*; but he ignored them all. There was also the belief that in the event of Monmouth succeeding to the Crown his bastardy would be automatically cancelled.

Like his father, Monmouth gained an unenviable reputation as a gallant. Among his many conquests could be counted the lovely Eleanor Néedham, younger sister of the incomparable Jane Middleton, a noted beauty of the early Restoration. By Mistress Néedham, Monmouth had four children, two sons and two daughters viz: Brig-Gen James Crofts and Capt Henry Crofts, RN. *'For Debauchery and Irreligion he was one of the vilest Men that has set foot in Boston'* claimed Judge Sewell. Henrietta, Duchess of Bolton – who accompanied the ladies of the condemned Jacobite peers with a petition to the House of Lords in 1716 and in doing so earned the condemnation of Lady Cowper viz: *'The Duchess of Bolton went with the ladies, to make believe she was one of the Royal Family: though that won't do; it's too plainly writ in her face that she's Penn's daughter, the quaking preacher'*, *'She said Lady Derwentwater came crying to her, when the Duke was not at home, and persuaded her to go to plead for her Lord'* and Isabella, who died an infant.

After Monmouth's death, Mistress Néedham married a commissioner of the Inland Revenue and bore him a daughter. She also received regular payments from the Treasury to help with the expense of her children's upkeep and education. Monmouth also had a daughter, Mary Hicks, by, it is said, Elizabeth, daughter of the poet Edmund Waller. This young lady was married at the age of thirteen, in 1689, to James de Cardonnel, who served as secretary to the Duke of Schomberg during the Jacobite Wars in Ireland, and she had by him eleven children. The present day representative of this family is Charles Boyd Findlay, of Alton, Hampshire (see *Burke's Landed Gentry of Scotland*).

Monmouth also had an intrigue with Mary Kirke, a Maid of Honour to the Duchess of York (Mary of Modena) but appears to have shared her favours with the Duke of York and Lord Mulgrave. Warned of Mulgrave's interest in his mistress, Monmouth had him placed under house arrest in the palace guard house. Mulgrave retaliated by challenging one of the Duke's adherents, Mr Felton, to a duel, Lord Middleton and Mr Buckley being seconds. Nine months later, in May/June 1675, the unfortunate maid '*had the ill fortune to become the mother of a boy, which however, died within 3 or 4 hours*'. '*It was not said yet to which father it belongs*'.

After the child was born, her brother Capt Percy Kirke challenged Mulgrave to a duel '*for having debauched and abused his sister*' despite the fact that '*ye Earle purged himself before hand of any injury he had done of ye nature & though shee herself does not accuse him either of getting ye child or any other act that we heare of*'. Again Lord Middleton acted as Mulgrave's second and Kirke was seconded by Capt Charles Godfrey, who later married James II's ex-mistress Arabella Churchill. Mulgrave was severley wounded but Mrs Kirke '*persists to protest that she does not know whether he be man or woman*'. Mrs Kirke, who was aunt to the 1st Duchess of St Albans, subsequently married, as his second wife, Sir Thomas Vernon, Bt, and by him had several children. However, the greatest love of Monmouth's life was Henrietta, Lady Wentworth, whom he took as his mistress in 1680. There were no children of the union, but the relationship was strong and lasted until his death.

Unlike his cousin the Duke of Berwick (*see* page 99), Monmouth was not a naturally gifted soldier or commander. But that did not prevent his father from making him Captain General of all the Armed Forces in England, Wales and Scotland. His victory over the covenanters at Bothwell Bridge in 1679 was due mainly to the experience and abilities of his more able subordinates, in particular John Graham of Claverhouse, subsequently known as 'Bonnie Dundee'. Nevertheless he displayed conspicuous bravery on a number of occasions during his military career. The most notable was at the siege of Maestricht in 1673, on which occasion Louis XIV wrote to King Charles

'*I ought not to forget to mention that the day after, the besieged having made a sortie upon the hald moon by means of a small mine, the Duke attacked their guard in hand upon the first alarm of the sortie, and dislodged them*'.

He also took part in the naval battle of Sole Bay in 1665 when the English Fleet under the command of the Duke of York defeated the Dutch. Having seemingly reached such dizzy heights of favour, he then earned the King's displeasure in 1683 by becoming implicated in the Rye House plot to kill the King and Duke of York and was banished the kingdom. Nell Gwyn (*see* page 75) tried to act as an intermediary, but to no avail. The King never spoke his name again and even on his deathbed, he did not mention him.

In the post Restoration years, the rumour that Charles had married Lucy was so strong and persistant that the King was eventually forced to make several public declarations denying it. The belief that he could be legitimate, clearly played on Monmouth's mind for the whole of his life, but what evidence did he have to support it? The unofficial marriage certificate drawn up by his ex-tutor, Thomas Ross, was obviously a key factor in leading him to commit, in the eyes of some of his contemporaries, the ultimate folly of rebelling against his uncle James II. However, whilst his father remained alive, his ambition was held in check and of all the King's bastards, he was the most loved and indulged. Had he been content to be the first noble in the land after his uncle James, a long and fruitful career in government could have been his for the taking.

During his lifetime Monmouth enjoyed a princely income of over twenty-one thousand pounds per annum, far more than any of King Charles's other bastards. Only the Duchess of Cleveland had an income that surpassed his, due mainly to the number of children she had borne the King. In addition to his pensions etc., Charles also purchased John Ashburnham's house at Chiswick for him at a cost of seven thousand pounds and later Moor Park at a cost of thirteen thousand, two hundred pounds from the Duke of Ormonde.

When Charles II died in 1685, Monmouth finally took the fateful step of landing at Lyme Regis on the south coast of England with a handful of supporters and munitions and was proclaimed King at Taunton. Within a short time four thousand men had flocked to his standard, most of whom were weavers and artisans. After a brief and unsuccessful attempt to take the city of Bristol he attacked the Royal army at Sedgemoor and suffered an ignominious defeat. He was later captured in the New Forest and imprisoned in the Tower of London, where he was beheaded (at the 5th blow) in 1685. Although all his honours were forfeited, his wife was able to pass on her own title as Duchess of Buccleuch to their children, and indeed their grandson was restored to the English honours of his grandfather, excepting the Dukedom of Monmouth.

On his deliverance by water to the privy stairs at Whitehall for his fateful interview with King James, he was observed by the Earl of Ailesbury, who dearly loved him and afterwards wrote of him that he

'was a fine courtier, but of a most poor understanding as to cabinet and politics, (who) gave himself wholly up to flatterers and knaves by consequence'.

The image of the poor Duke ascending the stairs *'lean and pale with a disconsolate physiognomy'* haunted him for the rest of his life. But even King James was forced to admit that *'from the very beginning of this desperate attempt'* the Duke *'behaved with the conduct of a great captain and had not made one false step'*. Praise indeed!

Neither of Monmouth's legitimate sons resembled their royal grandsire but the younger Henry Scott, subsequently created Earl of Deloraine by Queen Anne, was renowned for his good breeding and was a personal friend of George, Prince of Wales, later George II. His mother, the Duchess of Buccleuch, complained repeatedly about his extravagance stating that she had given him £20,000 plus another £4,000 for the building and furnishing of his house at Leadwell, thus leaving him just £5 in her will. His second wife Mary, daughter of Charles Howard, a grandson of the Earl of Berkshire, became mistress to George II and was also governess to the Princesses Mary and Louisa.

Their affair began in the winter of 1734 following the dismissal of Lady Suffolk, the King's previous mistress of some twenty years standing.

'About nine o'clock every night the King used to return to the Queen's apartment from that of his daughters, where, from the time of Lady Suffolk's disgrace, he used to pass those evenings he did not go to the opera or play at quadrille,

*constraining them, tiring himself, and talking a little bawdy to Lady Deloraine,
who was always of the party', claimed Lord Hervey.*

On the death of her husband, Lady Deloraine had married again in 1734 to Mr Wyndham, six years her junior, and by him had at least one son whose paternity was called into question by none other than Sir Robert Walpole. According to Lord Hervey:

*'Sir Robert one day, whilst she (lady Deloraine) was standing in the Hall at
Richmond with her little son of about one year old in her arms, said to her:
'That's a pretty boy, Lady Deloraine; who got it?' To which her Ladyship,
before half a dozen people, without taking the question at all ill, replied: 'Mr
Wyndham, upon honour'; and then added, laughing, 'but I will not promise
whose the next will be'*

If Lord Hervey is to be believed, she had:

*'one of the prettiest faces that ever was formed, which though she was now five
and thirty, had a bloom upon it, too, that not one woman in ten thousand has
at fifteen and what is more extraordinary a bloom which she herself never had
till after she was twenty five and married. She was of a middle stature, rather
lean than fat, neither well-made, nor crooked, not genteel, and had something
remarkably awkard about her arms which were long and bony, with a pair of
ugly white hands at the end of them.'*

When the affair ended is unclear, but Lady Deloraine died in 1744.

The present representative of the family is Richard Walter, 10th Duke of Buccleuch and 12th Duke of Queensberry, KBE, DL (born 1954), one of the largest landowners in the country. It is interesting to note that through his grandmother, Mary (Molly), *née* Lascelles, he (and his cousin the Duke of Northumberland) also descend from Nell Gwyn and Charles II through the Dukes of St Albans (*see* page 75).

Although the Duke's father was officially recognised as Chief of the Name and Arms of Scot, his surname is in fact Montagu-Douglas-Scott, thus representing the great alliances and inheritances that have been made by his ancestors over the centuries. The complicated arms matriculated at the Court of the Lord Lyon are firstly his paternal

Royal quartering, being the arms of King Charles II, *debruised by a baton sinister argent* as Earl of Doncaster; secondly for the Dukedom of Argyll; thirdly for the Dukedom of Queensberry; fourthly for the Dukedom of Montagu; and in the centre of the shield an inescutcheon with the arms of Scott. The family motto *Amo* (I love) certainly seemed appropriate enough when granted.

Charlotte Jemima Henrietta Maria Howard, later Countess of Yarmouth (née Boyle , later FitzRoy) (1650–84)

Charlotte was born in about 1650 in Paris, the daughter of Charles II by Elizabeth, daughter of Sir Robert Killigrew, Vice Chamberlain to Charlotte's grandmother, Queen Henrietta Maria. Elizabeth had been married in 1638, at the age of sixteen, in the Chapel Royal at Whitehall to Francis Boyle, the 4th surviving son of the 1st Earl of Cork. Francis was later created Viscount Shannon, the original patent was dated 1654 at Paris and sold at Sotheby's in 1965. According to the Duke of Ormonde, Viscount Shannon was '*a plain, honest gentleman*' and from his surviving letters would seem to have been '*a kindly and fair-minded man*'.

At the time of her daughter's birth Elizabeth Boyle was twenty-eight years old and Charles just twenty years old. The age difference is interesting simply because it is the only recorded case of Charles having an older woman as his mistress. Charlotte grew up to be very like her father in looks and her portraits display a lively intelligence and a merry disposition. At the age of thirteen she was married to James Howard, who died in 1669 aged nineteen, (grandson of Theophilus Howard, 2nd Earl of Suffolk, KG, PC) and by him had a daughter Stuarta, who became a Maid of Honour to Queen Mary II; she died in 1706. Charlotte married again in 1672 William Paston, subsequently 2nd Earl of Yarmouth, a stalwart supporter of King James II to whom he remained loyal at the Revolution, even at the cost of several periods in the Tower of London. Unfortunately Charlotte died suddenly in 1684 at her house in Pall Mall, aged only thirty-four, and was buried in Westminster Abbey, leaving two sons (who predeceased their father) as well as two daughters. She died '*Without any Arms of her own, the King, her father, not having assign'd her any in her Life-time.*'

Although Charles never publicly acknowledged Charlotte or granted her the royal arms, he did grant her and her husband a modest pension of £500 in 1667, which continued to be paid to her even after the death of her husband in 1669. The King's failure to recognise her may have been due to her mother's desire to hide her indiscretion. Legally she was the daughter of Lord Shannon and was named as such in official documents as is evidenced by the following entry in the parish registers of Heston, Middlesex:

> *1662/3 9 March   Jacobus Howard, Thoma Howard, Armigero Patre*
> *praenobili Suffolccie Comite & Charlotta Boyle,*
> *Patre Francisco Vicecomte Shannon*

In her naturalisation papers granted the same year, she was once again described as Lord Shannon's daughter:

> '*Charlotte Boyle, born at Paris in France, daughter of Francis,*
> *Viscount Shannon, brother to Earl of Corke*'

William Paston was not created Earl of Yarmouth, for that honour had already gone to his father Robert in 1679. William '*a Non Juror all King William's reign, but a man of sense and knowledge in the affairs of his country*' was not so fortunate when it came to managing his own finances. By 1708 it was said of him that he

> '*is as low as you can imagin; he hath vast debts, and suffers every thing to run to extremity; soe his goods have all been seised in execution and his lands extended, soe that he hath scare a servant to attend him ... And yet cannot be perswaded to take any method of putteing his affairs in a better posture, wch they are still capable of*'.

None of the Earl's sons survived him, the eldest Lord Paston, a godson of Charles II, died at the age of 45 in 1718 and his younger brother William at the age of 35 in 1717. The former earned some notoriety in 1700 when he

> *'shot the Ld Portland for refusing to marry his sister Mrs Howard, to whom he had promised marriage. My Ld Paston challenged first but he refused, and so was shot'.*

Lord Portland, then British Ambassador to France, was of course a favourite of William III and the affair caused quite a stir. When Lord Paston eventually married, it was to a lady who was described by one historian as '*the daughter of a porter and an apple woman*'. The union produced only a daughter, who died unmarried in 1731.

Of Lady Yarmouth's daughters, the eldest, Charlotte, married firstly Thomas Herne, of Heverland, Norfolk and secondly Thomas Weldon. By her first husband Lady Charlotte had seven sons one of whom bore the unusual name of Hanover Herne, no doubt named in honour of the House of Guelph. The child was born in 1712, before George I came to England, and one wonders what the other descendants of Charles II thought about this honour. Lady Yarmouth's younger daughter Rebecca married Sir John Holland, Bt and died in 1726, having borne her husband three sons and three daughters.

The modern day representative of the family is Sir Charles John Buckworth-Herne-Soame, 12th Bt, who is descended from Lady Charlotte's eldest son Paston Clement John Herne.

Charles FitzCharles, Earl of Plymouth (1657–80) and Catherine FitzCharles

Catherine Pegge was the daughter of Thomas Pegge, the squire of Yeldersley Old Hall, Derbyshire and a staunch Royalist, by his wife Katharine, daughter of Sir Gilbert Kniveton, Bt of Mercaston, another brave cavalier who paid a high price for his loyalty. Catherine had met King Charles II in Bruges whence the Pegges had fled, and it was not long before she was the mother of two of his illegitimate children, Charles and Catherine. Subsequently she married in 1667, as his 4th wife, Sir Edward Green, 1st and last Bt, of Sampford, Essex and died in 1678. By her husband she had had another daughter Justinia, who died unmarried in Pontoise, France in 1717, aged fifty, and a son William who died before his father. Sir Edward had died in 1676 in Flanders a ruined man who

'by his extravagance and love of gambling, entirely ruined his estate and his large inheritance passed from his family'.

Charles FitzCharles, as her son was called, was born in 1657 in what was then the Spanish Netherlands and as he was rather swarthy like his father, he soon became known as as Don Carlos and sometimes as Mr Green. At the age of eighteen, he was created Earl of Plymouth in 1675 and the arms granted to him were those of his father, debruised *by a baton sinister vair*. On his first appearance in England in 1672 a contemporary noted:

'A new gentleman begins to appear, one Mr Green, who hath been bred some years in Flanders. The King hath not seen him yet, much less owned him'.

Another Sir Charles Lyttelton also wrote

'There was a fine youth wth the King, by the name Don Carlos, who the King ownes by my Lady Greene, who has bine bred in Flanders. They say he has a great deal of witt and is finely bred'.

Cromwell's spies had also been well aware of this latest addition to the Royal family and had sought to make mischief by spreading rumours that Catherine was loose living woman and/or that Charles II had heartlessly seduced her.

The timing of their son's appearance in England was obviously designed to remind the King of his existence and the néed for him to make adequate provision for his education and future. Lady Green's assessment of her son mirrored that of many an anxious mother and she wrote to Lord Danby of her concerns viz:

*'knoweing his nature perfectly good, but easily drawne to liberties pleasing to
youth if he have not a constraint put upon him by one he valwes'.*

However, her main concern was *'to see him well educated'* and to this
end, in 1674, the King appointed Sydney Lodge as his tutor and
Robert Cheeke his governor. The effect on the young man was
remarkable, for within several months his education had come along
by leaps and bounds and King Charles considered the possibility of
sending him up to Cambridge, only to change his mind.

It would seem that this young man was very spoilt and ran up
huge debts, particularly tailors' bills, which his father ultimately had
to settle. But Don Carlos's visit to England was all too brief, for
in late 1674 he returned to the continent with his tutor in the
royal yacht *Portsmouth* for a period of study in France, accompanied
by Robert Paston, the younger brother of his brother-in-law Lord
Paston. They were royally received by the Governor of Calais, the
Duc de Charrost, and all the garrison towns that they passed before
heading for the south of France. Once there, Paston wrote to his
mother that Don Carlos

*'is most altered in everything for the better, as it cannot be imagined; insomuch
that the last post Mr Cheeke writt to the King, and did give him a very good
character of him, wch I hope will make the King more kind to him'.*

Paston's praise was endorsed by his tutor

*'My Lord has made a considerable improvement; I endeavour to make his
Ldsp knowing in ye latine; to yt end I have advis'd him to ye reading of
Tullies offices; wherein he'll meet with instructions fitting to his quality; he
is now reading besides Tullie, Sallust, Aurelius Victor etc. I intend shortly to
invite his Lordsp to ye reading Caesar's commentaries etc'.*

After several years in France, Plymouth became restive and wrote
to Lord Danby expressing his hope that the King would send him
on campaign, but nothing came of the appeal. Instead he became
embroiled in an incident with the Duke of Somerset which made
King Charles very angry and determined that the young man should

be sent home. The result, however, was gratifying in many ways for him because the King allowed him to serve as a volunteer in the Prince of Orange's army. On his return he further tarnished his reputation by fighting a duel with Sir George Hewitt in 1679, Lord Mordaunt being his second. His behaviour, so reminiscent of his half brother Monmouth during his early years at court, angered the King who declared '*he shall make him know he hath no rank but what he has given him*'. Nevertheless, in July 1680 he was appointed Colonel of the 4th Regiment of Foot.

As he had done with the Duke of Monmouth, King Charles took great care to select a suitable wife for his son. By the end of 1678 the negotiations for his marriage to Lord Danby's daughter were completed and they were married at Wimbledon in Surrey. Lady Bridget Osborne, was the second daughter of Thomas (Osborne), Duke of Leeds, better known as Thomas Danby, Lord Treasurer to Charles' father. A document relating to their marriage and signed by Charles II emerged recently when sold in Nottingham in February 2003. The marriage was described by Robert Paston in the following manner

> '*I have to give my Lord Plimouth joy, who was this day sennight married at Wimbledon very privately; his settlements are yet to make, for there is but 4,000 l a year more yet given him, which is out of the excise; he has his apartment at the Cockpit & lies it out every day till 12 o'clock*'

Shortly thereafter the King allowed the Earl to serve as a volunteer at Tangier, acquired by King Charles in 1661/2 as part of Catherine of Braganza's dowry. In return for which he (Charles) was obliged to

> '*take the interest of Portugal and all its dominions to heart, defending the same with his utmost power by sea and land even as England itself*'.

In June 1663 Charles had duly fulfilled his obligations to the full when a force of three thousand men, mainly Cromwellian veterans, defeated the army of Don Juan of Austria, illegitimate son of Philip IV of Spain, at the battle of Amegial, thereby greatly assisting in securing Portuguese independence from Spain.

The chief command for this expedition had been given to the Earl of Mulgrave, who later married Plymouth's cousin Lady Katherine Darnley, but the decision to send the Earl to Tangier was to have fateful consequences for in October 1680, aged only 23, he died there of a '*bloody flux*' whilst the garrison was repulsing the forces of the Alcaide of Alcazar, commander of the Moorish army, sent to capture the town. It was a sad and premature end to what had promised to be a glorious chapter in this young man's life. In Tangier he had been described as '*a fine youth with a great deal of witt and is finely bred*' and he even rated a mention in Pepys' diary. His body was returned to England and was buried at Westminster Abbey, whereupon, having no children, all his honours became extinct.

There are conflicting reports about his younger sister, Catherine FitzCharles, who is often confused with her half-sister Cecilia FitzRoy (*see* page 73), the daughter of Barbara Villiers. Catherine died young, whilst Cecilia, became a nun at Dunkirk under the name Dame Cecilia OSB.

Anne, Countess of Sussex
(*née* Palmer, later FitzRoy)
(1661–1722)

Anne FitzRoy, was the eldest daughter of the notorious Barbara Villiers or Palmer, later to become Countess of Castlemaine and Duchess of Cleveland (1641–1709). Her mother, a notable beauty had an unenviable reputation as a very promiscuous woman, with a dozen or more known lovers to her credit, including, it is alleged, Philip Stanhope, Earl of Chesterfield, Charles II, Harry Jermyn, Charles Hart (the actor), Jacob Hall (tightrope dancer), John Churchill (the soldier) and many many more.

Anne was born on 25 February 1660/1, almost exactly nine months after the glorious restoration of King Charles II. However, she was not conceived in London on the night of the Restoration, 28 May 1660, as has always been alleged, but at the court of the exiled King Charles on the continent. Anne's date of birth indicates that she was probably conceived at The Hague whither Charles had gone on 14 May 1660 in preparation for his return to England. Barbara and her husband Roger Palmer arrived at the exiled court in February 1660, with an offer of £1,000 to the King, for which Palmer expected a percentage as he had a gay wife and a small income. Within weeks her '*sinister and exotic beauty*' had captivated and ensnared the King. Thomas Hearne the antiquarian wrote of her:

> '*The Dutchess was certainly a Lady of admirable beauty and in all other respects very fit for so accomplished a Prince as K. Charles II was, had her Extract been equal to his, and her virtues been greater. Yet she writ but a very bad Hand, nor were the Things she writ done with much spirit. She was so little versed in the Art of inditing, that she could not spell. She could talk as well as any body, and write, even at best as badly. Her Thoughts were gone when she come to take time to committ them to writing, but nothing was more gay and pleasing as they came in Discourse from her Mouth.*'

When she met Charles, Barbara was a bride of just thirteen months, but he was not her first love; that prize went to Philip Stanhope, Earl of Chesterfield. He is often credited with the paternity of Barbara's first child, but as the following account shows the assertion cannot be true. In January 1660, at the height of his affair with Barbara, the Earl was obliged to flee England after killing another gentleman in a duel over '*a sprightly mare*'. On reaching the Continent he went straight to Paris where he wrote to Charles offering his services. Eventually, on receipt of a favourable reply, he then travelled to Breda, to which Charles had moved with his meagre court in April 1660. Once there, he obtained the King's pardon and immediately returned to France. In the meantime Barbara's passion for Chesterfield had cooled considerably, and her fateful meeting with Charles killed it completely.

However, contemporary gossip still attributed Anne's paternity to the Earl of Chesterfield, but as he was in France at the time of her conception he cannot have been her father. In fact he did not return to the King and Court again until the day he departed from Holland for England – 23 May 1660 – and Anne was conceived during his absence. Barbara had no doubts about her paternity and many years later wrote to Charles

> '*that as she is yours, I shall allwayes haue som remains of that kindness I had formerly for I can hate nothing that is yours*'.

Legally, however, she was the child of Barbara's husband, Roger Palmer, shortly to become Earl of Castlemaine, in recompense no doubt for his timely donation to the King's coffers and the services of his wife to the king. As he had not yet separated from his wife, Anne therefore bore his surname. In an officially recorded pedigree, the Palmer family declared that

> '*The Lady Anne Palmer daughter to the Earle of Castlemaine & Barbara, Countess of Castlemaine, was borne 25 Feby being Shrove Munday about 10 of the clock 1660.*'

However, Charles acknowledged her paternity in 1673 when he granted arms to both her and her younger sister, Charlotte (*see* page 63), together with the surname of FitzRoy. In the patent, he described them as '*his dear and natural daughters by the Duchess of Cleveland*', and granted them the precedence as daughters of a duke, all of which helped to cement their mother's position at Court. But despite this, Roger Palmer always regarded Anne with affection and made her his trustee and chief beneficiary under his will.

At the age of eight Barbara sent her daughter to the Queen Mother's monastery at Chaillot in France for her education, but Henrietta Maria's death the following year cut short her visit. In 1671 her mother tried again and this time sent Anne to the Abbey of Pontoise, in Normandy, where Lady Neville was Abbess, only returning to London in November 1672. On her return there was a new arrrival in the nursery, another sister Lady Barbara FitzRoy, born the previous June. Two years later aged only thirteen, Anne was married at Hampton Court, with a dowry of £20,000 from the King, to Thomas (Lennard), 15th Lord Dacre, who was created that year Earl of Sussex; unfortunately the dowry was never paid.

The young Earl 'was Lord of the Bedchamber to King Charles & coming very young to Court fell (as was natural enough to do at his age) into the expensive way of living he found the fashion there, and through this unlucky setting out, and the neglecting afterwards to tak a proper care of his affairs from an easiness & Indolence in his disposition: not to be excused (as he neither wanted parts or capacity), and by great losses at Play, he was so much entangled and distressed that at different times he was obliged to sell several of his estates etc'

Of Lady Sussex's character there is an abundance of evidence. She had by all accounts inherited her mother's beauty, but she was wilful and extravagant. Only three years later her behaviour had so enraged her husband, in particular her intimacy with the Duchess de Mazarin, that he decided to retire into the country. The cause of his displeasure was twofold. The first related to her friendship with the beautiful Hortense Mancini, Duchess de Mazarin, who had been introduced to court by Ralph Montagu with the intention of her making her the King's mistress. She had arrived at the beginning 1676 and within seven months had befriended Lady Sussex whose apartments, formerly her mother's, were immediately above the King's, with entry by a private staircase. Soon the French Ambassador was able to inform his master that:

'The King goes nearly every day to visit Madame Sussex, whom Madame Mazarin is nursing. I happened to be there the day before yesterday when he came in. As soon as he came in Madame Mazarin went and whispered to him with a great air of familiarity, and she kept it up all the time the conversation was general, and never called him Your Majesty once. At the end of a quarter of an hour His Britannic Majesty sat on the end of the bed, and as I was alone I thought it proper to retire. But I remain convinced that it is not without foundation that the most enlightened courtiers believe that the King their master desires to profit by his opportunities'

Lord Sussex was naturally dismayed by his wife's role in bringing the King and Madame Mazarin together, and was even more so, after an incident in St James's Park when it was reported that:

> '*She and Madam Mazarine have privately learnt to fence, and went down into St James's Park the other day with drawn swords under their night gowns, which they drew out and made several fine passes with, to the admiration of several men which was lookers on in the Park*'.

> '*Lady Sussex is put by her mother into a religious house in France, and she means certainly to come hither in the spring either to ajust things better between her and her Lord or to get his consent that her daughter may goe into orders*'.

But within a short time Lady Sussex had managed to win the sympathy of the English Ambassador and his wife, who promptly offered her the hospitality of their home in Paris. The Duchess of Cleveland was incensed by her daughter's behaviour and put the worst possible interpretation on the whole affair. When the news reached England the Duchess's version of the whole affair became common gossip:

> '*After amusing herself for a time with hunting, hawking, nyne pins, crekkit matches etc, she became quite tired both of the country and of her husband and before the end of the year definitely left him to go and live with her mother in Paris. During that lady's temporary absence she supplanted her in the affections of Ralph Montagu [afterwards Duke of Montagu], then ambassador there, who lived with her 'in open scandal' to the wonder of the French court and the high displeasure of this.*'

However, Henry Savile's account was hotly denied by the ambassador's wife, who leapt to the defence of Lady Sussex and claimed that she had been cruelly slandered, because she had invited her into her Paris home on account of her ill health and depleted finances. Unfortunately for the ambassador, Ralph Montagu, the Duchess of Cleveland wrote furiously to King Charles complaining of his behaviour. The end result was that he was recalled from his post and banished from Court. Four years later Lady Sussex returned to England and went back to her husband, only to be ungenerously referred to in Rochester's poem:

'And here would time permit me I could tell
Of Cleveland, Portsmouth, Crofts & Arundel,
Moll Howard, Su---x, Lady Grey and Nell
Strangers to good but bosom friends to ill,
As boundless in their lusts as in their will.'

Fortunately the reunion was a success and Anne duly presented her husband with three more children, the first of which was a son Charles, who was baptised at Windsor Castle in June 1682, with the King as sponsor. Despite her past behaviour the King continued to be kind to her, and a week after her confinement, it was reported that he had bought Lord Falkenbridge's house for her.

At the revolution in 1688 Lady Sussex finally separated from her husband, a staunch Protestant, and joined her uncle King James in exile at St Germain-en-Laye, where she attended the Queen as one of her Ladies in Waiting. She took her two daughters with her despite the non payment of her annuity. The Earl, who was a Gentleman of the Bedchamber, was eventually forced to sell his Hurstmonceux and other estates in 1708 as a result of excessive litigation, reckless extravagance and gambling losses. He died aged in 1715, aged 61, without male issue at Chevening, Kent, when the earldom became extinct, but the much older barony of Dacre fell into abeyance between his two daughters and co-heirs, Barbara and Anne, his sons having died young. His widow, who, judging from her portraits at Belhus and by the Swede, M. Dahl, was a very handsome woman, died in 1722. Her senior representative today is Anthony, 6th Viscount Hampden and Rachel, the Baroness Dacre (27th), widow of William Douglas-Home, the playwright.

Sir Charles FitzRoy, formerly Palmer, KG, 1st Duke of Southampton & 2nd Duke of Cleveland (1662–1730)

Of all the King's illegitimate issue the Duke of Southampton was the least blessed with those qualities that could equip him to make a mark in the world. He would, according to Dean Prideaux, '...*ever be very simple, and scarce, I believe, ever attain to the reputation of not being thought a fool'*. This want of intellect was due, if John Aubrey is to be believed, to an unfortunate incident in his youth:

> '*The Duke of Southampton who was a most lovely youth, had two foreteeth that grew out, very unhandsome. His cruel mother caused him to be bound fast in a chair and had them drawn out; which has caused the want of his understanding'.*

One of '*Barbara's Brats'* as Nell Gwyn was to describe him, he was the eldest son of King Charles II by Barbara Villiers, the daughter of William, Viscount Grandison, who had earlier married Roger Palmer, later Earl of Castlemaine; she was later created Duchess of Cleveland in 1670. Not all of her contemporaries admired her character, one in particular Antoine Hamilton castigated '*the crudeness of her manners, her ridiculous haughtiness and her perpetual suspicions and petty passions'*. Another Bishop Burnet wrote of her

> '*She was a woman of great beauty, but most enormously vicious and ravenous; foolish but imperious; very uneasy to the King, and always carrying on with other men'.*

Charles FitzRoy first saw the light of day in June 1662, shortly after the marriage of his father King Charles to Catherine of Braganza. Initially baptised by a Roman Catholic priest at the behest of Lord Castlemaine, he was subsequently baptised on 16 June 1662 at St Margaret's Westminster, with the King as his sponsor, declaring '*He is my son'*. The other sponsors were the Earl of Oxford and Lady Suffolk. However, he was entered in the register as the son of Lord Castlemaine:

*'1662 June 18 Charles Palmer Ld Limricke s to ye right honorble Roger Earl
of Castlemaine by Barbara'.*

As Barbara was married to Roger Palmer at the time, Charles was
passed off as Castlemaine's son, with his legal father's courtesy title
of Lord Limerick. His real paternity was not recognised by King
Charles II until 1670, when he took the surname of FitzRoy and
was styled Earl of Southampton, the courtesy title of his mother,
who had been created Duchess of Cleveland. Young Charles himself
had to wait until 1675 to be created Duke of Southampton in his
own right, although he had been appointed a KG and granted arms
two years earlier.

Of his education little is known other than that he was educated at Oxford, but his mother's attitude to learning in general was
unequivocal

*'I care for no education other than what nature and I myself can give him
which will be sufficient accomplishment for a married man'.*

Indeed her meddling was notorious. On one occasion Humphrey
Prideaux reported that

*'My friend Mr Bernard, who went into France to attend upon two bastards
of Cleveland, hath been so affronted and abused there by that insolent woman
that he hath been forced to quit that employment and return'.*

When the Duke reached the age of nine in 1671, his mother decided
that he should be married. She chose as his bride Mary, the daughter
and heiress of Sir Henry Wood, Bt, Clerk of the Green Cloth, who
possessed extensive landed estates in Suffolk producing an income
of approximately £4,000 a year. This ceremony had to be repeated
in 1677 when both parties were of age, but only three years later, in
1680, the young bride died of smallpox at the age of sixteen, without
any issue. After much litigation, her great fortune passed to her
husband who remained a widower for the next fourteen years until
he married in 1694 Anne, the daughter of Sir William Pulteney.

The latter was one of the leading members of the House of Commons during the reign of King Charles II, and his grandson and namesake was created Earl of Bath in 1742 despite being an opponent of the government then in power under Sir Robert Walpole. By his second wife, the Duke, who as his mother's eldest son and heir, had succeeded her as Duke of Cleveland upon her death from dropsy in 1709, had three sons and three daughters. The eldest son William, duly succeeded to his father's dukedoms, but both became extinct upon his own death in 1771, his other brothers having died young.

Unlike his sister Lady Sussex, (*see* page 50) the Duke of Southampton did not follow his uncle King James to France in 1688. Indeed it would have been folly to have done so given that all of his income came from the state. Nevertheless he, together with the Dukes of Grafton and Northumberland plus the Earls of Lichfield and Yarmouth, opposed the offer of the Crown to William of Orange in 1689, and he was suspected of intriguing for the restoration of his uncle James II in 1691. However, he signed the 1696 Association following the attempt by Jacobite agents to assassinate William, and thereafter, to all intents and purposes, he accepted the new regime, despite his oath of allegiance to King James.

Like his sister Lady Lichfield, (*see* page 63) no scandal appears to have sullied the Duke's good name and to all appearances he was a sober and happily married man. However, the character of his second wife was the subject of much ridicule and derision on more than one occasion. The first, whilst her husband was still alive, occurred in 1727, when she developed an overwhelming passion for her husband's nephew Lord Sidney Beauclerk, 5th son of the 1st Duke of St Albans (*see* page 75). The event was recorded by Lady Mary Wortley Montagu in a letter to Lady Mar:

> '*The Man in England that gives the greatest pleasure and the greatest pain is a youth of Royal Blood with all his grandmothers beauty wit and good qualitys; in short he is Nell Guinn in person with the sex altered and occasions such a fracas amongst Ladies of Gallantry that it passes belief. You will state to hear of her Grace of Cleveland at the head of them. ... In good ernest she has turned Lady Grace & family out of doors to make room for*

him and there he lies like leafe gold upon a pill. There was no so violent &
so indiscreet a passion'.

At the time the Duchess was 63 and Lord Sidney was 25. The Duke's
reaction to this affair is not on record. That the Duchess was indeed
a woman of strong passions is further illustrated by her treatment
of her eldest daughter Barbara, whom she disowned. The reason for
this is unknown, but the poor woman died at the age of 38 and was
buried in the choir of the collegiate church of Manchester. Buried
with her was a gentleman named William Dawson, who in his will,
explained his reasons why

*'to testify his gratitude to a kind benefactress, but because his fate was similar to hers;
for she was disowned by her mother, and he was disinherited by his father'.*

Her Grace was singularly unfortunate in her relationships with her
daughters. When she married for a second time in 1733, none of her
children were made aware of her intention to marry again or invited
to the ceremony. Her second daughter Lady Grace discovering the
truth in the following manner:

*'I din'd to day at Capel More's with Lady Grace Vanes, who cryed at relating
Her mother's marriage which she did not know till last Saterday when she
din'd with her grace. As she was going away she desir'd Mr Southcoute to
carry him (sic) home, but he answered that he was at home already, for the
Duchess had done him the honour to marry him. As the Duchess had ask'd
her to return the next day to meet the Duke and Duchess of Cleveland, she
went and when she told the Duke that her mother was married to Mr Sout.,
he cry'd pho pho, it cant be I am not such a fool neither as to believe that;
and she says that all she do will never make him believe it.'*

A few months later in 1733, Her Grace's youngest daughter Anne
dishonoured the family name further by marrying her footman, John
Paddy. Fortunately the Duke was spared all of these problems for he
had died three years earlier in 1730, in his 69th year and was buried
in Westminster Abbey. His widow and sole legatee, was to survive
him for another sixteen years.

Sir Henry Fitzroy, KG, formerly Palmer, 1st Duke of Grafton (1663–90)

The Duke of Buckingham described his King as *'father of his people'* adding *sotto-voce 'of a good many of them'*. Rather in the same vein, Rochester dared to write:

> *Nor are his high Desires above his strength;*
> *His sceptre and his – are of a length.*
> *And she that plays with one may sway the other,*
> *And make him a little wiser than his brother.*

Charles II had no less than five children by Barbara Villiers, and no less than thirteen prime ministers descend from Villiers stock as indeed does the present Queen.

Henry was born in 1663, but in view of his mother's fearsome reputation, Charles delayed in recognising him as his son for some time and it was not until 1675, aged twelve, that he was created Duke of Grafton. Three years earlier in 1672, he had been created Earl of Euston, in recognition of his marriage to five year old Lady Isabella Bennett, the only daughter and sole heiress of 1st Earl of Arlington, (which included the Euston estate), from which Henry's earldom was taken. Despite some opposition from the Arlington family, they were re-married in 1679, when Evelyn described it as the union of *'the sweetest and most beautiful child'* to a *'boy that had been rudely bred'* He was appointed a KG the following year.

Despite Charles II's alleged reluctance to accept young Henry as his child, portraits of him show a strong resemblance to the King. The rumours that Charles Berkeley was the father of another of *'Barbara's Brats'* as Nell Gwyn described him, have no foundation whatsoever. That Charles Berkeley spent a great deal of time with Lady Castlemaine is beyond dispute, he was, after all, a favourite of the King and the Duke of York. According to Bishop Burnet his relationship with the King and Lady Castlemaine was of an exceedingly dubious nature for the said gentleman and Sir Henry Bennet *'had the management of the mistress* [Lady Castlemaine] *and all the Earl of Clarendon's enemies came about them, chief of whom were Buckingham and Bristol'*. Others, including

Dr Clerke, simply declared that the gentleman's greatness '*is only his being pimp to the King, and to my Lady Castlemaine*'.

Henry was '*a kockish, idle boy*' who displayed all of his mother's tempestuous and arrogant nature in his youth. In character he was well suited to the military and naval life, and surprisingly in time developed into, according to one contemporary:

> '*A man of good sense and extreme good nature, affable to all, without partiality, and ready to support men of worth without regard to the unhappy factions in the fleet with which he served, for he judged only of each man according to his capacity and because he himself was educated to the sea. A very gallant man, his courage and skill extremely recommended him to the esteem and affection of all the seamen, with whom he was very familiar, and by who he was extremely beloved, for he was always well disposed towards them and often joined with them in their rough sports*'.

Clearly he had his father's common touch, but on occasions he was prone to the excesses of character displayed all too readily by his mother. One notable instance was the episode of his brother Northumberland's marriage (*see* page 67) to the beautiful widow Catherine Lucy. No sooner was he married to her, than Grafton persuaded him to spirit her away to a convent in Ghent, much to her anger and the consternation of the Court. In two duels he also killed both his opponents – namely, Jack Talbot, brother of the Earl of Shrewsbury and Mr Stanley, brother of the Earl of Derby. Both events took place in 1686, the latter because Mr Stanley had stated that the Duchess of Cleveland, had just given birth to a son by her then lover, Cardell Goodman.

Young Henry, described by one contemporary as '*exceeding handsome, by far surpassing any of the King's other natural issue*' became, as we have seen, a brave and resourceful sailor. Evelyn described him as '*a plain useful and robust officer, and were he polished, a tolerable man*'. Although serving as Colonel 1st Foot Guards from 1681–88 and promoted to Brigadier General of Foot, Henry served predominantly at sea and took part in a number of expeditions. He served as Vice Admiral of England from 1682–89 upon the death of Prince Rupert, an Elder Brother of Trinity House and sometime

Master, Governor of the Isle of Wight and Lord High Constable
for the Coronation of James II as well as carrying the Orb at
William III's Coronation.

In 1683 he became captain of the *Grafton* and the following year
visited King Louis XIV, and at some personal danger gained military
experience at the Siege of Luxembourg. He distinguished himself
by commanding a part of the King's forces which suppressed the
rebellion of his half brother the Duke of Monmouth (*see* page 36),
and he narrowly escaped with his life at Philips Norton in Somerset
in 1686 and was present at Sedgmoor the following month.

Although openly supporting his uncle James II, acting as conduc-
tor to the Papal Nuncio D'Adda on his public entry to London in
1687, and accompanying his uncle on a march against William, he
soon turned against him when Dartmouth had been given command
of the fleet in preference to him. Thereafter he excited discontent and
joined the conspiracy, later running away with John Churchill, later
1st Duke of Marlborough, to join William of Orange at Axminster
in 1688, who duly restored him to his regiment. Henry, along with
most of his other half-brothers, supported the cause of the Prince of
Orange and he was one of the first to desert his uncle King James
II when William III landed in 1688.

His brilliant action in *Grafton* at the Battle of Beachy Head in
1690 saved the Dutch from the French and was much praised. But
only three months later, as a volunteer under Churchill, now Lord
Marlborough, he was mortally wounded during the storming of the
City of Cork, dying a fortnight afterwards, aged only 27.

Grafton was regarded as the most popular and ablest of the sons
of Charles II, his strong and decided character, his reckless daring,
and rough but honest temperament, caused him to be widely
lamented. His widow, by whom he had an only son and heir,
was painted by Kneller and Lely and was among the 'Beauties of
Hampton Court'. She went on to marry Sir Thomas Hanmer, a
Tory statesman, but having become Countess of Arlington in her
own right upon her father's death, it was in this title that she was
thereafter known.

However, the family motto: *Et Decus et Pretium Recti* (the orna-
ment and recompense of virtue) does not seem particularly apt but

accompanies the Royal arms of King Charles II *debruised by a baton sinister,* which were granted to him.

Of Charles's three sons by Barbara Villiers, only one, Henry founded an enduring and direct noble line. His descendants include Augustus Henry, 3rd Duke who became Prime Minister from 1766–70 and thereafter Lord Privy Seal. The present male line descendant is Hugh Denis Charles, KG, 11th Duke, (born 1919), who has been actively involved in preserving historic buildings and churches and cathedrals and still lives at the ancestral seat, Euston Hall in Suffolk. His wife continues to serve as Mistress of the Robes to HM The Queen as she has done since 1967.

Lady Charlotte FitzRoy, formerly Palmer, later Countess of Lichfield (1664–1718)

Lady Charlotte FitzRoy, a notable beauty in her day, was the fourth child of Barbara Villiers by Charles II, and reputedly the King's favourite daughter. She was born in 1664 with the surname of Palmer, but was not formally recognised by the King until she was eight, when with her older sister Anne (*see* page 50), she was granted in 1673 the surname of FitzRoy, the rank of a duke's daughter and granted arms. In the patent they were described as '*his dear and natural daughters by the Duchess of Cleveland*'.

Charlotte had an angelic face as shown in Lely's painting of her *ca* 1672 with an unidentified servant. Two years later, aged only ten, she was married to Sir Edward Henry Lee, Bt, who, in anticipation, had been created Earl of Lichfield. The King provided her with a dowry of £18,000 together with an annual allowance of £2,000. In 1676 she accompanied her mother to France and was placed in a convent for her education, but returned the following year, aged only twelve, to marry her husband for the second time.

Lichfield was a Gentleman of the Bedchamber and Colonel of the 12th Foot and 1st Foot Guards and Lord Lieutenant of Oxfordshire, but being a staunch Tory, he retired from office at the Revolution. When James II retired to France in 1688, Lichfield was one of the few loyal peers of the realm to attend him during his last days in

England – the others were Lord Ailesbury, the Earl of Dumbarton and Lord Arran, subsequently Duke of Hamilton. The event was recorded by Lady Dartmouth who wrote to her husband that '*Lord Midleton and Lord Alsbery and Lichfield attended him* (James II) *to the last with great tendernesse...*' Like her husband, the Countess was a staunch Jacobite and immediately wrote to the Queen, offering her services to which she replied:

> '*I hope you do not think I am so unreasonable as to expect you should leave your husband and children to come to me. I am in too miserable a condition to wish that my friends should follow it, if they can be in their own country ... No change or condition shall ever lessen the real kindness I have for you*'.

The Countess had also been present at the birth of the Princess of Wales prior to the Queen departing for France and could thus vouch for his legitimacy. Lord Lichfield was universally regarded as a man of honour and principle a fact that was noted by Mackay in his *Characters*:

> '*A man of honour, never could take the oaths to King William; hath good sense; is not yet come to Queen Anne's court; 50 years old.*'

However, in 1702, Lady Lichfield did ask Queen Anne if she could attend Court but was told not until her husband had taken the oaths.

As a young girl Charlotte was ill used by her mother. On one occasion she

> '*being in her mother's coach in the park happened to break the glass of the coach and thereupon her father the King passing by in another coach, happened to stop and asking his daughter what made her cry so (for she cryed as soon as the glass was broke) she answered, because she was afraid that her mother would beat her soundly. Upon this the King took her into his own coach and shewed a particular dislike of the Duchess's ill usage, by sending an express message to her never to strike her more, under pain of loosing his sight and favour for the future, if she should offer any such thing*'.

Lady Lichfield proved to be a model wife and presented her husband with thirteen sons and five daughters during their thirty year marriage, but like all large families, not all survived the rigours of childhood – three sons and one daughter died in infancy. All of their births and the names of the godparents were recorded by their mother. King Charles stood godfather to the eldest son and daughter. The Duke of Northumberland (Lady Lichfield's brother – *see* page 67) was also a godfather to two of the children as was his brother the Duke of Grafton (*see* page 60). Several of the Countess's half-brothers and sisters also stood as godparents viz: The Duke of Richmond (*see* page 88), the Earl and Countess of Derwentwater (*see* page 92) and the Duke of St Albans (*see* page 75). But even this was not enough to secure the Lichfield line which was extinct by 1776 with the death of her 13th son, the 4th Earl, who died as a result of a fall from his horse when hunting. Her present day representative is the 22nd Viscount Dillon (born 1973).

Like her mother, of whom King Charles used to say that if *she had had as much sense and wit as she had beauty, she had certainly ruined mankind*, Charlotte was not spared the traumas of parenthood. Her eldest child and namesake, born when she was just fourteen years old, married at a very early age the eldest son of Lord Baltimore. She was according to a contemporary account a *'comely, portly fair woman' 'of a sweet and courteous humour and disposition'* and *'a tender and affectionate mother to her children'*.

In later life, despite her large girth, she was still considered to be very handsome. In the first six years of their marriage Lady Baltimore bore her husband four sons and two daughters, but unfortunately after the birth of the second child, his attitude towards her changed. Initially he was *'so fond of her that tis said he scars sturs out of her chamber'*, however after the birth of their son in 1699, he took a mistress and began to beat her. In an attempt to please her husband Lady Charlotte became a Catholic to the intense grief of her father Lord Lichfield, who declared that

> *'my joy in the birth of this little boy is quallifyed by ... my daughter turning papist being a great affliction to me who had taken the utmost care to have her well grounded in the Protestant religion'.*

In the style befitting her grandmother, Lady Baltimore retaliated by taking several lovers, among them her grandmother's husband Robert 'Beau' Feilding, Count Briancon and Count Castelli, each of whom fathered a child on her. The relationship with Beau Feilding began during the five months she stayed with her grandmother, the Duchess of Cleveland, from November 1705 to March 1706. Her presence there was surprising given the latter's reputation. In March 1706 she moved to lodgings in Westminster where Feilding visited her amost every day and it was not long before she became pregnant. In September she was ejected from her lodging by her landlady and found alternative accommodation in Stratton Street, Westminster where Feilding continued to visit her. However, shortly after she had settled in, she began to receive visits from '*a tall lusty brown man and a very civil well bred gentleman*' called Count Briançon. Charlotte's child, a daughter, was born in April 1707 and maintained by Feilding but their relationship was to all intents and purposes over.

The following year, Charlotte presented Count Briançon with a son who died shortly thereafter. At the end of the year the Count also died suddenly and Charlotte found herself without a protector and with only £200 a year to live on. However, by the end of 1709 she had found another in the person of Count Castelli. She eventually remarried and died in her 42nd year after a bout of dancing, being six feet tall

> '*yet withall very nimble and active*' having shown '*great agility that night in dancing, tho' she went to bed extraordinary well, and slept extraordinary well, yet an alteration followed next day, and she continued languishing more than a month, and then died*'.

Lady Lichfield was famous for her beauty when young, and later for her '*very great sense and virtue*'. She was painted by Lely and Simon Verelst and engraved by Peter Vandebanc and in miniature by Richard Gibson. Thomas Hearne describes how she used (at the request of His Majesty) to scratch the King's head, when he slept in the elbow chair.

Sir George FitzRoy, formerly Palmer, KG, 1st Duke of Northumberland (1665–1716)

George was the third and youngest son of the infamous Barbara Villiers and King Charles II. He was born in 1665 'in a Fellow's chamber' at Merton College, Oxford, and like his brothers and sisters was given initially the surname of Palmer. He was not recognised by the King as his son until 1673 when he was granted arms in the surname of FitzRoy and put in special remainder to his elder brother's earldom of Euston. The following year he was created Earl of Northumberland in his own right and in 1683 Duke of Northumberland and a KG.

If John Evelyn is to be believed he was

> *'the most accomplished and worth owning of Charles II's children, and 'a young gentleman of good capacity, well bred, civil and modest…extraordinarily handsome and well shaped and skilled in horsemanship'.*

His portrait by W. Wissing (as engraved in Doyle's *Official Baronage*), supports this, and Mackay describes him as *'a tall black man, like his father, the King'* adding that *'he is a man of honour, nice in paying his debts'*.

When Northumberland reached his eleventh year, the King sought to arrange his betrothal to a great heiress Lady Elizabeth Percy, but her grandmother objected on the grounds that he was a bastard. Annoyed by the grandmother's opposition and impatient at the delay, the Duchess of Cleveland took it upon herself to call on Ralph Montagu the English Ambassador in Paris, Lady Betty's stepfather, and in order to assist her endeavours, proceeded to befriend his wife, a task in which she was eminently successful. So much so, that Lord Danby was able to write to Montagu and declare that as

> *'The Duchess of Cleveland and your lady are upon such good terms with one another … He believes the notion might perhaps now be agreeable to your lady, though it hath not been so formerly'* [He then concluded] *'If yet the same*

difficulties remain … His Majesty will look upon it as a good service if your Excellency can procure it for Lord Plymouth.'

However young George was not without competition as Montagu related:

'All the [Villiers] family do reckon that the King has engaged himself to My Lady Duchess of Cleveland to do all he can to procure this match for my Lord Northumberland, who himself is already cunning enough to be enquiring of me after My Lady Betty Percy, and has taken such an aversion to My Lord Ogle about the report, that when they meet at my house he is always ready to laugh or make mouths at him, so that the governor now will never scare let them meet'.

Unfortunately despite all her best endeavours, the Duchess's carefully laid plans came to naught when she discovered that the Ambassador had been sheltering her errant daughter Lady Sussex, whom she had placed in a convent. Naturally the Duchess put the worst possible interpretation on this situation, and wrote furiously to the King demanding Montagu's recall. As a result Northumberland did not marry Lady Betty and for a good number of years afterwards all thoughts of making a splendid marriage were put aside.

In 1681, at the age of sixteen, Northumberland made his first trip to the Continent without parental supervision, on this occasion taking with him a Mr Cornwallis and a Mr Lewis, his chaplain Mr Wickail and governor, a Frenchman, one Monsieur Lachevaye. He travelled to Venice in 1682, when he was in receipt of Secret Service funds, and joined the Army in 1683 being present as a volunteer at the Siege of Luxembourg. On the journey there he had the mortification of seeing one of his companions, a nephew of Richard Rigby, killed when a cannon ball blew off his head whilst sitting down to dinner with his fellow officers. His gallantry and bravery were duly noted at the siege by Lord Preston:

'The Duke of Northumberland is given a very honourable account by all those here of his behaviour at Courtnay where he was all the first night at the head of those who opened the trenches'.

The following year, 1684, Lord Preston again sent to the King a report of his progress:

> *'This King [Louis XIV] hath on all occasions honoured him [Northumberland] with particular marks of his esteem and since the business of Courtnay hath never failed to speak very advantageously of him and I do not believe that any one hath in so short a time gained more the value of this Court (which as your Majesty knoweth is not over favourable to strangers) than hath his Grace done...'*

Northumberland became Colonel of the 2nd troop of Horse Guards from 1685–89 and 1712–15. He was Colonel of the Royal Horse Guards in 1702 and became successively Brigadier General, Major General and finally Lieutenant General in 1710.

He was also a Gentleman of the Bedchamber to James II and under William III was appointed Lord Lieutenant of both Surrey and Berkshire, Constable of Windsor Castle and Ranger of Windsor Park, acting Great Chamberlain, Chief Butler of England and a Privy Councillor.

The sudden death of his father, King Charles, in 1685 affected the fortunes of all his bastard children, including Northumberland. On his deathbed he particularly recommend the young Duke to his uncle the Duke of York saying '*I desire brother, that you will be kind to George, as I am sure he will be honest and loyal.*' He was according to Thomas Hearne, the antiquary '*the only son who did not degenerate from good principles*'.

The following year, 1686, aged just twenty-one, Northumberland secretly married Catherine Lucy, a Catholic, described by the Countess of Norton as:

> *'rich only in beauty, which though much prized, will hardly maintain the quality of a Duchess'.*

She was the widow of Thomas Lucy, of Charlecote, and daughter of Robert Wheatley, of Bracknell, Berkshire who was allegedly a poultry merchant, but for which there is not a scrap of evidence. He had seen all his three daughters make good marriages, the first, Anne, to the

Earl of Dumbarton, whilst the second, Elizabeth, became sister-in-law of the Duke of Berwick. King James was extremely angry having just negotiated a marriage for his young nephew with a daughter of the Duke of Newcastle, a sister of the Lord Ogle, who had been his rival in the affections of Lady Betty Percy.

In response to this, Northumberland and his brother the Duke of Grafton attempted to redeem the situation by conspiring to place Catherine in a convent. The episode caused a major stir in Court circles, and the events surrounding it were reported avidly by numerous correspondents to Sir William Trumbull, the then English Ambassador in Paris. The first was John Mountstevens who reported that:

> 'The Duke of Northumberland went abroad in his coach this morning to take the air with his new Duchess and about Chelsey (sic) the Duke of Grafton met with them and they all went aboard a barge that lay there for Gravesend. It is said that she intends to put herself into a nunnery beyond sea'.

Six days later Dr Wynne wrote to Sir William informing him that '*The King is said to have expressed his concern for the Duke, that he should be imposed upon by the lady*'. On the 3rd of April 1686 the arrival of the errant Dukes was duly noted in a newsletter:

> 'The Dukes of Northumberland and Grafton after having landed and disposed of the Lady at Ostend; her relations are mightily concerned at it and are resolved to prosecute the matter to the utmost, which if they do, it is believed they will be obliged to fetch her back again'.

Dismayed and angered by his brother's folly, the Duke of Grafton made enquiries '*to see if a way could have been found for a divorce*' but he did not receive any encouragment from the party he approached. Once they had placed the unfortunate Duchess in a convent, the two Dukes arrived incognito in Brussels and presented themselves to Sir Richard Bulstrode. They were then brought

> 'privately to his Excellency, who received them with all possible respect and did what the Duke of Grafton desired in commanding the Lady Abbess by

letter not to suffer the Lady to go out of the cloister without his particular
order'.

Realising by now that the Lady had been done a great injustice, King James ordered Grafton to bring her back immediately. But although Northumberland took his wife back, he refused to live with her and took as his mistress the woman whom he was to make his second wife. Whilst his uncle James was King, George remained loyal, and unlike his brother Grafton, did not actively intrigue to have him replaced with his son-in-law William of Orange. Indeed when William of Orange first landed, the Duke refused to join him, but the following year, due to the non payment of his pensions, he was forced to go cap in hand to that Prince and make his peace. By May 1689 it was reported that he

'is now mightily in his Majesty's favour and has received his arrears and has
3,000 l per annum settled'.

Unfortunately the royal favour did not last long, for the Duke did not receive any office under that Prince until the very last year of the reign, when he was appointed Lord Lieutenant of Surrey and Constable of Windsor Castle. William's opinion of him as being '*a great blockhead*' clearly influenced his initial decision to keep him out of government.

At the end of Queen Anne's reign, the Duke was made a Privy Councillor, but this was small recompense for his having been kept out of office for the previous two reigns. However, this may have been due to his preference for an army life. Nevertheless he seems to have been singularly unfortunate because on the accession of George I he was dismissed from all his posts. The reason was almost certainly due to the ill nature of the Prince of Wales, as illustrated by the occasion when

'the Duke coming one day into Court, happened to touch the prince as he
passed; upon which, the Prince turning said, What can't a Man stand still for
a Bastard; upon which the said Duke readily and aptly replyed, Your Highness
is, tho', the son of no Greater a King than my father, and as for Mothers, we
will neither of us talk upon that Point'.

Although Northumberland did not have any legitimate issue, he is credited with at least one illegitimate child who was born shortly before his first marriage. The child, a son John, was baptised in 1685/6 at St Margaret Westminster, the son of Jane Leviston (*sic*); the Duke's name was also given in the register. Nothing further is known of the child and the mother's identity is uncertain. For instance it is not known if she was a spinster or a married woman. However it is possible that Jane Leveson-Gower (1670–1725), daughter of Sir William Leveson-Gower, Bt., and wife of Henry Hyde, Lord Clarendon, could be a contender. For she was a celebrated beauty, was for a time the mistress of firstly Henry Boyle, Lord Carleton by whom she had a daughter, Catherine, Duchess of Queensberry (1701–77); and secondly, allegedly Matthew Prior, the poet and diplomat.

Northumberland's wife, Catherine, died without issue in 1714 and the following year he married again his lover Mary, daughter of Henry Dutton, with whom he had lived during the lifetime of his first wife. But just over a year later, George himself died suddenly without any legitimate issue and was buried in Westminster Abbey when all his honours became extinct. Following his second Duchess's death in 1738, her will excited so much curiosity from her deceased husband's relatives, that her immediate heirs became seriously alarmed, as Lady Mary Wortley Montagu commented:

'*The Duchess of Northumberland's will raises a great bussle among those branches of the royal blood. She has left a young neice very pretty, lively enough just fifteen to the care of Captain Cole who was the director of Lady Bernard (Grace FitzRoy, dau of 1st Duke of Cleveland). The girl has 300 pound per annum allowed for her maintenance till she marries which she is not to do without his consent and if she died without issue her 20,000 pounds to be divided between the children of the Duchess of St Albans (Ladies Diana and Caroline) & Lord Lichfield (Ladies Harriet and Anne, daughters of the 2nd Earl). The heirs-at-law contest the fantastical will etc'.*

Dame Cecilia FitzRoy (1670/1–1759)

Dame Cecilia, her real name is unknown, is often confused with Catherine FitzCharles, sister of the Earl of Plymouth, (*see* page 46) who actually died an infant, according to Francis Sandford's *'Genealogical History of the Kings & Queens of England'*.

Cecilia, according to the archivist of the Benedictine congregation, was just a little older than her sister Barbara, (*see* page 85) who was born in 1672. If taken literally, this could mean that she may have been born 1670/1, thus making her 87 years old when she died in 1759. Such an age would thus account for the reference to her being '*very aged*' at death. However, there is the possibility that she was in fact born even earlier. Curiously, none of King Charles's bastards lived to a great age, the Countess of Sussex and the Duke of Southampton living the longest, dying at the age of 69 (*see* page 50). Dame Cecilia's long lifespan makes her unusual amongst the children usually attributed to Charles, and this very fact could be used to argue against her being a royal bastard.

On the possibility of her having been born even earlier, it should be remembered that Lady Castlemaine was certainly pregnant with a child in July 1667, when King Charles declared

'that he did not get the child of which she is conceived at this time, he having not as he says lain with her this half year'.

However, Lady Castlemaine insisted that the child bear the name FitzRoy, rather than her husband's name of Palmer, and demanded of the King *'God damn me but you shall own it. Whoever did get it, you shall own it'*. By this date the distracted Charles was taking his pleasures elsewhere, most notably with Nell Gwyn and Moll Davies.

This child, possibly the fruit of the Countess's brief affair with Harry Jermyn, is not heard of again. The news of her pregnancy is recorded in the pages of Samuel Pepys' Diary under the date 27 July 1667 and for a short time, about a week, caused a rupture in her relations with the King. However by the end of the first week of August, she and the King were friends again and he resumed his visits to her, going two days a week. If she did carry the child to its full term, then the birth must have taken place by the end of December 1667, because she was back at Court on 14 January 1668 attending a performance of '*The Indian Emperor*'.

Little is known of Cecilia's life except that she entered the Dunkirk monastery of the Benedictines about 1713. Her mother had died four years earlier in 1709, and Cecilia was professed in or about 1715. The little that is known is due to the lucky survival of some of the Congregation's archives during the French revolution. It is recorded of her that she was an excellent musician and a number of her books survive with her name on the fly leaf. One was given by her '*dear cosen John Darral*' September 1725 and another by Sister Gertrude Darrell, novice; grandchildren perhaps of Marmaduke Darrell, of Fulmer, Bucks and his wife Catherine Palmer, who was sister of Roger, Earl of Castlemaine, the husband of Dame Cecilia's mother Barbara.

In some of Dame Cecilia's books, appears the mysterious cipher CH and it is probable that the letters relate to Charles Hamilton, the alleged illegitimate son of her sister Barbara (*see* page 85). This discovery, plus the knowledge that Cecilia was still in England when Charles was born in 1691, unlike her sister Barbara, suggests quite strongly that he was Cecilia's child and not hers – the fruit of Cecilia's liaison with James Hamilton, Earl of Arran (later Duke of Hamilton). It is clear that the Earl's intentions were less than honourable from the fact that he was married at the time, as well as already being the proud father of several bastard children.

Dame Cecilia's eventual entry into the Dunkirk community was almost certainly influenced by the unfortunate death in 1712, of the Duke of Hamilton in a duel with Lord Mohun. The prospects of a good and suitable marriage for her had always been slim, given the uncertainty surrounding her paternity, but the delay in entering a religious community does perhaps suggest that she did entertain some hope of finding a husband.

There are two theories about the upbringing of her son Charles, which are not incompatible with each other. One is that he was brought up by his grandmother in Chiswick, and the other that he was placed in the household of the Earl of Middleton at St Germain-en-Laye. After his father's death in 1712, he went to Antwerp and then Switzerland (where he was known as the Count of Arran and devoted himself to classical studies) before dying in Paris in 1754 and leaving issue of at least one son.

Dame Cecilia is not mentioned by Sandford as one of King Charles's children, indeed her very existence is ignored by him. However, she is mentioned in a French work of reference of the late eighteenth century as King Charles's daughter: *Dictionnaire de la Noblesse*, by M de la Chenaye-Desbois (pub. 1773).

Sir Charles Beauclerk, KG, FRS, 1st Duke of St Albans (1670–1726)

'Come hither you little bastard' was how his mother Nell Gwyn endearingly summoned her six year old son, Charles, in the presence of his father King Charles II, because as she said, she had no other name or title by which to call him. It is also said, unlikely though it be, that she threatened to throw her son into a river, lake or moat unless he was immediately ennobled and given a surname. But whatever the truth of these stories, it was not long before he was named Charles Beauclerk and created Earl of Burford (1676) and Baron Heddington and eight years later Duke of St Albans (1684) – the last Dukedom to be created by King Charles II. He was also given two colourful appointments; Hereditary Master Falconer of England and Hereditary Registrar of the Court of Chancery (worth £1,500 pa).

Described by Evelyn as *'a very pretty boy'*, Charles was the only surviving son of King Charles II and his favourite mistress, the actress *'Pretty Witty Nell'*, who paradoxically was appointed a Lady of Queen Catherine's Privy Chamber and was the subject of King Charles's deathbed wish *'let not poor Nelly starve'*. Nell Gwyn was never ennobled, although it was said on good authority that the King was planning to create her Countess of Plymouth which did not materialise, and later Countess of Greenwich, which was thwarted by his death. Nevertheless she was the mother of a duke and the founder of a dynasty.

Madame de Sevigne when writing to Madame Grignan in 1675 commented that

'She [Louise de Keroualle, later Duchess of Portsmouth, another rival
mistress of Charles II, of whom more anon – see page 88] *had not
counted on the advent of a young actress whose charms bewitched the King,
and from whom she finds herself unable to detach him. In pride and resolution
the actress is her match. If looks could kill Keroual would no longer be alive,
the actress makes faces at her, often manages to inveigle the King, and boasts
of his favours. She is young, untamed, bold, agreeable and dissolute, and she
plies her trade with a will.'*

Nell Gwyn, about whom no less than sixteen biographies have
been written over the last three centuries – the most recent, by
her descendant Charles Beauclerk, Earl of Burford and heir to the
Dukedom, and published last year – as well as at least thirty four
portraits and miniatures painted, (including those by Kneller, Lely
and Verelest), captured not only the King's heart, but the people's too.
Her life was the classic rags to riches story and her wit and sense of
fun was infectious and would fill a volume.

Although neither her date nor place of birth are known with
any certainty, nor even her father, it is clear that she was brought
up in Covent Garden, London, where she first became an orange
seller at the newly founded King's Theatre. There she caught the
eye of Charles Hart, its manager as well as one of the best known
actors of the day, and it was he who introduced her to the stage and
into his bed. In seven short years, she played at least twenty major
roles and rose to become one of the most successful and best loved
comic actresses of the day, before catching the Royal eye. The top
playwright, John Dryden, wrote parts especially for her and would
rather delay his productions than see them put on without her. She
was indeed great box office as well as being the darling strumpet
of the crowd.

In fact the meeting of Charles II and Nelly seems to have been
very contrived. Pepys records in July 1668 that *'my Lord Buckhurst
hath got Nell away from the King's House, and gives her £100 a year, so
she hath returned her scripts to the house, and will act no more.'* Finding
yourself a rich nobleman to keep you – as Nelly had done, was
pretty much the ideal for actresses and Nelly had done rather

well! Charles (Sackville), Lord Buckhurst, later Earl of Dorset and of Middlesex was described by Horace Walpole as '*the finest gentleman in the voluptuous court of Charles II.*' At this time, however, Buckhurst was mainly a man of pleasure, best known for his life of debauchery, although he was also well known as a poet and for his ballads. Later on he was to become a patron of the arts. This, then, was the man who took Nelly from her adoring public to settle her down in the spa town of Epsom. It was a happy and pleasant enough interlude.

One of the remarkable things about Nelly is that she always appears to have always been faithful to the man she was with – a sort of serial monogamy. This was unusual given the times and the company she kept, quite apart from her upbringing. She was truly loyal and being such a public figure, she could never have kept any lovers secret. But her move to Epsom was shortlived and within six weeks, Nelly was back in London, embarrassingly asking for her old job back. Buckhurst was not a man of bottomless funds and Nelly had been simply too expensive for him, although they were to remain friends for the rest of their lives. Nelly now looked to regain her old place at Drury Lane but this was awkward, for she had walked out on the Company and on her lover, its manager. Despite her box office appeal, it is hard to imagine any great welcome back. Yet despite Hart's hurt feelings for Nelly, he had a business to run and she was certainly good for business.

But although Nelly was soon back on stage, unbeknown to her, a new chapter of her love life was about to open up. As Nelly's career in the public eye had started in the King's Company, little did she realise that it would be in the company of the King that she would continue for the rest of her life. For one of Nelly's friends was the notorious Barbara Castlemaine, (*see* page 50), the King's chief mistress and a patron of the arts and the friend of many an actor and actress. Barbara had been introduced to Charles Hart in 1668, and as Pepys records:

> '*my Lady Castlemaine is mightily in love with Hart, of their house: and he is much with her in private, and she goes to him and do give him many presents*'.

In doing so, Barbara broke with her cousin the Duke of Buckingham, who then set about driving a wedge between her and Charles II by introducing a rival, and who better than Nelly. But mistresses néeded installing and compensation for her current noble lover was required. There is good evidence that Buckhurst did indeed receive compensation for giving up Nelly to the King; he was sent on Royal business to Paris, on three occasions between 1669–70, and was also appointed a Gentleman of the Bedchamber – with its salary of £1,000 a year besides being granted land.

A story published at the time had Charles and Nell on their first date. The King had seen her at the theatre and had asked to meet her in a tavern for dinner afterwards together with her companion, Charles Villiers and his brother, James, Duke of York. At the end of the evening, the bar keeper presented Charles with the bill, but he carried no money. So Charles passed the bill on to his brother, who did not have enough money on him and he duly passed it on to the unfortunate Villiers who had to pay the whole bill. Whereupon Nelly cried out *'Oddsfish! sure this is the poorest company that I ever kept!*

In January 1668, Pepys was told that *'the king did send several times for Nelly, and she was with him'* but her unique attraction was her sharp mind and wit that set her apart from all others. An example of this wit was the name Nelly gave her King. Because her two previous lovers had been called Charles (i.e. Hart & Buckhurst) she called her king *'my Charles III'*. Even the French ambassador so enjoyed the sparkle of Nelly's *'buffooneries'* that he wrote to Louis XIV, saying how the king's spirits would rise when he was with Nelly.

Charles and Nelly had two sons, but her only surviving son, St Albans, as he became, was born in May 1670 at her house in Lincoln's Inn Fields. Charles acknowledged the child straightaway who was called Charles after him, the third of his natural sons to be so-named. A portrait by Lely, painted at the King's command, shows Nelly as Venus, with her son Charles as Cupid. Motherhood would now confer some financial security upon Nelly, for as the mother of the King's son, neither she nor he would starve for as long as the King lived.

Although Nelly's will shows clearly that she did not become a Catholic, as Charles had done, it does seem clear that after Charles' death in 1685, Nelly was subjected to a great deal of pressure from James that her son should become a Catholic and that his Protestant tutor should be replaced by a Catholic one. However, despite it all, the young Duke remained firmly Protestant and a Whig and was to support King William III.

After St Albans had spent some years in Paris, he became a soldier and later Colonel of Princess Ann of Denmark's Regiment of Horse, now the 8th Hussars. According to the *London Gazette,* he distinguished himself greatly at the taking of Belgrade in 1688 (aged eighteen) for which James II made him a special grant of £2,000, but only two months later The Duke of St Albans' Regiment was one of the first to defect to William of Orange and, having been decimated at Steenkirk in 1692, it was disbanded. In 1693 the Duke served in Flanders and took part in the Battle of Néerwinden. He returned there several times more with King William III and was present when he received Peter the Great at Utrecht and at the Treaty of Rijswijk, after which William presented him with a *'sett of coach horses finely spotted like leopards'*. Later that year he served as an Ambassador Extraordinary to France in 1697 to offer the King's congratulations on the marriage of the Duke of Burgundy with Marie Adelaide, daughter of Victor Amadeus II of Savoy, at a time when diplomatic relations had not been restored between England and France. On his departure Lord Portland wrote to the King:

> *'I am annoyed to have to tell your Majesty that the Duke of St Albans left this place without making the usual present to the introducers, which has made a very bad impression, even as regards your Majesty. He has left debts unpaid in the shops, and borrowed 150 pounds from Lord Paston (his nephew) to avoid having his baggage seized. He promised to pay when he got home, and has forgotten both'.*

St Albans subsequently held various important Court appointments under William III and George I, including Captain of the Band of Gentlemen Pensioners, a Lord of the Bedchamber, Lord Lieutenant of Berkshire and was appointed a KG in 1718 and elected Fellow of the Royal Society in 1722, which had been founded by his father.

Having only very limited means of his own, St Albans relied upon a number of pensions he received – extraordinarily £2,000 from Queen Catherine of Braganza, his mother's pension of £1,500 which was transferred to him upon her death in 1687, £800 from the parliament of Ireland and £2,000 from the Crown. He had had to sell his mother's house at 79 Pall Mall in order to settle her debts, but he still owned Burford House in Windsor as well as Bestwood Lodge in Nottingham, the mortgage of which had been paid off by James II. He was, however, considerably poorer than most of his half-siblings, whose mothers had been more grasping and avaricious.

A number of paintings and engravings of him by Kneller, Lely and others still exist and in 1704 he was described as *'of a black complexion, not so tall as the Duke of Northumberland, yet very like King Charles'*..

He married in 1694, the beautiful Lady Diana de Vere, whose portrait by Kneller (and Lely and others) is one of the '*Hampton Court beauties*'. She later became Mistress of the Robes and Lady of the Stole to Queen Caroline, formerly Princess of Wales, and was the only daughter and heiress of the 20th and last Earl of Oxford, KG and the last of the long and distinguished family of de Vere. The de Veres, who were created Earls of Oxford in 1142, were Lords Great Chamberlain of England for 500 years, and one of whose members may even have written the plays of Shakespeare. But whilst her blood may have been blue, she brought with her little or no dowry, other than twenty-two heraldic quarterings and her fertility. For they had a total of nine sons and three daughters from whom descend some 2,000 living members of the family, chief of which is Murray, 14th Duke (born 1939), a chartered accountant, who lives quietly in London with his third wife.

His father, Charles, 13th Duke was only ninth in succession to the dukedom when he was born in 1915, so by the time he succeeded his second cousin in 1964, eight male heirs had to have died. He had the same problem, therefore, as the Duke of Chalfont in that delightful film *Kind Hearts and Coronets*, in which Alec Guinness played six separate roles as sons of the duke. However, although it is not suggested that Charles dealt with the problem in the same way, he did take four years proving his succession and persuading the Lord Chancellor to issue him with a Writ of Summons.

In fact Lady Diana was not the King's choice of bride for his son, for in 1684 it was rumoured that Sir John Cutler's daughter was his intended. However, this young lady married the Earl of Radnor, and being her father's only child, took his estates elsewhere.

Despite the Duke's obvious delight in his wife's charms, he still found the time to frequent the establishment of Mother Elizabeth Whyburn where *'only the crème de la crème of harlotry'* were gathered. It was here that he became *'besotted with the charms of Sally Salisbury,'* a notorious prostitute, and competed with Lord Bolingbroke, the Earl of Cardigan and his own half brother the Duke of Richmond for her favours. This amazing creature was born in 1692 in Shrewsbury of poor parents who came to London to seek their fortune. Whilst very young, she was debauched by the infamous Colonel Francis Charteris, known as *'the Rapemaster General of the Kingdom'*. Later she was to claim that she had lain *'with the noble Augustus just over from Germany'* the Prince of Wales (later George II). St Albans's association with her did him no credit, but it was perhaps too much to expect the son of Charles II and Nell Gwyn not to display a want of judgement in matters of the heart.

The eight surviving sons born to the Duke and his Duchess are a striking example of public service. Of these six became Members of Parliament for Windsor, where their grandfather King Charles had commissioned a house to be built for Nelly close to the Castle which he named Burford House. This is now part of the Royal Mews and was sold back to George III by 3rd duke in 1778 for £4,000 to help house his large family.

St Albans' eldest son, Lord Burford, described by Lord Hervey as '*one of the weakest men either of the legitimate or spurious brood of Stuarts*' was an MP from 1722–26, having previously held Bodmin. On his succession to the Dukedom in 1726 his career in the House of Commons ceased, but he went onto become Constable and Governor of Windsor Castle, High Steward and Warden of Windsor Forest, KG and KB. The chapter describing him in the official family history is headed '*The Insupportable Labour of Doing Nothing*'.

Lord William, the second son, with the support of his cousin the 2nd Duke of Richmond, was elected MP for Chichester serving there for seven years becoming Vice Chamberlain of Her Majesty's Household, only to die at the early age of thirty five.But the most able of the sons was the third son, Lord Vere, who served as MP for Windsor from 1726–41 and was created a peer in 1750 as Lord Vere of Hanworth. His career in the Navy saw him rise from Captain in 1721 to Admiral in 1748, besides serving as Lord Lieutenant of Berkshire.

The fourth son, Lord Henry was a professional soldier and Colonel of the 31st Foot, who distinguished himself at the Siege of Gibraltar. During the 1745 rebellion his regiment, the 31st Foot, formed part of the forces commanded by Lt Gen Sir John Ligoner to defend the Midlands from the advancing Jacobite army. Fortunately his regiment took no part in the final battle at Culloden, but he subsequently fell foul of 'Butcher' Cumberland when he refused to alter his vote at a court martial brought by the Duke against a soldier he would have condemned. For this act his was roundly persecuted by Cumberland, earning for himself much sympathy and Cumberland almost universal condemnation. He also served as MP for Thetford for twenty years, having been given his seat by his cousin the 2nd Duke of Grafton.

However, the most interesting and colourful sprig of the ducal house was undoubtedly Lord Sidney, the fifth son. He too was MP for Windsor and served as Vice Chamberlain of the Household to King George II and was appointed a Privy Councillor. He was also a notorius fortune hunter and, according to Lady Mary Wortley Montagu, '*Nell Gwyn in person, with the sex altered*' whose pursuit of the Duchess of Cleveland, his aunt by marriage, was immortalised in the verses:

> '*Her children banished, age forgot,*
> *Lord Sidney is her care;*
> *And, what is a much happier lot,*
> *Has hopes to be her heir*'.

He also paid court to the elderly Lady Betty Germain who was forced to part with £1,000 in order to get rid of him.

The sixth son Lord George shared a pension of £800 on the Irish establishment with his brother Lord Henry, and for a short period in 1745 he was aide-de-camp to George II. He ended his military career as a Lieutenant General and Commander in Chief of the King's Forces in Scotland from 1756-67 and a member of the Royal Company of Archers (now the Sovereign's Body Guard for Scotland), having earlier been Lieutenant Governor of Gibraltar. During the '45 rebellion he served as a Lt Colonel of the 1st Regiment of Foot Guards, which formed part of Ligonier's forces in the Midlands.

The seventh son, Lord Seymour died an infant and the eigth son, Lord James, served as Bishop of Hereford for forty-one years and as chaplain to George II. He is largely responsible for maintaining the tradition that his grandmother was born in Hereford. The 9th and youngest son, Lord Aubrey, a Captain in the Royal Navy and Captain of *Prince Frederick*, died a hero's death at the Battle of Carthagena in 1740.

The family coat of arms, granted in 1676, are the Royal Arms of King Charles II, *debruised by a baton sinister gules charged with three roses proper*, and were subsequently quartered with the ancient arms of de Vere, Earls of Oxford. The family motto, still unfulfilled, reads '*Auspicium Melioris Aevi*' (a pledge of better times to come), for which the family is still waiting patiently.

James, Lord Beauclerk (1671–80)

James was born on Christmas Day 1671 and was named after his uncle the Duke of York, who, together with the King visited Nelly later that day. James was the younger son of Nell Gwyn by Charles II, and the French Ambassador complained that the political business of the Court had all but stopped in order to celebrate his birth.

Like his elder brother Charles (*see page 75*), James had to wait for five years before he was given a surname and arms and was officially acknowledged by his father. Although he was granted the appellation of Lord Beauclaire/Beauclerk in 1676 '*with the same place and precedence as is due unto the eldest son of an earl*', and was in special remainder to his brother's titles of Earl of Burford and Baron

Headington, he himself was the only son of King Charles II not to have been separately ennobled in his own right.

But if Charles had intended to ennoble James, as probably he did, he was in fact prevented from doing so by James's early death in 1680 when he died in Paris '*of a sore leg*' aged only eight. He had been tutored there for the previous two years, where education and deportment were regarded as the best in Europe, and while very little is known about him, at least he is remembered in a number of paintings and engravings by Kneller, Lely, Abraham Blooteling, Henri Gascar and C. Netscher.

Worse too was that Nelly hadn't been there at his death, nor did she go to his funeral or even visit his grave, and indeed no one knows where he was buried. Naturally, Nelly was heartbroken and went into deep mourning, shutting herself away for many months. She was devastated by his death and never quite recovered from it, compounded, as it was, by her mother's death the previous year and Charles II's death only five years later. However, it is extraordinary that so little is known about the death of a son of the reigning king by one of the most famous women in the land, for there was little reference to him and still no one knows exactly how or where he died.

However, one of the most likeable aspects about his mother, Nelly, was that she alone, actually loved the king for the man himself and not for what she could get out of him. Nelly was totally loyal to the king as his subject and his lover. She was simply and truly overjoyed at whatever time he chose to spend with her. Nelly's philosophy was, perhaps, summed up by the inscription on her bedpan:'*Fear God and Serve the King*'. Indeed she also has the distinction of being the only Royal mistress to have an annual Newmarket race named after her: *the Nell Gwyn Stakes* which is a trial race for fillies.

Lady Barbara (Benedicta) FitzRoy, formerly Palmer (1672–1737)

Barbara, who was her mother's youngest daughter, was born on 16 June 1672 (and not 16 July as claimed by the editors of the *Complete*

Peerage), in Cleveland House, St Martins in the Fields. She is generally reputed to have been the fruit of Barbara Cleveland's liaison with John Churchill, the great Duke of Marlborough.

Like the rest of Barbara's children, she was given the surname of Palmer upon birth, although Charles II did later informally recognise her as his own daughter, by giving her the surname of FitzRoy. In the surviving records of the Benedictine Nuns of Pontoise, France she was declared to be

> '*natural dau of our latt soueraine King Charles ye 2nd … her mor was the Dutchess of Cleavland*'

But although Charles never publicly acknowledged her or granted her arms, when Barbara was appointed Prioress of St Nicolas's Hospital, Pontoise by the Duc d'Bouillon in 1720, she took out letters of naturalisation in which she was described as Charles's *legitimised* daughter; and in the preamble was also addressed by King Louis XV as '*our dear cousin*'.

Contemporary opinion, however, favoured young Churchill as the father, King Charles allegedly declaring

> '*You may tell my lady that I know the child is not mine, yet I will acknowledge it for old times' sake*'.

This was an extraordinary declaration on his part, considering that Barbara had had several lovers prior to the child's conception. The first was the poet William Wycherley, whom Barbara met secretly at the home of Mrs Knight, the famous singer, during Lent (1671). When word was brought to the King of the affair, he determined to catch them *in flagrante* and one day suddenly arrived unannounced only to pass Wycherley on the stairs muffled in his cloak. On taxing the Duchess for being abed she replied '*It is the beginning of Lent and I retired hither to perform my devotions*'. Where upon he replied '*Very Likely and that was your confessor I met on the stairs*'. The affair only lasted a few months.

Young Churchill arrived back from Tangier in the winter of 1670–1, and before the year was out had fought two duels. The first reported in a newsletter from London in February 1670–1 stated that:

> *'Yesterday was a duel between Mr Fenwick and Mr Churchill esquires who
> had as their seconds Mr Harpe and Mr Newport son to my Lord Newport; it
> ended with some wounds for Mr Churchill, but no danger of Life'.*

The second, a more serious affair, took place in August 1671, the
details of which were reported by Sir Christopher Lyttleton:

> *Landguard August 21 1671*
>
> *I have yr Lordships of Augst 3d, in wch you give mee a worse account of Mr
> Bruce then by yr former, and for wch I think you could not be too severe with
> him. His captaine had not had much better luck at home, for hee has bine
> lately engaged in a reencounter with youg Churchill. I know not ye quarrel;
> but Herbert rann Churchill twice through the arme, and Churchill him into
> ye thigh, and, after, Herbert disarmed him. But wht is ye worse, I heare yt
> Churchill has so spoke of it, that the King and Duke are angry wth Herbert.
> I know not wht he has done to justify himself.*

What these letters clearly show is that despite the commonly
held belief, that during the years of his army service, Churchill
only returned in the winter months, he was in fact in England
on the above dates. Nevertheless, as in the Wycherley affair, King
Charles again attempted to catch the Duchess unawares with her
lover. On doing so he taxed her with her lack of discretion and
to the fleeing ensign declared '*I forgive you, for you do it for your
bread*'. His continuing interest in her affairs and his unannounced
visits, betray on his part a certain jealousy or, perhaps, a desire to
protect her reputation, such as it was, she being the mother of
a good number of his children. Either way, his visits continued,
only tailing off in March of the following year when Barbara was
heavily pregnant with her latest child, conceived in the autumn
of 1671 (end of August/beginning of September), when the Court
was at Windsor and King Charles was wooing the future Duchess
of Portsmouth.

Not content with Churchill as a lover, the following year Barbara
took up with the Earl of Mulgrave (John Sheffield, a notorious roué,

who later married James II's illegitimate daughter). Indeed it was reported by Lord Conway in November 1673 that Barbara was '*with child by Mulgrave and in no favor with the King.*' Her situation was very reminiscent of the Emperor Augustus's daughter Julia, who when she took a lover, would always liken herself to a merchant ship which only took on passengers when it had a full cargo! In this way Julia was able to preserve the legitimacy of her children. So for King Charles to acknowledge the child in the knowledge that her mother had had at least two lovers prior to her conception, was extraordinary indeed and only makes sense if he (Charles) was still having intermittent carnal relations with her.

Despite her mother's proclivities and reputation, the young Barbara grew up to be a modest and well bred young lady. However, this has not prevented historians from accusing her of being the mother of an illegitimate child by the Earl of Arran (James Hamilton, subsequently 4th Duke of Hamilton). This allegation is strongly denied by the archivist to the Benedictine congregation of which Barbara was a member. Indeed the facts, once again, appear to contradict the popular belief of a double illegitimacy, certainly in Barbara's case.

Her alleged illegitimate child, Charles Hamilton, was born 30 March 1691 at Cleveland House. As Barbara FitzRoy became a novice at the Benedictine convent at Pontoise on 22 November 1689 and was professed there 2 April 1691, under the name Benedicta, it is clearly impossible for her to have been the child's mother.

Dame Benedicta spent thirty years as a member of the Benedictine congregation at Pontoise only leaving on 27 Aug 1721 to take up her post as Prioress of the Royal Priory of St Nicolas, where she eventually died in 1737 aged 65.

Sir Charles Lennox, KG, 1st Duke of Richmond & 1st Duke of Lennox (1672–1723)

Referred to by John Evelyn, the diarist, (with Charles Beauclerk) as '*very pretty boys who seem to have more wit than the rest (of Charles'*

progeny)', he was born in 1672 and created Duke of Richmond and
Duke of Lennox (in Scotland) at the tender age of three. Charles
Lennox was the son of Charles II by the French spy Louise Renée
de Penancoet de Keroualle (1649–1734), who was created Duchess of
Portsmouth for life in 1673, and Duchesse d'Aubigny in France. In
that year Charles was also granted by his father a pension of £2,000
per year. Evidence of her undoubted hold over King Charles can be
found in the words attributed to him on his deathbed '*I have always
loved her and I die loving her*'.

Madame de Sevigne when writing to Madame Grignan in 1675
commented

> '*Keroual has every reason to be satisfied with the treatment she has received in
> England; she has achieved her purpose which was to be the King's mistress. He
> spends all his nights with her with the full knowledge of everyone at Court;
> her son has been acknowledged and has received two dukedoms and withal
> has amassed great wealth and has succeeded in being feared and respectewd,
> at any rate by some persons.*'

But Louise does not come over very well. She was French, Catholic,
driven, manipulative, greedy and hungry for power. Lord Halifax
described her as '*scheming, aloof and heartless*'. However, she obviously
had her attractions and clearly Charles II was devoted to her, call-
ing her 'Fubbs' – an amalgation of 'fat' and 'chubby'. She became a
marvellous target for Nell Gwyn's wit, with her broken English and
her French pretensions.

In 1681 Richmond was appointed a KG and Master of the Horse
(although he was replaced as the latter by James II) and Governor
of Dumbarton Castle. He also became High Steward of the City of
York. It was said that his mother introduced the young KG with
the blue ribbon over his left shoulder instead of round his neck
and with the George appendant on the right side instead of on the
breast. Charles II is said to have been so pleased with this conceit
that he commanded all other knights to follow suit and so they still
do. However this story is not believed by Beltz in his *Order of the
Garter*. But what was the character of this youngest bastard son of
the King? Mackay describes him

'when not Thirty Years old [as] *Good natured to a fault, very well bred, and hath many valuable Things in him; is an Enemy to Business, very credulous, well Shaped, Black Complexion, much like King Charles....*

Thomas Hearne writes in 1723 that he was

'a man of very little understanding, and though the son of so great a king as Charles II, was a man that struck in with every thing that was whiggish and opposite to true monarchical principles'.

He even declared to the Earl of Wharton that he was a '*staunche Whig*'. So it is easy therefore to understand his mother's surprise that he should have embraced such principles as the theory of contract and mixed monarchy, when he was the son of a monarch such as Charles II. The idea that a

'monarch stood in a contractual relationship to the community as a trustee who ruled upon conditions, the breach of which rendered his crown forfeit'

was completely repugnant to her.

Prior to the death of his father, the Duke's mother saw fit to have him naturalised as a French subject, but even she was taken aback by the King's sudden death a few months later. Uncertain about her future in England, she took the young Duke to France, where he was professed a Catholic later that year. Aged only thirteen, he was ceremoniously received at Fontainebleu by King Louis XIV of France just one day before the French King rejected the Edict of Nantes.

When old enough, he later served for a time in the French army firstly as an ADC to the Duc d'Orleans, the King's nephew, and then as commander of his own cavalry regiment. Curiously however, he did not serve in any of the regiments that accompanied King James to Ireland in his attempt to win back his kingdoms. Instead King Louis sent him to serve in the Low Countries from whence he wrote to his mother:

'Although you were angry with me when I left, because I applied myself to nothing, I can assure you that you will be very pleased with me during this campaign'.

To the consternation of his mother and surprise of King Louis the young Duke then suddenly decided that he wished to return to England, and with no more ado, promptly left France without telling anyone. He claimed that he would enjoy a far higher rank in England and greater revenues. He then formally renounced his Catholicism at a ceremony at Lambeth Palace in May 1692. Two years later, he was appointed Lord High Admiral of Scotland and in 1696 Grandmaster of the Freemasons of England.

Despite renouncing his Catholic religion, William III initially suspected the Duke was a Jacobite and was privy to the plans of the Jacobite Court. However, by serving as the King's ADC he was able to convince him otherwise. When asked to sign the Assocation of 1696, he promptly did so, and thus gave further proofs of his allegiance to King William. However his Whiggish principles always sat awkwardly on his shoulders and on more than one occasion he was forced to justify his stand to his mother.

The rumours of the Duke's drinking and debauchery, which had reached the ears of his mother in France, were, according to his wife, put about by his enemies:

'All those that are so handsome as His Grace will have enemies upon the account of envie'. 'His Grace, he had never bin from me twice after nine o'clock at night (wch is far from leading a debauch'd life)'.

Despite her protestations, however, his contemporaries knew otherwise. Like his half brother the Duke of St Albans he enjoyed the favours of the notorious prostitute Sally Salisbury and their affair was the talk of the town, the lady twitting him with the remark *'As a whore she was good enough for a Garter'.*

Eventually the Duke's dissolute way of life caught up with him and the year before his death his wife wrote to her eldest son:

'Your poore papa brought from London an intermitting feaver and with it a most violent Histerick Fits, that he has been all this Fortnight that he has favoured Goodewoode most extreamly ill. Mr Peakhame with the Barke has stoped the Feaver, but his other Fits were attended with such convulsions that I sent for a Doctor from London, who assures Lord Duke unless he interely leaves of strong waters he recovery is impossible. I hope this will prevaile else I fear you will hear very ill news, for indeed I never remember Lord Duke so broke and decayed as he is at present: in his Fits he raves after you and says he is sure if he did but see his Dear Boy he should be well'.

Later that year the Duchess wrote to her son again:

'our friend drinks not less than three pints a day notwithstanding his late illness. God keep you from having the same passion'.

He died in 1723, a year after his wife, Anne, whom he had married before 1692 and who had remained loyal throughout. She was the 2nd daughter of Francis, Lord Brudenell, sister to the 3rd Earl of Cardigan and widow of Henry Lord Belasyse of Worlaby, and they had one son and two daughters. The present representative of this family, which is unique in that it is the only issue of Charles II to have descended from father to eldest son in an almost unbroken male line over nine generations, is Charles Henry, 10th Duke of Richmond and Lennox and 5th Duke of Gordon and Duc d'Aubigny – a duke four times over (born 1929), who still lives at his ancestral estate at Goodwood in West Sussex. He is a chartered accountant and has given much public service, including holding high office in the Church of England as as a member of its General Synod and as a Church Commissioner. However, according to the newspapers in 1994, he had to pay off his own mistress in the sum of £10,000, before resigning as Lord Lieutenant of West Sussex.

His complicated arms include in the first grandquarter the Royal arms of King Charles II *within a bordure compony argent and gules, charged with eight roses of the 2nd,* the Scottish mark of bastardy, with an inescutcheon bearing the arms of the French dukedom of Aubigny; the 2nd grandquarter is for the Dukedom of Lennox

and the third grandquarter for the Dukedom of Gordon quarters
Gordon, Badenoch, Seton and Fraser with the motto '*En la rose je
fleuris*' (I flourish in the rose).

Lady Mary Tudor, later Countess of
Derwentwater (1673–1726)

Mary Tudor was born in 1673, the daughter of Moll or Mary Davies,
actress and singer, by King Charles II. She is said to have caught
the King's eye when she sang '*My Lodging It is on the Cold Ground*'
in the play *The Rivals* and it was not long before she was warming
herself in the King's bed and was thereafter provided with a house
in Suffolk Street.

Moll's origins are uncertain. One source claims she was the illegitimate daughter of Col Charles Howard, son of the Earl of Berkshire,
and another the daughter of a blacksmith from Charlton, near the seat
of the Howard family in Wiltshire. Her chief talent was dancing and
she was, according to Pepys, far superior in this regard to Nell Gwyn.
Pepys claimed that Col Howard '*do pimp for her for the King … but
Pierce says that she is the most homely jade as ever he saw, though she dances
beyond any thing in the world*'.

Moll's portrait painted by Kneller, shows an attractive woman with
a fine figure but her liaison with Charles did not last as long as Nell's.
She was also painted by Sir Peter Lely, William Pawlett and Gerald
Valck. Her rivalry with Nell Gwyn led to one notable incident when
having boasted of her Royal conquest, Nelly invited her to tea and
then fed her with sweetmeats doctored with a purgative drug, with
disastrous results in the Royal bed! In 1681 she is recorded as singing
at Court in John Blow's *Venus and Adonis* '*I give you freely all delights,
with pleasant days and easy nights*'.

Mary, who was the youngest of Charles II's fifteen officially recognised bastards, was almost certainly born in Suffolk St, where her
mother lived from 1667–76 and from 1676–81 she lived in St James's
Square. After the birth of her daughter, Moll received a pension
of £1,000 and after the King's death she married James Paisible,

later court musician to Prince George of Denmark. Paisible, a Frenchman, arrived in England about 1674 and was described by one contemporary as '*indolent, but with easy and agreeable manners*'. When King James II left England in 1688, the Paisibles followed him to France but were given permission to return in 1698. James Paisible died in 1721/2 leaving a will but making no mention of a wife. However, he did have a son and namesake who was apprenticed in 1717 to a London weaver and then granted the freedom of the City in 1726.

Mary was acknowledged by her father in 1680, when she was granted a warrant of precedence as the daughter of an earl, with the surname of Tudor and in 1683 as a duke's daughter. She was granted the royal arms, with due differences, by King James II in 1687 viz; *within a bordure quarterly erminois and counter compony argent and gules.* Her first husband, whom she married aged only fourteen in 1687, was Edward Radcliffe, 2nd Earl of Derwentwater (who died 1705), and they had three sons and a daughter. For the last five years of his life, however, the Earl was separated from his wife, and within two weeks of his death, she had married again to Henry Graham, of Levens, MP for Westmoreland '*with whom she had lived in her husband's lifetime*'. Unfortunately Lady Derwentwater's second husband died within eighteen months of the marriage, but she found another, James Rooke, only eight months later who outlived her, she having died in Paris in 1726. On the occasion of her third marriage a contemporary noted that:

> '*This town is full of nothing but of ... and Lady Deringwater (sic) whoe last Tewsday cam and went in her moarning coach for Mr Grims (sic) to church, and was marryed to Jamse Roock, Coll Roock's son. Grims has been dead not thre qrs of a year yet; she turned Lady Tuften's children out of the church, and said she would not be marryed tel they went out. She was marryed in whit satin. She has settled fower hundred a year upon him for her life, and the rest she keeps for her self and hous. She ows a great deal of money hear; Twickenham, August 28 1707'.*

Although Lady Mary's marriage had been arranged by her uncle, King James, there is no evidence to suggest that she felt herself beholden to him for the honour, or that she showed any attachment to his cause when in exile. The same, however, could not be said for her sons James and Charles. They quite literally gave their lives for the Stuart cause.

James, the eldest son, who became the 3rd Earl on the death of his father, was brought up at the court of King James and was a companion of the young Prince of Wales. With the Dukes of Burgundy, Anjou and Berry, Louis XIV's grandsons, and the young Prince of Wales, he hunted boar and stag in the forests surrounding Versailles. However, in 1705, at the age of sixteen he left St Germain in order to complete his education by making the Grand Tour, and only returned to England in 1709/10.

Within two years he had made a splendid marriage with a Catholic heiress, and had settled down to what, at first, seemed happy domesticity. Unfortunately, however, within five years his situation changed completely, the Government suspecting him of being an active Jacobite. Naturally in the run up to the 1715 uprising in Scotland, his Jacobite connections made him a natural figurehead for Catholics in the north of England and the Government issued a warrant for his arrest. The rest is history. He commanded a troop of horse in the Jacobite army consisting of 1,500 foot and 600 horse under General Thomas Forster, despite having no military training. After their defeat at Preston, he surrendered himself and was imprisoned in the Tower of London where, despite entreaties from many of his kin, he was beheaded, aged just twenty-six, in 1716, a year when the *aurora borealis* shone especially bright. Just before his execution he wrote these words to his mother:

> *'Within four hours of the time of execution, I write these lines to ask your blessing; to assure you, that though I have not been brought up with you, I have all the natural love and duty that is owing to a mother, who has shewn her tenderness, particularly in my last misfortunes…' 'I wish Mr Rooke very well too; he is a man of great honour, and I hope you will bear with one another, as married people must and make each other happy'.*

He had been found guilty of high treason and was attainted when all his honours were forfeited. His younger brother was also arrested and condemned to death, but managed to escape to France. However, upon returning to England thirty years later, he too was arrested and beheaded on Tower Hill. Although the male line of the family survived until 1814, Moll's descendants are still to be found in the Petre family.

Chapter V
The Bastards of James II
(1633-1701)

Henrietta, Baroness Waldegrave, later Viscountess Galmoye, *née* FitzJames (1667–1730)

Henrietta FitzJames, was born in 1667, the eldest surviving daughter of the Duke of York later King James II and Arabella Churchill. Her mother, despite Gramont's comments, was not an ugly woman; she was in fact very beautiful as her portrait at Althorp shows. She captured the Duke's attention in the mid 1660's, whilst a Maid of Honour to his first wife Anne Hyde, and gave birth to her first child at the age of twenty. She went on to present the Duke with three more children before making a respectable marriage with Charles Godfrey, a Captain in the Life Guards. During her liaison with James she received a yearly allowance of £1,000 and a freehold house in St James's Square, which she later sold for £8,000.

At the age of sixteen, Henrietta married her first husband Henry Waldegrave, the eldest son of Sir Charles Waldegrave, Bt, who three years later was created 1st Baron Waldegrave of Chewton. When King James retired to France in 1688, Lord and Lady Waldegrave followed him and settled at St Germain-en-Laye, but shortly afterwards Lord Waldegrave who was Comptroller of the King's Household, died at the young age of twenty-eight.

Of Lady Waldegrave's character little can be discovered, but what is known points to a headstrong young woman. However, in her youth she was a dutiful and obedient daughter and it seems that James was very fond of her. In 1682, before her marriage, she visited the Continent and reports of her good conduct reached James from his cousin, the Abbess of Maubuisson (Louise of the Palatine). In his letter to her he declared how glad he was to hear that

> *'you behave yourself so well and that she gives you so good a character. I hope you will do nothing to give her reason to alter her opinion of you, and that you will do nothing to make me less kind to you as you can desire'.*

However, she struggled to come to terms with her sudden widow-hood and angered her father in 1695 by becoming pregnant, as the Marquis de Dangeau declared:

> *'Madame de Waldegrave, fille naturelle du roi d'Angleterre, et qui etoit a Saint Germain avec lui, est par son ordre dans un convent a Paris. On l'accuse d'etre dans un etat ou une femme veuve ne doit pas etre; elle ne veut point dire qui l'a mise dans cet etat.'.*

Her father promptly ordered that she should retire to the Benedictine convent at Pontoise, until she had given birth. Rumour had it that the father was Richard Talbot, Duke of Tyrconnell, but in reality it was almost certainly Piers Butler, Viscount Galmoye, whom she later married. However, she left him a few months later, returning to England, and never saw him again. Despite having served in the Irish campaign and being created Earl of Newcastle by King James, the latter did not approve of the match. Nevertheless, this disgrace did not prevent Galmoye from becoming a Lieutenant General in the French army.

Lady Waldegrave had three children by her first marriage, two sons, James and Henry, plus a daughter Arabella, who became a nun. James was brought up as a Catholic at the court of St Germain-en-Laye, but, like his cousin Derwentwater, returned to England to marry an heiress with a portion of £10,000. On her death in 1719, he renounced his Catholic faith, and was then allowed to take his seat in the House of Lords. He rose high in the favour of George II, was appointed Ambassador to the Court of Vienna and created a KG and then Earl Waldegrave.

Unfortunately the amorous proclivities of his mother and grand-mother re-appeared in his eldest daughter, Henrietta, who, when the widow of Lord Edward Herbert, fell in love with John Beard, the actor and singer, and wished to marry him. The episode caused grave concern to her father who threatened the unfortunate pair with the direst of consequences. To their credit they ignored the threats and were eventually married. However, in an attempt to break up the union, the bride's brother sought to besmirch his character by claiming that

> *'her lover had the pox and she would be disappointed of the only thing she married him for which was her lust for that he would continue to lie every night with the player that brought them together and give her no solace. But there is no prudence below the girdle'.*

Her extraordinary behaviour led Lady Pomfret to declare that

> *'Her relations have certainly no reason to be amazed at her constitution but are violently surprised at the mixture of devotion that forces her to have recourse to the Church in her necessities which has not been the road taken by the matrons of her family'.*

Lady Henrietta was not the only member of her family to exhibit the amorous proclivities of Lady Waldegrave and her mother Arabella. For Arabella Dunch, Lady Waldegrave's neice, the daughter of her half sister Elizabeth, wife of Edmund Dunch, was rusticated (*sic*) for 'gallantrys' by her husband Edward Thompson in 1727. Miss Dunch's father Edmund had died in 1719, aged forty, and was well known for his predilection for gaming having been drawn into it purely to please his lady (Elizabeth, the daughter of Charles and Arabella Godfrey). When Lady Waldegrave died in 1730, at the age of sixty-three, she was immediately followed a month later by her mother Arabella, at the age of eighty-three, who was buried in Westminster Abbey in the grave of her brother Admiral George Churchill.

James FitzJames, 1st Duke of Berwick Upon Tweed (1670–1734)

Born in France in August 1670 at Moulins in the Bourbonnais, James was the eldest illegitimate son of James, Duke of York, later King James II and Arabella Churchill. He was perhaps the most accomplished and renowned of all the royal bastards who appear in this book. His military talents – for he was a superb tactitian and strategist – were clearly inherited from his Churchill forebears and after his death Montesquieu wrote

> *'such indeed was the fate of this House of Churchill that it gave birth to two men who were destined, at the same time, each of them to shake, and to support, the two greatest monarchies of Europe'.*

He first displayed his considerable military talent when his father sent him to fight for the Emperor Leopold I against the Turks, in 1686. He was just sixteen years old but the Emperor made him welcome and declared

> *'here we have a new volunteer who is a natural son of the King of England but who is less remarkable for his birth than for his good sense and ideals and who, I am sure, will distinguish himself in the future by his exploits'.*

Berwick served *'with remarkable gallantry'* at the seige of Buda under the Duke of Lorraine, Commander in Chief of the Imperial Forces and returned to England the following year to be created Duke of Berwick with an allowance of £5,000 per annum.

His apprenticeship under such a distinguished and capable commander as the Duke of Lorraine would prove invaluable to Berwick throughout the remainder of his life. The benefits were first displayed during his service in the Jacobite War in Ireland, between 1689 and 1691, when he was initially given the commission of a Major-General and placed under the command of Lieutenant-General Richard Hamilton. His finest hour, however, came in 1690 when at the age of twenty he was left in sole command of all King James's forces after his father left the country to raise reinforcements in France. During the period that he was in sole command he sought to check the progress of the forces under the command of his uncle Lord Churchill, re-establish the morale of the army, dissipate any factions within it and consolidate the Jacobite position within the kingdom. He succeeded in all of these endeavours and greatly increased his reputation and prestige by doing so. It was during the Irish campaign that he learnt the three cardinal rules of battle, to only fight on ground of his own choosing, always develop a good intelligence of the enemies' movements and strength and make sure that your soldiers were well fed, well paid and supplied with plenty of ammunition and arms.

After the Treaty of Limerick, however, Berwick withdrew into France where he soon joined the French Army, rising to become a Marshal of France (1706), a fitting honour for a man of his undoubted military talents but which necessitated him becoming a naturalised Frenchman. In all he served in twenty-nine campaigns, commanding fifteen some on the opposite side to his uncle the Duke of Marlborough. The pinnacle of his career, however came in 1707 when he soundly defeated an English army sent to oppose him at the Battle of Almanza.

> *'the only battle recorded in which an English general at the head of a French army defeated an English army commanded by a Frenchman (Henri de Ruvigny)'.*

His victory drew the praise of none other than Frederick the Great who considered Berwick's tactics at Almanza a classic example of a text book battle. His campaigns and victories in Spain also ensured the survival of the fledging Spanish Bourbon monarchy during the War of the Spanish Succession between Louis XIV's grandson Philip and the Archduke Charles. *'We are very foolish to get ourselves killed for these two simpletons'* commented Lord Peterborough after the battle of Almanza.

Following the debacle of the Monmouth Rebellion it is remarkable that Berwick was even considered as a possible candidate for the crown. But his situation during the brief period of his father's reign was similar in a number of respects to that of the Duke of

Richmond, Henry VIII's bastard son. Between 1670 and 1688 James II had no surviving legitimate male heir, only two illegitimate sons. The succession to the crown appeared to be securely vested in his two legitimate daughters Mary and Anne. Rumours did circulate, however, that James wanted the Pope to legitimize Berwick and place him first in the succession or alternatively after his sisters much the same as Louis XIV did with his bastard sons the Duc de Maine and the Comte de Toulouse. In the event that this had occurred there is no doubt that he would have made an excellent monarch. Fate, however, decreed otherwise and Mary of Modena proceeded to give James II a legitimate son.

Throughout his father's lifetime Berwick was the model of a dutiful son but after his father's death he faced a dilemma of major proportions. In his quest to provide for his growing family he was forced to become a subject of the King of France a move that had the approval of his half brother James but only with the proviso that Berwick would be available to command any Jacobite forces in the event of a rebellion or invasion of England. It was a scenario that would bedevil many Jacobite emigres and in Berwick's case would have catastrophic consequences. There is no doubt that had Berwick accepted his half-brother's commission to command the forces raised to fight his cause during the 1715 rebellion, the course of English history would have taken a very different turn. Initially Louis XIV did give Berwick permission to lead the expedition but later changed his mind, possibly as a result of pressure from the English Ambassador Lord Stair. As it was, his considerable abilities were placed at the service of the French king, who benefited enormously and his half brother and true sovereign, rued the day that he allowed him to become a naturalized Frenchman. Berwick undoubtedly suffered a crisis of conscience over the whole affair but eventually common sense prevailed and a number of years later he set down his views on paper to his son the Duke of Liria who faced a similar situation:

> 'The King's letter to you is very strange. He always speaks of duty, as if he
> were master to allow people making their fortunes, and seems to mean that
> he consents to your establishment in Spain only upon condition that you will
> abandon all whenever he will be pleased to call upon you: this is following

*his maxim again with me. Methinks that he should caress people, and not
always speak of duty, of which perhaps he knows not the extent. We ought to
always wish him well, and even render him service, but it is out of principles
of honour, and we are not obliged to abandon all our establishment, and leave
our children to starve for his projects or fancy…'*

Berwick was a brave, highly-principled man who, according to some,
was cold, reserved, sarcastic and exceedingly haughty. However, he
did have a sardonic sense of humour. At the funeral oration of his
father James II in 1701, the preacher declared that the deceased James
had never committed a mortal sin. To this Berwick replied *'And what
of me?' 'I am then a venial sin!'*

In recognition for his considerable military talents James received
many honours. In 1707 Philip V of Spain created him Duke of Liria
and Xerica, as a reward for winning the battle of Almanza and driving
out the forces of the Archduke Charles. In France he was created Duke
of FitzJames in 1710, with special remainder to the issue of his 2nd wife
having already been appointed a Marshal of France in 1706.

James married twice – firstly in 1695 to Honora de Burgh, (d. 1698),
the widow of Patrick Sarsfield, Earl of Lucan (in the Jacobite Peerage)
and daughter of William, Earl of Clanricarde. They had a son, before
she died in 1698. He married again two years later in 1700 Anne
(who died 12 June 1751), dau. of Hon. Henry Bulkeley, 4th son of
Thomas, 1st Viscount Bulkeley, and had further issue. Berwick was
killed at the siege of Philippsburg in 1734, when his head was blown
off by a cannon ball, his passing lamented by the whole of France
where he was regarded as a hero. *'One could say with truth'*, wrote
Montesquieu his great friend, *'that he had in him more grandeur than
he had occasion to let appear, acting, as he did, always in the simplest way
and never seeking estimation'.*

In England, however, he was regarded as an embarrassment.
Although the Duke was outlawed in 1695 it has not deterred his
descendants from using his various titles. A present day descendant in
Spain is Maria Rosario Cayetana FitzJames Stuart y Silva, Duchess of
Alba, Duchess of Liria and Xerica, Duchess of Montoro, Duchess of
Arjona, Duchess of Hijar, Duchess of Olivares and forty-three other
titles. If the outlawry were to be reversed, the present heir male to the

Dukedom of Berwick would be Jacobo Hernando FitzJames Stuart Gomez, Ducque de Penaranda de Duero. The Duke of Berwick's descendants in France, the Ducs de FitzJames, are now extinct in the male line.

Henry FitzJames, Duke of Albemarle (1673–1702)

Henry FitzJames was created Duke of Albemarle by his father King James II on 13 January 1696. He had been born in August 1673, the younger of James's sons by Arabella Churchill and he and his elder brother James were educated at the Colleges of Juilly, near Meaux, Plessis and La Fleche under the care of Father Gough (sic) a Jesuit, who had performed a similar service for the Duke of Monmouth, Charles II's eldest illegitimate son.

He was by all accounts a very headstrong young man and would prove to be something of a liability to his father. He had a strong fondest for the bottle and was the complete opposite to his brother in this regard. They spent most of their early years in France but their reception at the English Court in 1685 caused quite a stir and angered the Queen, Mary of Modena. The Florentine Ambassador Terriesi observed:

'She spent the whole of last week weeping bitterly; the reason alleged is that the King has received his two sons by the sister of Lord Churchill, at Court, and, in a measure, has begun to recognise them'

A week later he wrote:

'There are no signs of abatement in the passionate emotion aroused in the Queen … by the report that the King has re-taken Madam Sedley into favour and meets her in the house of Mr Grime when he is hunting … But the true reason may be the coming to Court of Madam Churchill's two sons contrary to the King's promise…He is sending them back to France shortly for their education'.

In December 1686 the King recalled them again and the younger Henry was sent to sea on HMS *Sedgemoor* under the command of Capt David Lloyd *'to observe the motions of the Algerines'*.

Henry appears to have had his fair share of mishaps during his youth. In 1684, on one of his visits to England – during the reign of his uncle Charles II – he had an accident which threatened to disfigure his face.

> *'I was very sorry to hear this morning of the accident which happened to your brother Harry'* [wrote his father], *'and send this footman on purpose to you, to have an account from you how he does. They tell me his face will not be marked with it … Remember me to your brother James, and tell him I am sorry his journey should be stopped for some days, especially by such an accident; and tell Harry I Hope he will be carefuller for the time to come, and now that he do what the chirurgeons will have him….'*

When William of Orange invaded England in 1688 and King James withdrew to France, his illegitimate sons James and Henry joined him at St Germain. However, within two months they all sailed from the French port of Brest with the French expeditionary force commanded by Lieutenant-General Rosen and landed in Ireland in March 1689. The expedition conveyed by fourteen ships of the line, eight frigates and three fireships commanded by the French Admiral Jean Gabaret, landed at Kinsale.

Young Henry, only seventeen years old, was made Colonel of a Regiment of Infantry but his conduct did not impress the French ambassador d'Avaux who thought him *'a very debauched young man, who burst himself daily with brandy'*. Curiously this did not prevent King James from writing to the Grand Master of the Order of St John of Jerusalem and obtaining the title of Honorary Grand Prior of England for his son. Another example of this young man's behaviour was again recorded by the French Ambassador:

> *One day the Duke of Berwick and his brother entered a room where Lord Dungan (son of the Earl of Limerick) and four or five sparks of the army were cracking a bottle of claret. Presently an Officer blamed the Grand Prior for having broken a certain captain of his regiment. Henry FitzJames replied*

*offensively, Berwick good humouredly suggested that instead of wrangling
they should drink to the health of all true Irishmen, and confusion to Lord
Melfort, who had well-nigh lost them the kingdom. Whereupon the Grand
Prior angrily protested that Melfort was a right good fellow, and a friend of
his, and if anyone dared drink such a toast, he would pitch a glass of wine in
his face. Some of the gentlemen remarked that FitzJames had no business to
fall into a passion if they chose to drink the toast; and then, raising an empty
goblet, made the usual reverence. Instantly the ill-conditioned Prior flung his
wine into Dungan's face, the glass cutting his lordship's nose in two places.
The bystanders rushed between the parties. However, Dungan, though a high
spirited young man, treated the insult with contempt. 'Never mind' he said,
'the Prior is not only a child, but the son of my King'*

Unlike his brother James, Henry was not created a Duke whilst his
father was still in possession of his kingdoms, for he had to wait until
he was an exile in France. At the beginning of 1695 it was rumoured
that young FitzJames had married in Paris *'a Mrs Rogers, the daughter
of his father's tailor'*. The rumour was, of course, untrue but his brother
James did propose marriage to one of the daughters of the Count
d'Armagnac without the knowledge of his father but was promptly
turned down. St Simon's assessment of this young man's character
was less than flattering, he considered him *'the stupidest man on earth'*.
However, if true, that did not prevent him from being placed in
command of the French fleet at Toulon in 1696 whilst his father
was waiting on the coast of Normandy to invade England. That he
had some ability is clear because he was promoted to the rank of
Lieutenant General and Admiral in the French service in 1702.

Henry eventually married on 20 July 1700 Marie Gabrielle (who
married secondly on 25 May 1707 John Drummond, 2nd Earl of
Melfort and died 15 May 1741), the only child of Jean D'Audibert,
Count de Lussan. Her dowry was twenty thousand pounds with free
board and lodgings at Versailles. Only two years after their marriage,
Henry died suddenly on 27 Dec. 1702, at Bagnols in Languedoc, leaving
a daughter, Christine Marie Jacqueline, who was baptised on 22 May
1711 at St Germain-en-Laye, and whose godparents were James III and
his mother Mary of Modena.

Arabella FitzJames (1673–1704)

Berwick's and Albemarle's younger sister, Arabella, was born year in February 1672/3, the youngest child and only daughter of James, Duke of York, later King James II, by Arabella Churchill, whose name she was given. Her mother later went on to marry Colonel Charles Godfrey, Master of the Jewel Office who died in 1714, whereas she survived him for another sixteen years, dying in 1730 and having further children.

Meanwhile, in April 1689 Arabella became a novice in the Benedictine congregation at Pontoise and was professed there a year later on 30 April 1690, taking the name Dame Ignatia; the ceremony being witnessed by Queen Mary of Modena. Fourteen years later, she died in November 1704, unmarried and aged only 32. According to the nuns

> *'She was ever pious and ye fear of God rul'd all her actions; sickness and infirmity grew up with her, which was a great hinderance to her zeal in all common observances ....'.*

Katherine, Countess of Anglesea, later Duchess of Buckinghamshire & Normanby (1681–1742) and James Darnley (1685–86)

The Lady Katherine Darnley, as she was styled on her marriage licence, was allegedly born 1681/2, the third and youngest surviving illegitimate daughter of James, Duke of York, later King James II.

Her mother Catherine, Countess of Dorchester, became James's mistress in the late 1670s and bore him a number of children, of whom the only survivor was the Lady Katherine. The birth of their first child was heralded by a contemporary in the following terms:

> *'The daughter of Sir Charles Sedley, being reputed a maid, was brought to bed of a child and layd it to ye Duke of York, before he went beyond the*

seas; which, together with the thought of departing out of England, made his Duchess very melancholy'.

If the dating is correct the child was born in fact shortly before 9 March 1679, when the Duke and his wife departed for Flanders following the Exclusion Crisis. The Duke was again banished to Scotland in October 1680. The Duchess went with a heavy heart, her situation being reported by Henry Sidney as follows:

'The Duchess is very melancholy; but whether it proceeds from the apprehensions of making another journey or seeing the Duke so publicly own Mrs Sedley, I cannot tell'.

Mrs Sedley's association with James continued to cause his wife acute embarrassment. When he succeeded to the throne in 1685, he attempted to send her away, but before long had renewed his relationship with her, plunging his wife into a deep melancholy: *'The Duchess ... prays all day almost She is very melancholy; the women will have it for Mrs Sedley'.* Mrs Sedley's hold over James was because of her wit and frankness, characteristics she inherited in abundance from her father Sir Charles Sedley. At the revolution, when taxed with his ingratitude to King James, he wittily replied that: *the King having made my daughter a Countess, it is fit I should make his daughter a Queen'.* When Queen Mary cut her dead at a Court function on one occasion, the Countess declared

'Why so haughty madam? I have not sinned more notoriously in breaking the seventh commandment with your father, than you have done in breaking the fifthe against him'.

On her one time royal lover's choice of mistresses, she commented, *'We are none of us handsome, and if we had wit, he has not enough to discover it'.*

Once canvassed as a possible wife for John Churchill, the celebrated Duke of Marlborough, Mrs Sedley lost out to the beautiful Sarah Jennings. She eventually married, aged almost forty, Sir David Colyear, who was created Earl of Portmore in 1703 by Queen Anne.

Initially the Countess was violently opposed to William III's usurpation of the crown, and when the Earl of Ailesbury, a known Jacobite,
was asked to carry the Sword of State before him at his Coronation,
she retorted '*Did you not wish the sword in his body*'. However, in 1696,
the year of the assassination plot, she fell into a dispute with Lord
Ailesbury and shouted at him '*I will make King William spit on you!
Go to your ----King James*'.

Lady Katherine inherited her mother's quick temper and was
described by Horace Walpole as '*more mad with pride than any Mercer's
wife in Bedlam*'. In an attempt to cure her of this, Lady Dorchester
informed her that she was in fact the daughter of Colonel James
Graham, of Levens, to whose legitimate daughter, the Countess
of Berkshire, she is alleged to have borne a striking resemblance.
However, she was most unfortunate in her choice of husbands. The
first whom she married in 1699 was James (Annesley), 5th Earl of
Anglesey (who died without any male issue early in 1701/2), but
they had been separated after a few months on account of his cru-
elty. Their only child Catherine was born in 1701 and she married
William Phipps from whom descend the Marquesses of Normanby.
In his will the Earl gave his daughter a dowry of £15,000 but with
the proviso that she was never again to see her mother and grandmother, the Countess of Dorchester. He also placed her under the
guardianship of Lord Haversham

Katherine married again in 1705/6 at St Martin in the Fields,
as his 3rd wife, John (Sheffield), 1st Duke of Buckinghamshire and
Normanby (who died in 1720/1), a nobleman with a very colourful
and scandalous past The only son of the 2nd Earl of Mulgrave, he had
been a Gentleman of the Bedchamber to King Charles II, whose sentiments towards the opposite sex he shared. In 1673 it was rumoured
that he had got Barbara, the Duchess of Cleveland, the King's ex-
mistress, with child and the following year he was involved in a love
triangle with Mary Kirke, a Maid of Honour to the Duchess of York,
who was also sharing her favours with the Duke of Monmouth and
the Duke of York. The child born of these proceedings, a boy, died
a few hours after its birth. To his credit the lady never accused him
'*of getting ye child or any other act*' therefore the paternity must be laid
at the door of one of the other participants.

In Bishop Burnet's estimation, Buckingham was

'a nobleman of learning, and good natural parts, but of no principle; violent for the High Church, yet seldom goes to it; very proud, insolent and covetous, and takes all advantages'.

It is recorded of him that when James II had just returned to London after his first ineffectual attempt to leave the country, Mulgrave, as he was then known, produced a warrant ready drawn for signature by the unfortunate King which would have created him a Marquess, whereupon the irritated King exclaimed '*Good God, what a time you take to ask a thing of that nature*'. Unsuccessful in his attempt he had to wait until 1694, when William III created him Marquess of Normanby. He received his Dukedom from Queen Anne in 1703, an honour perceived by some as just reward for his courtship of her some twenty years previously.

Although the Duchess bore her second husband several children, only one survived to adulthood. When her first son was born in 1710 and died an infant, her mother accused the Duke of killing it with over care because

'he wou'd not let it suck from the apprehension he had that there was no sound woman to be mett with, nor fed with a spoon because he designed the Dutchess when she was well enough shou'd give it suck herself, so he had an invention of a sucking bottle wch was so managed in short the child was starved…'

Their only surviving child Edmund, who succeeded his father as Duke of Buckinghamshire, served under his uncle the Duke of Berwick during his last campaign in Germany, and died in 1735, of consumption.

The Duchess, who survived until 1742, was an assiduous supporter of the rights of her half brother the Old Pretender and visited him often in Rome. On one occasion, in 1731, upon her return, she met with the King's first minister Robert Walpole in an effort to convert him to the cause, only to find herself unwittingly betraying to him her plans for a restoration. Her haughtiness was a byword, and after hearing Whitefield preach, wrote to Lady Huntingdon in the following words:

'I thank your ladyship for the information concerning the Methodist preachers. Their doctrines are most repulsive, and strongly tinctured with impertinence, and disrespect towards their superiors. It is monstrous to be told that you have a heart as sinful as the common wretches that crawl the earth. I cannot but wonder that your ladyship should relish any sentiments so much at variance with high rank and good breeding'.

Katherine's younger full brother, James Darnley Fitzjames, was born in 1685, but died the following year when he was buried in Westminster Abbey.

Chapter VI
The Bastards of Charles Stuart
(1720–88)

HRH Charlotte Stuart, LT, Duchess of Albany (1753–89)

Charlotte was the illegitimate daughter of Charles Edward Stuart, *de jure* King Charles III, known to history as Bonnie Prince Charlie, the hero of the 1745 Jacobite Rising and the eldest grandson of King James II in the legitimate male line. Of her Robert Burns wrote:

'This lovely's maid's of Royal blood, that ruled Albion's kingdoms three, but oh, Alas, for her bonnie face, they've wronged the Lass of Albany. We'll daily pray, we'll nightly pray, on bended knée most fervently, the time will come, with pipe and drum, we'll welcome home fair Albany'.

Wronged poor Charlotte certainly was. The famously unlucky star which afflicted the Stuarts began its malign influence with her birth and waned only with her death.

It was in December 1745, during the Highland Rising, that Charles met Charlotte's mother, shortly after the retreat from Derby to Glasgow. She was Clementina, daughter of the ardent Jacobite, John Walkinshaw of Barrowfield and Camlachie by Catherine, daughter of Sir Hugh Paterson of Bannockburn and Lady Jean Erskine, daughter of Charles, 5th Earl of Mar.

Charles, conspicuous for his lack of womanising, formed an attraction for Clementina at Bannockburn House whilst she nursed his severe fever after the victorious Battle of Falkirk. The attraction was mutual, but the relationship platonic, overtaken by events culminating in Charles' defeat at Culloden, the legendary five months on the run in the Western Isles and his eventual escape to France. Once on the continent Charles vented his anguish by a descent into alchoholism and the high emotion of two passionate love affairs. The first was with Louise de Rohan, Duchess de Montbazon, his first cousin on his maternal Sobieski side. It produced the elder of his two illegitimate children, a little boy named Charles who was born weak and died in early 1749 aged nearly six months. Immediately afterwards, Charles fell into the arms of another Polish cousin, Marie-Anne Jablonowska, Princess de Talmont – an explosive relationship which ended without issue.

In May 1752, desperate for the warmth of domesticity, Charles sent for Clementina Walkinshaw with whom he set up home. They lived together as Count and Countess Johnson in Liège where their daughter, Charlotte, was born in 1753 and christened in October in the Church of La Bienheureuse Vierge Marie des Fonts. It was this open demonstration of a family life, which gave rise to the doubtful view that it constituted marriage under Scots Law. Concern that they had actually married provoked Charles' younger brother, Cardinal Henry, into demanding from Clementina a written declaration to the contrary on pain of forfeiting her allowance. She had little option but to agree. Yet that was in 1767, after the couple had separated, and was designed to clear the way for Charles to marry and produce the legitimate male heir who was never to be.

Although Charles adored his little '*Pouponne*', his relationship with Clementina was deteriorating because of his heavy drinking, justified fear of assassination by the Hanoverians, and constant travelling in desperate attempts to rescue something of the Stuart Cause. Towards the end of 1755 and until 1756 the family lived together in Basle as Dr and Mrs Thompson – the Hanoverian minister in Berne described their appearance as: '*persons of easy fortune, but without the least affection of show or magnificence*'.

Charles' condition reached rock bottom upon the death knell of the Stuart Cause when, in November 1759, a French naval force under his nominal command, led by the Duke d'Aiguillon and the Count de Conflans, was destroyed in Quiberon Bay by Admiral Hawke during an attempt to invade Ireland. The much abused Clementina could take no more and in July 1760 fled with Charlotte from the Château de Carlsbourg to Paris with the help of Charles' father and the protection of Louis XV. Charles was beside himself with grief but, unable to get his beloved daughter back, could only cope with this loss by cutting off all contact with her and Clementina.

In Paris, mother and daughter lived quiet lives under the care of the Archbishop of Paris at the Convent of the Nuns of the Visitation whilst Charles isolated himself at Carlsbourg until succeeding his father in Rome upon the latter's death in 1766.

The French then produced a young bride for Charles – Princess Louise von Stolberg-Gedern. The couple were married in early 1772 and the bride's single task was to produce a male heir to keep the Stuart card in play. But Louise proved barren whereupon, having recovered his health, Charles relapsed into drinking. Finally, Louise began an infamous affair with the young playboy, Count Vittorio Alfieri, and she and Charles were formally separated in 1784.

This marriage and its failure to produce an heir had a profound effect on Charlotte Stuart's life. Upon his father's death, Charles angrily refused to maintain Clementina and Charlotte's allowance, maintaining his total silence towards them, refusing to answer a single letter from either. So his brother Henry took this duty upon himself, though reducing their pension from 6,000 to 5,000 livres and demanding from Clementina her written declaration that she and his brother had never married. Mother and daughter had to leave Paris for cheaper lodgings in the Convent of Notre Dame de la Miséricorde in Meaux-en-Brie.

Horrified by the implications of her father's marriage, Charlotte travelled with Clementina to Rome in 1772 to appeal for recognition, bravely refusing to see her father without her mother. Forced back to Meaux by Henry, he at least agreed to allow them to move back to Paris where Charlotte's petition to Louis XVI for material assistance was refused because, as Horace Walpole observed: '*The House of FitzJames, fearing their becoming a burden to themselves, prevented the acknowledgement of the daughter*'.

The next blow came in early 1775. Despite having ignored his daughter for so long, Charles decided he néeded to keep Charlotte in reserve as the Stuarts last hope. Though at her most eligible age, he forced her to promise neither to marry nor take the veil. These orders were communicated to her by Abbé Gordon, Principal of the Scots College in Paris who wrote back to Charles that:

'Your letter touched her to such a degree that I was sorry I had spoken to her so freely ... She was only six years old when she was carried off, so that she ought not to be entirely ruined for a fault of which her age hindered her to be anybody's partner ... She deserves better, being esteemed by all who know her as one the most accomplished women in this town ...'

It was this most impossible of social situations which convinced Charlotte in early 1776 to resign herself to the drab life of an honorary canoness at a convent in Franche-Comté. On her way she was invited to dinner by Lord Elcho. She was twenty-two, outgoing, full of common sense and very patient. She had dark blond hair and bright blue eyes, being described by Horace Mann as having: '*a good figure, tall and well made*'. There she met and fell in love with her relation, the handsome, thirty-seven year old Prince Ferdinand de Rohan. Like Charlotte he too was neither free to marry nor have a family. For as the youngest son of the Duke de Montbazon he had been pushed into a church career and become the Archbishop of Bordeaux.

Changing her plans, Charlotte returned to Paris where Ferdinand leased a house for her and her mother on the same Rue St Jacques upon which stood the convent in which they lived as lady pensioners. He also acquired a country home for them south of Paris at Anthony. Having given up all hope of ever being recognised by and reconciled with her father, Charlotte began a secret family with Ferdinand. Between 1779–84 she bore him three children, Marie Victoire, Charlotte and Charles. For years their fates remained one of the mysteries of late Stuart history.

Yet it was precisely at this time that Charles' relationship with Louise von Stolberg was breaking up and his robust health beginning to fail. This prompted him to perform an astonishing *volte face*. In a document dated March 23rd with a codicil dated two days later, Charles decided to make Charlotte his sole heir. In addition he created her Duchess of Albany, a dukedom traditionally reserved for the heirs of Kings of Scots. Five days later he raised her to the status of legitimate child with the additional title of Her Royal Highness and secured recognition of all this by the Vatican as well as the King and Parliament of France. Ultimately he invested her with the Order of the Thistle and even passed to her the right of Royal Succession. Yet it wasn't until Charles recovered from his second near-fatal stroke in early 1784 that he wrote to Charlotte, telling her of his decisions and asking her to come and live with him in Florence. It should have been the answer to her prayers. But she had long given up hope for such a thing and was at that time pregnant with her third child.

Charlotte was unable to breathe a word of her secret family to either her father Charles in Florence nor uncle Henry in Rome. So she left her three children in Paris under the care of their grandmother, Clementina Walkinshaw as well as Ferdinand de Rohan and left for Italy, assuming their separation would not last too long.

Arriving in Florence on October 5th, 1785 Charlotte managed to nurse both her father and his finances back to health, bringing him greater happiness than he had known at any time since the Highland Rising. She also became the only woman to win and keep the heart of her uncle with whom she reconciled the notoriously difficult Charles after decades of estrangement, and returned her father into the bosom of the Roman Catholic Church of his birth, winning praise from the Pope himself. Charlotte finally managed the unthinkable – Charles began to write warm and courteous letters to her mother. In her own to Clementina she revealed how badly she missed her family, openly hoping they would soon be reunited.

Her friends called her '*the angel of peace*' and '*her father's guardian angel*'. As the author of Charles' happy twilight after her own long years of denial, Charlotte deserved much when her father finally died in 1788. But she had contracted a malignant cancer of the liver. Her last weeks of life were lived out in the knowledge she would never see her children, mother nor Ferdinand again, and in desperate concern for their safety in Paris with the outbreak of the French Revolution. In October 1789 Charlotte wrote to Clementina:

> '*Don't worry. I am well. I love you and will send news as soon as possible. Please kiss my dear friends for me*'.

She died in Bologna one week later, at the house of the Marchesa Giulia Lambertini-Bovio who wrote to Henry that: '*So blessed was her death, that the tears I pour out from grief are tears of tenderness*'.

SECTION III

HANOVERIAN BASTARDS

1714–1901

Chapter VII
The Bastards of George I
(1660–1727)

Anna Louise Sophie, Grafin Von Delitz
(1692–1773)

Unlike their Stuart predecessors, the early Hanoverian Kings of England did not publicly acknowledge any of their illegitimate children. However there is enough contemporary documentary evidence to attribute paternity, and most modern German historians now believe that George I was the father of at least three illegitimate children: Anna Louise Sophie, Grafin von Delitz, Petronelle Melusine, Countess of Chesterfield (*see* page 120) and Margaret Gertrude, Grafin zu Schaumburg-Lippe (*see* page 122).

Anna Louise Sophie was born in January 1692, and registered as the child of Friedrich Achaz von der Schulenburg and his wife Margarethe Gertrud. The latter, a daughter of Gustaf Adolf, Baron von der Schulenburg, was a sister of the celebrated Ehrengard Melusina, Duchess of Kendal and mistress of King George I. By attributing the paternity of his child to another, George was simply following accepted convention and one only has to remember the example of the Countess of Castlemaine, all of whose children bore her husband's surname until acknowledged by King Charles.

Anna Louise Sophie's mother was in fact Ehrengard Melusine, but for the duration of her mother's life she was officially passed off as her niece. Why George never acknowledged her is unknown, but it might have been because she was born before his divorce, and the scandal that was attached to it, plus the discretion demanded by his father in all matters of the heart, did not encourage him to do so. However this was in strange contrast to the honour accorded to George's half sister Sophie Charlotte von Kielmansegg, who was granted the Brunswick arms, by George, with the obligatory baton sinister to denote illegitimacy.

By not publicly acknowledging Anna Louisa Sophie as his daughter, there was much speculation about her origins and status. Some of her contemporaries assumed that she was George's mistress, and others (Lord Hervey) claimed that she performed a similar service for George II and Frederick, Prince of Wales. Lord Hervey said of her:

> *'Madame d'Elitz was a Schulenburg, sister to my Lady Chesterfield, a very handsome lady, though now a little in her decline, with a great deal of wit, who had had a thousand lovers, and had been catched in bed with a man twenty years ago (1716) and been divorced from her husband upon it. She was said to have been mistress to three generations of the Hanover family; the late King, the present, and the Prince of Wales before he came to England ...'*

Except for a minor indiscretion in his youth, George did not take another mistress after Ehrengard Melusine. Indeed in many ways she, together with their three girls, made the happy family unit that George himself lacked, and upon arriving in England in 1714, he lost little time in arranging their passage from Hanover. By this time Anna Louise Sophie had been married off to the noble Ernst August Philipp von dem Busshe-Ippenburg, a relative, it would seem, of Johann von dem Bussche, brother-in-law of the Countess von Platen und Hallermund, sometime mistress of George I's father, Ernst August. Sadly the marriage did not last as has been explained above. She was by all accounts a witty and accomplished young woman and, despite her behaviour, George remained fond of her, so much so that he bought her a beautiful palace at Herrenhausen in Hanover and arranged with the Emperor that she should be granted the title of Grafin von Delitz in 1722.

Eventually she sold the palace and bought a house in Paddington instead. She was not her mother's favourite child, for that honour went to her younger sister Petronelle. Of her mother it is reported that upon her arrival in England, she was mobbed and booed by a crowd whilst riding in her carriage. Frightened she cried out '*Goot peoples, ve haf come only for your goots!*' The crowd replied wittily '*Yes! And for our chattels too*'.

The Grafin von Delitz eventually died in 1773, aged eighty-one, without issue, requesting that her body be buried with that of her mother Ehrengard in South Audley St Chapel, London. *The Complete*

Peerage records that at her death, she was known as the Hon Lady Dallet, presumably a corruption of the name Delitz.

Petronelle, Countess of Chesterfield (1693–1778)

Petronelle was the second daughter of King George I by his favourite mistress Ehrengard Melusine von der Schulenburg, in Germany, a Maid of Honour to the Electress, Sophia of Hanover, later she was created Duchess of Kendal for life in 1716 in the English Peerage, and was also created by the Emperor, Princess of Eberstein in 1723.

Ehrengard was appointed a Lady in Waiting to the Electress Sophie in 1690 and within a short time had captured the heart of her son George. She came from a very illustrious Altmark family, who could trace their ancestry back to the 13th century. Her eldest brother, later a Field Marshal, was in the service of the Duke of Brunswick-Wolfenbuttal. She was tall and thin, thus earning her the nickname 'Malkin' (scarecrow/hoppole). In temperament she was pliant and patient and shared with George an interest in music and the theatre. Her future son-in-law the Graf zu Schaumburg-Lippe praised her desire '*to do all the good she can*'.

Petronelle was born in 1693, a year before her father's marriage was dissolved. Like her elder sister, she was registered as the child of Friedrich Achaz von Schulenburg and his wife Margarethe Gertrud. However, like her sisters she was never publicly recognized by her father by the usual means of a grant of the royal arms, duly differenced. Contemporary sources speak of Petronelle as good looking and spirited enough to speak her mind to George on issues where she disagreed with him. Like her mother she was appointed a Lady in Waiting to her grandmother the Dowager Electress.

Why she chose to marry Lord Chesterfield is unknown. His reputation did not stand up to close scrutiny. He was after all a member of the Hellfire Club and had taken as his mistress the notorious Elizabeth Dennison, a celebrated bawd, who ran a bawdy house in Covent Garden in the 1730s. Although known as 'Hell-fire Stanhope' she was a woman of '*Pleasant manners, humour and wit*'. Chesterfield also took a fancy to George Anne Bellamy, a celebrated actress, the illegitimate daughter of James O'Hara, Earl of Tyrawley, whose '*beauty, wit and intelligence, --- talents, --- generosity and refined manners irresistibly attracted everyone to her*'.

As a prospective son-in-law he was less than appealing. He was also the grandson of Philip, Earl of Chesterfield, the first love of Barbara Palmer, subsequently Lady Castlemaine.

In 1722 Petronelle was created Countess of Walsingham for life, but after her marriage in 1733 to Philip Dormer (Stanhope), 4th Earl of Chesterfield, KG, she adopted the title of her husband and died without children in 1778. 'Her portion', according to the *Complete Peerage* was said to have been '£50,000 *down and* £3,000 *per annum payable out of the Civil List revenue in Ireland during her life*'.

Her mother, the Duchess of Kendal, who died in 1743, left her a part of her immense wealth, but according to one source (Lord Hervey), both mother and daughter had been defrauded out of the money left to them by George I as a result of his successor (George II) burning the will. When the Earl threatened to take legal proceedings, George II gave him £20,000 as a *quietus*. However a copy of George's will has survived and in it he left his mistress almost £23,000, thus seemingly disposing of the rumour that she was defrauded out of her bequest

The earl held a number of important appointments and served twice as a Lord of the Bedchamber to King George II, as Captain of the Yeoman of the Guard, as Ambassador to The Hague (where he distinguished himself by the magnificence of his entertainments), as Lord Steward of the Household and as Lord Lieutenant of Ireland. He was the author of the *Chesterfield Letters* written to his illegitimate son, which, according to Dr Johnson '*inculcated the morals of a Strumpet and the manners of a dancing master*'. He died in 1773 '*of a slow decay*' at Chesterfield House, Mayfair aged seventy-eight.

Margaret Gertrude, Countess von Schaumburg-Lippe (1701–26)

Margaret Gertrud was the youngest daughter of King George I by his favourite mistress Ehrengard Melusine, Baroness von der Schulenburg and was born in 1701. The gap between her birth and that of her elder sisters is curious, given that their father was not absent on campaign. However, like them she was registered as a child of different parents: Rabe Christoph von Oeynhausen and his wife Sophie Juliane von der Schulenburg, sister of the Duchess of Kendal.

'Trudchen' – Gertrud's nickname – was her father's favourite and at the age of twenty was married to Albrecht Wolfgang, Graf zu Schaumburg-Lippe, who succeeded his father as ruler of Schaumburg-Lippe in 1728. She was by all accounts a beautiful and accomplished young woman, but one that was not destined to survive her husband, dying in 1726 of tuberculosis, having borne him two sons. She was also trilingual and able to speak fluent German, French and English as could her two sons.

Her husband and his brother had both been educated in England because of their parents estrangement, and in 1720 the elder had entered George's service before being chosen as Margaret's husband. That it was a political marriage that later turned into a love match, is clear from the knowledge that George I stated in their marriage contract, that he would defend Schaumburg-Lippe against all its enemies and the affection in which they held each other.

However, their elder son died young, having been killed, it was rumoured, in a duel whilst studying at Leiden University. The younger, who succeeded his father, was an ally to Britain during the Seven Years War and was entrusted by the Portuguese King with the reorganisation of that monarch's army; he also wrote treatises on the art of war. All in all, a very accomplished young man.

Chapter VIII
The Bastards of George II
(1683–1760)

Field Marshal Johann Ludwig, Count von Wallmoden (1736–1811)

Johann Ludwig von Wallmoden is believed to have been the illegitimate son of King George II by Amalie Sophie Marianne von Wallmoden, the daughter of Johann Franz Dietrich von Wendt, a general in the Hanoverian Service by his wife Friederike Charlotte von dem Busshe, first cousin of Sophia Charlotte von Kielmansegge, George I's illegitimate sister. As he was born three years before his mother's divorce in 1739, for propriety's sake Johann was given the surname of her husband, Gottlieb Adam von Wallmoden, Oberhauptmann of Calenberg (by whom she had already had a son Franz Ernst). Like Johann's aunts, the illegitimate daughters of George I, he was never publicly acknowledged or granted the royal arms with due differences. He therefore used the arms of Wallmoden, whose name he bore.

Madam von Wallmoden first caught the King's eye in 1735 during a visit to Hanover. Surprisingly, the King then wrote to his wife, the Queen, describing his conquest in some detail. The result of this intimacy, Johann, was born in April 1736. He was brought up at the English Court, to which his mother had been brought by the King. She was installed at St James's Palace and was created Countess of Yarmouth on 24 March 1740. Her arrival was hailed by Walpole, in the hope that her influence might be politically helpful, but in the event, Lady Yarmouth proved entirely unfit for the role of a Pompadour, and she had the good sense to abstain from meddling in Court intrigues. Prior to Madam Wallmoden, the King had Lady Suffolk as his mistress after whom he enjoyed the favours of Lady Deloraine, governess to the Princesses Mary and Louisa.

Lady Deloraine was the widow of Henry Scott, Earl of Deloraine, younger son of the ill-fated Duke of Monmouth, illegitimate son of King Charles II. She was his second wife and was made a widow by his sudden death in 1730, aged fifty-five, the same age as his grandfather King Charles, when he died. At the time of her affair with King George, she was the wife of William Wyndham, of Ersham, Norfolk. Although described by Lord Hervey as '*very handsome*', Sir Robert Walpole's description of her was less than flattering: '*very dangerous, a weak head, a pretty face, a lying tongue, and a false heart, making always sad work*'. By her first husband she bore two daughters.

After the death of the King in 1760, whose affections she never lost, the Countess of Yarmouth, returned to Hanover, where she died on 19 October 1765. Meanwhile Johann entered the Hanoverian Service where he bore high command, in the war with the French (1793-1801) albeit with no great distinction, even though he was a Field Marshal. He also became Count Wallmoden of Hanover and died some ten years afterwards in Hanover in October 1811.

Chapter IX
The Bastards of Frederick, Prince of Wales, son of King George II (1707–51)

Cornwall FitzFrederick (1732–36)And Amelia FitzFrederick (*b & d.* 1733)

Both children were the illegitimate issue of Frederick, Prince of Wales and The Hon. Anne Vane. She was the daughter of Gilbert, 2nd Baron Barnard and the sister of Henry, 1st Earl of Darlington as well as the sister-in-law of Grace FitzRoy, daughter of Charles, 1st Duke of Southampton and 2nd Duke of Cleveland, (*see* page 56), the illegitimate son of King Charles II. Anne was well known from Dr. Samuel Johnson's line '*Yet Vane can tell what ills from beauty spring*', but she died unmarried in Bath on 11 March 1735/6, outliving both her children.

Her son, Cornwall FitzFrederick was born on 4 June 1732 and baptised on 17 June following at St James Piccadilly. He died on 23 February 1736 and was buried on 26 February in Westminster Abbey, aged only three.

His sister, Amelia FitzFrederick, was born on 21 April 1733, but she died the following day on 22 April 1733.

Chapter X
The Bastards of George, Prince of Wales, later King George IV (1762-1830)

Major George Seymour Crole
(1799–1863)

George Seymour Crole, was born 23 August 1799 in Chelsea, the illegitimate son of George, Prince of Wales, later George IV, and Elizabeth Fox, alias Crole. He was never officially recognised by his father, although there is evidence to show that he admitted to it privately, but he was provided for throughout his life by his father as well as William IV and Queen Victoria.

George's mother had been born about 1770, the daughter of Joseph and Eleanor Fox. Joseph had been a tavern keeper in Bow St, Covent Garden before acquiring the lease of the Brighton theatre, and was described by one contemporary as *'a very odd character ... he could combine twenty occupations without being clever in one ... He was actor, fiddler, painter etc'* and by another as *'a low person at Brighthelmstone'*.

Mr Fox died in 1791, leaving considerable debts of £2,700, whereupon his widow sold the theatre for an annuity of £70 and a free benefit performance. It was about this time that Elizabeth adopted the name of Crole, although no one seems to know why. She also became the mistress of George, the 3rd Earl of Egremont, who installed her in a house in Hans Place, Chelsea. She bore him four children, Mary, born about 1792, Charles Richard, born 1793, Elizabeth Eleanor, born 1796 and William John, born 1797. The elder son became an officer in the army and the younger son became a clergyman.

Young Crole's date of birth suggests that Elizabeth's relationship with the Prince of Wales began in late 1798, although there is evidence to suggest that it may have begun earlier in the year. Egremont had settled on her an annuity of £400 per annum, whereas the Prince promised her an annuity of £1,000 plus a house in Pall Mall. Sadly neither materialized and Elizabeth was forced to remain at Hans Place. However, she did eventually receive an annuity of £500 from the Privy Purse which was paid to her for the rest of her life.

Although the young 'prince' did not like the army life '*I never had much partiality for it, as it neither suits my habits nor inclinations*', he declared, he entered the service as an Ensign in the 21st Dragoons (1817), having first been to the Royal Military Academy at Sandhurst where he studied arithmetic, French, mathematics, fortification and military drawing, the fees for which were paid from the Privy Purse. In 1818 he was transferred to the 11th Dragoons and then promoted to Lieutenant (1820). For ten years he served in India where he became ADC to the Marquess of Hastings, Governor of Bengal, and subsequently Earl Amherst, living sumptuously in Government House. In 1823 he became a Captain by purchase in the 41st Regiment of Foot and then purchased the rank of Major (1826) for £1,400. He then returned home, before being sent off to the Ionian Islands with the 28th Foot.

According to his mother he was '*a very gentlemanlike young man quiet and unpresuming – having been all his life accustomed to consider himself as the natural son of the King*'. On the death of his alleged father King George IV in 1830, he was left a capital sum of £30,000 plus a cash payment of £10,000. The capital sum earned him an annuity of £300 which enabled him to quit the army the following year and sell his commission, being '*heartily sick of the service.*' He then settled down to civilian life and spent the remainder of his years living at Chatham in the Sun Hotel where he had gone to spend just one night, but instead remained there for thirty years. He was regarded as a generous, if somewhat eccentric character; he died there unmarried on 18 June 1863 and was buried in Highgate Cemetery. All of his assets passed to his younger half brother the Rev William John Crole Wyndham. His only surviving sister, Mary, married Mrs Jordan's eldest son the Earl of Munster (*see* page 129). His mother, who never married, died on 15 February 1840, aged sixty-nine.

Chapter XI
The Bastards of William, Duke of Clarence, later King William IV (1765–1837)

William Henry Courtenay (1788–1807)

William Henry Courtenay, was born around 1788, the eldest known illegitimate son of William, Duke of Clarence, later King William IV by an unknown mother. One source speculates that he might have been born near Lake Courtenay in Nova Scotia, or to be more precise Shelburne, which the Prince had visited in October 1788. By the following year, the latter was back in England and had taken up in quick succession with two young women, Sally Winne, the daughter of a Plymouth merchant, and Polly Finch, '*a handsome young woman who plied her trade in London*'. Not surprisingly the Prince's reputation suffered a great deal with this type of behaviour, and indeed his army friend Lieutenant William Dyott recorded of him that he '*would go into any house where he saw a pretty girl, and was perfectly acquainted with every house of a certain description in the town* (Shelburne)'. He was known by his friends as 'Silly Billy'. Other sources have suggested that William was conceived and born in Hanover.

It was not until the Prince met Mrs Jordan and settled down to a decade of cosy domesticity, that his reputation improved somewhat. That the Duke and Mrs Jordan were intimate prior to 1793 it clear from the fact that she miscarried the Duke's first child by her on 6 August 1792, the Duke declaring '*the papers have on this occasion told the truth, for she was last week for some hours in danger, but now, thank God, she is much better and I hope in a fair way of recovery*'.

Young Courtenay first appears in the Prince's household in 1794 and was cared for by Mrs Jordan, despite the fact that she was not his mother. Indeed he was very fond of her and she of him: '*I left*

William at school' she wrote on one occasion '*who cried on my leaving him, and told Mrs Sketchley that he would rather live with Mrs Jordan...*' On another occasion Mrs Jordan wrote to the Prince that he was '*a very fine boy and will, I am sure, prove himself everything you wish*'.

Courtenay's first taste of the naval life came in 1803 when he joined the ship *Majestic* at Plymouth as a volunteer 1st class, aged fifteen. The ship's captain was none other than Lord Amelius Beauclerk, third son of the 5th Duke of St Albans and himself a great-great-grandson of King Charles II. The *Majestic* was part of the Channel Fleet that blockaded Brest and guarded the approaches to Ireland in order to prevent the French transports from invading England. His next assignment was a stint of service in the *Tribune* which took him to Gibraltar and on the homeward journey witnessed the capture of five small Spanish vessels. Next the Duke obtained for him the post of midshipman on the ship *Blenheim* which promptly sailed for the East Indies escorting a convoy of twenty-two East Indiamen. The ship arrived in India on 23 August 1805, and whilst there Courtenay was transferred to the frigate *Macassar* only to return to the *Blenheim* a short time after. In retrospect this was to be a fateful decision, because the *Blenheim* was not seaworthy, having run aground on a sandbank in the Straits of Malacca. On 1 February 1807 the ship was caught up in a squall six hundred miles east of Mauritius and lost with all hands on board, including young Courtenay – a loss keenly felt by his father and Mrs Jordan. Writing a year later to Thomas Coutts, the banker, the Duke speaking of his children, remarked '*I have lost one who was drowned in the Blenheim. I have one in the Army and at the Military College, the second in the Navy.*'

George Augustus Frederick FitzClarence, PC, FRS, 1st Earl of Munster (1794–1842)

George FitzClarence was born on 29 January 1794 at seven o'clock in the morning in Somerset Street, off Portman Square, London, the eldest of five sons and five daughters all born to the indefatigable Dorothy Bland *alias* Mrs Jordan (1761–1816), the well known comic actress, by her Royal lover the Duke of Clarence, later King William IV. This liaison was popularly described as '*his bathing in the River Jordan*'. George's date of birth differs from that given in *The Complete Peerage* and was taken from a list prepared by William IV and signed by him in the Archives of Wemyss Castle.

Dora, as she was known to William, the younger daughter of Francis Bland, an actor and stage hand, (and himself the third son of Nathaniel Bland, an Irish Judge), possessed many good qualities but chastity was not one of them, having previously had three illegitimate children by Sir Richard Ford, a police magistrate, and another son by Richard Daly, the manager of the Theatre Royal in Cork. Her fecundity was remarkable, and at her death she was survived by no less than thirteen of her fourteen children. Her family's motto *Nec Temere Nec Timide* (neither rashly nor fearfully) was not followed by the Duke and his lover, as their twenty year affair was conducted openly and all their children were given the surname of FitzClarence. She was described by Leigh Hunt (RA-GEO/Add/40/255) as '*so pleasant, so cordial, so natural, so full of spirits, so healthily constituted in mind and body, had such a shapely leg withal, so charming a voice and such a happy and happy-making expression of countenance*'

Nevertheless, the hundreds of letters in the Royal Archives between Mrs. Jordan and her royal lover from 1790–1814 testify to the strength and longevity of their relationship. Yet ultimately it seems to have foundered from lack of money as Mrs. Jordan's acting career came to an end and their debts began to mount. In 1811 the Duke of Clarence coldly began a seven year search to find a rich wife who emerged in the shape of Princess Adelaide Louisa Theresa Caroline Amelia (1792–1849), the eldest daughter of George I, reigning Duke of Saxe Meiningen. They were duly married in 1819 but had no surviving issue. Tonybee in his introduction to the actor *Macready's Diaries*, states that '*it is perhaps not surprising that in after years he (Macready) should have poured bitter contempt on the royal lover who, having profited for years by her splendid earnings, abruptly consigned her to poverty and neglect*'. For five years later, Mrs. Jordan died near Paris, in exile, alone, as well as in poverty and misery.

Meanwhile, George, their eldest child, became a soldier by profession and served in the 10th Royal Hussars. In the Royal Archives, there are literally hundreds of letters to him from both his mother and father and these give some account of his military experiences from the age of fourteen when he first sailed for Portugal. His father was obviously proud of him, especially with reports from Brigadier General Charles Stewart, (to whom he was ADC), describing him as a *'Gallant Fellow'* (RA-GEO/Add/39/07) and writing to *'express my continued satisfaction and approbation'* (RA-GEO/Add/39/20). His mother's letters were more critical urging him to pay more attention to his writing and spelling and referring to his bills which she thought *'extravagantly high'*.

He later fought at the battle of Corunna, was wounded and captured by the French at Fuentes de Onoro, but escaped, wounded again at Toulon and later served in India as ADC to the Governor General. On his return from his first term of duty his proud father wrote to his sister Princess Amelia in the following words:

'I am happy to inform you that George arrived last night in high health and spirits, after having established a perfect character with all ranks in our army'.
'General Stewart, (later 3rd Marquess of Londonderry), who certainly on one occasion saved his life, speaks of my son in such terms of commendation, that unless writing to you I would not mention the circumstances. Indeed in the event of the General going again he told me he would rather have George than any other for his aide-de-camp'.

Despite retiring on half pay as a Lieutenant Colonel of the Coldstream Guards in 1828, George was appointed Deputy Adjutant General of the Forces in July 1830 but resigned in high dudgeon the following December. Ultimately he was promoted to Major General in 1841 to command Western District, and was appointed Lieutenant of the Tower of London (1831–33), Constable of Windsor Castle (from 1833 with its annual salary of £1,300 and membership of the Privy Council), and ADC to his father and later Queen Victoria. However, after much lobbying, he had had to wait until the advanced age of thirty-seven before he was ennobled as Earl of Munster in 1831 following his father's accession. Nevertheless, he was disappointed that it was not a dukedom even though it was one of his father's former titles. He therefore spent the next ten years asking for more. However, despite all these honours and being described in the patent as '*Our dearly beloved natural son*', he and his brothers were constantly to plague their father for more honours and appointments and more cash, and indeed when George was asked who should carry the Crown at his father's Coronation, his retort was *'who is more fit that your own flesh and blood'*. The *Morning Post* was incensed at *'the impudence and rapacity'* of the FitzJordans, and in the next reign, Queen Victoria was to dismiss her cousins as *'ghosts best forgotten'*.

Much of his time in later life seems to have been spent in pursuit of fame, fortune and honours. He was constantly pressing both his father and afterwards Queen Victoria for financial help and for lucrative appointments for both himself and even his children. In the Royal Archives is a bound book of 113 pages, being *A Copy of correspondence between His Majesty King William IV and the Right Honble The Earl of Munster in April and May* 1837 *relative to a provision for the Earldom of Munster with a commentary thereon and An Appendix containing a copy of a former correspondence upon the same subject* (RA-GEO/Add/39/657). This shows in some detail and at great length, how the King had attempted to provide equally for all his children and how Munster was affronted by not having received more on the grounds of primogeniture and the need to endow his earldom. Indeed, at one stage, he even refused to accept payments on the grounds that they were not enough and for a time he estranged himself from his father.

Queen Victoria's diaries also make many references to this. On 24 January 1838 the Queen *'showed him* [Lord Melbourne] *a letter from Lord Munster to Lord Conyngham expressing his gratitude and wishing to see me to thank me in his own and in his brothers' and sisters' names for what I had done for them'* (VIC/QVJ/1838 24 January) – i.e. extending their annual allowances, originally granted by King George IV. Four months later, George was back seeing Lord Melbourne about their FitzClarence pensions from the Civil List. In the diary entry for 15 May 1838 it states that '*Lord Munster told Lord Melbourne that the late King always imagined that Lord Egremont* (his father-in-law) *would leave Lord Munster a great deal'* whereas in the event he gave Lord Munster £5,000 about a fortnight before he died. Egremont had long been suspicious that *'the King had promoted the match on account of the money'*. But in September that year, there is a reference to Egremont having given George a property in Somerset.

In 1819 George had married another bastard, Mary Wyndham, natural daughter of the Earl of Egremont (who regarded her as over-religious), by whom he had four sons and three daughters, and indeed one of his grandsons was to be awarded a VC and bar. George was soon busy promoting their interests as well as his own, when writing to his father and later Queen Victoria over the next twenty years, both of whom were remarkably generous and tolerant. Indeed there are many references in Queen Victoria's diaries to Munster dining at Windsor, including on Christmas Day 1838 when he '*was in high spirits and talking a great deal*' prompting Melbourne to comment '*I never knew such a wrong-headed man; he never sees a thing right; and then always thinks he is right.*' (VIC/QVJ/1838 26 December). There are also three large filing boxes of correspondence in the Royal Archives entitled *The Munster Papers* 1805–41 but they do not cast George in a favourable light.

Sadly George never came to terms with his lot and he was still writing to Lord Melbourne (RA-GEO/Add 39/629) about the possibility of succeeding Major General Sir Henry Frederick Bouverie as Governor of Malta in 1839, and to the Duke of Wellington about money or lack of it as late as 15 December 1841 (RA-GEO/Add 39/637). Three months later, on 20 March 1842, a disappointed man and aged only forty-eight, he shot himself at his home in Belgravia, just five years after his father's death, and with a pistol presented to him by his uncle George when Prince of Wales. Greville's Memoirs note that

'he was a man not without talent, but wrongheaded, and having had the folly to quarrel with his father and estrange himself from Court during the greater part of his reign, he fell into comparative obscurity and real poverty, and there can be no doubt that the disappointment of the expectations he once formed, together with the domestic unhappiness of a dawdling, ill conditioned vexatious wife, preyed upon his mind and led him to this act.

His will was proved at under £40,000 and his widow died nine months later in December 1842. One hundred and sixty years later the Earldom of Munster is now extinct in the male line upon the death in 2002 of the 7th and last Earl, Anthony Charles. He was a graphic designer and a stained glass conservator and he and his ancestors before him, bore the Royal Arms of King William IV, shorn of the escutcheon of the arch treasurer of the Holy Roman Empire and of the Crown of Hanover, but with *a baton sinister azure, charged with three anchors or*. However, descendants of Mrs Jordan and William IV still survive to this day through the marriages of their many daughters.

Sophia, Baroness De L'Isle & Dudley, *(née* FitzClarence) (1795–1837)

The eldest daughter of Mrs Jordan by her Royal lover the Duke of Clarence, later King William IV, was born on 4 March 1795 in Somerset Street, off Portman Square. At the beginning of their association the Duke had given Dora (as he called her) an annual allowance of £1,000, but on the instruction of his father, King George III, the Duke of Clarence then wrote suggesting that he should halve her allowance to £500. By way of reply, Mrs Jordan sent him the bottom half of a playbill bearing the words *'No money will be returned after the rising of the curtain'*.

Sophia was a great favourite with her father and there are many references to her in the letters written by both her father and her mother, all of which are preserved in the Royal Archives. In particular, from 1811 onwards, she spent a great deal of time with her father following the break up of her parent's long association. Mrs Jordan had negotiated a good settlement whereby the Duke paid £41,360 to produce £4,400 per annum (in a Deed of Covenant and Declaration of Trust, dated 23 December 1811 – RA-GEO/ADD/40/254). However, Sophia and her brothers were excluded, despite the fact that there was provision for her four younger sisters. Unlike her elder brothers, who enjoyed the company of their parents, Sophia seems to have taken her father's side over the separation, so much so, that Mrs Jordan was forced to declare:

'To say that Sophy's conduct towards me is reprehensible to too gentle a name for it. It is shocking to reflect how a young creature can without the smallest remorse break through the first and most sacred tie of human nature. Her selflove seems to have stifled every amiable and natural affection. Poor girl, I

1 Edward IV

4 Henry VII

2 Arms of Arthur Plantagenet, Viscount Lisle

3 Richard III

Left 5 Henry VIII

Below 6 His son Henry FitzRoy, Duke of Richmond & Somerset

Left 7 Charles II

His bastards: *Above* 8 and *Below* 9 Sir James Fitzroy, Duke of Monmouth & Buccleuch and his coat of arms

10 Charlotte Howard, Countess of Yarmouth

11 Charles FitzCharles, Earl of Plymouth

12 Anne, Countess of Sussex

Left 13 and 14 Sir Charles FitzRoy, Duke of Southampton & Cleveland and his coat of arms

Below 15 and 16 Sir Henry FitzRoy, Duke of Grafton and his coat of arms

Fitz Roy Duke of Cleveland.

Fitz Roy Duke of Grafton.

17 Lady Charlotte FitzRoy,
Countess of Lichfield

18 Sir George FitzRoy, Duke
of Northumberland

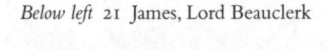

Beauclerk Duke of St Albans.

Left 19 and *above* 20 Sir Charles Beauclerk, Duke of St Albans and his coat of arms

Below left 21 James, Lord Beauclerk

Below 22 Lady Barbara FitzRoy

Lennox Duke of Richmond.

Left 23 and *above* 24 Sir Charles Lennox, Duke of Richmond & Lennox

Right 25 Lady Mary Tudor, Countess of Derwter

26 James II

Left and opposite: Three of James II's illegititimate offspring

27 Henrietta, Baroness Waldegrave

28 James FitzJames, Duke of
Berwick upon Tweed

29 Katherine, Duchess
of Buckinghamshire and
Normanby

30 'Bonnie' Prince
Charles Edward Stuart

Right 31 and *below* 32 His daughter
Charlotte Stuart, Duchess of Albany and
her coat of arms

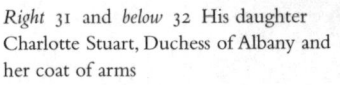

Right 33 and *Below* 34 George I and his coat of arms

35 His daughter Petronelle, Countess of Chesterfield

36 George II

37 Frederick Prince of Wales, son of
George II

38 George Prince of Wales, later George
IV

Left 39 William IV

His bastards:
Below 40 and 41 George Augustus Frederick FitzClarence, Earl of Munster and his coat of arms

Left 42 Sophia, Baroness De L'Isle & Dudley
Above 43 Henry Edward FitzClarence

44 Lady Mary Fox

45 Lieutenant-General Lord Frederick FitzClarence

46 Rear Admiral Lord Adolphus FitzClarence

47 The Rev Lord Augustus FitzClarence

48 Henry Carey, Baron Hunsdon

49 Catherine, Lady Knollys

50 Mary Walter

51 Count Blomberg or
The Rev Frederick William
Blomberg

Left 52 King Edward VII

Below 53 The arms of the House of Windsor

54 The Hon. Maynard Greville

Below 55 His coat of arms

Right 56 Sonia Rosemary Cubit

Below 57 The arms of the Earls of Albemarle

58 Prince Albert Victor Christian Edward, Duke of Clarence & Avondale

Left 59 David, Prince of Wales, later King Edward VIII and Duke of Windsor

Below left 60 (William) Anthony, 2nd Viscount Furness

Below 61 Timothy Ward Seely

lament and pity her, her disappointments must in proportion to her selfishness be severe. She never writes, and at a review, tho' within our carriage. She left the place to avoid speaking to me. It was taken notice of and mentioned in London. I don't think even her father could approve of such unprecedented conduct, and that is saying a great deal'

Mrs. Jordan was obviously very distraught about the split and wrote to the Duke expressing her feelings thus: '*on the eve of quitting this place for ever* (Bushey Park) *with sensations of regret and pleasure scarcely describable*'.

But at least the Duke, unlike his brother King George IV, did ensure that his children were publicly acknowledged upon his accession. As with her siblings, Sophia was granted by Royal Warrant in 1831 the precedence of a younger child of a Marquess and in 1818 all five sisters were granted a pension of £500.

Rather surprisingly, Sophia did not marry until she was thirty years old. Her husband Philip Charles Sidney, of an illustrious family, was five years younger than his bride, and it was not until 1835, ten years after their marriage, that he was raised to the peerage as 1st Baron De L'Isle and Dudley, of Penshurst He was successively an equerry to the King (William IV), a Lord of the Bedchamber and Surveyor General of the Duchy of Cornwall and had been appointed KCH and GCH.

Despite her advanced age, which curiously was the same as when her mother began her association with the Duke of Clarence, the marriage produced a number of children including two daughters. Of these, Adelaide, named in honour of the Queen, married her cousin Frederick FitzClarence but died without issue; and Sophia married Count Alexander Kielmansegg, a descendant of Sophia Dorothea Kielmansegg, half sister of King George I.

Sadly Sophia died at the early age of just forty-two, at Kensington Palace on 10 April 1837, having recently been appointed 'Housekeeper' thereof, and there is a brief reference to this in Queen Victoria's diaries. Indeed it was reported at that time that she was the favourite of her Royal father and that she had occasionally acted as his amanuensis. But only two months after her death, she was followed by her father King William. From her only son, descends the present representative of the Sidney family, Sir Philip John Algernon (Sidney) 2nd Viscount (born 1945), and Sophia's portrait is in pride of place at Penshurst Place.

Henry Edward FitzClarence (1797–1817)

Henry Edward FitzClarence, was born on 8 March 1797 at Richmond, Surrey, the third child and second son of William, Duke of Clarence and Mrs Jordan. His arrival in the world was noted in the 13 March 1797 edition of *The Times*:

> *'Little Pickle was brought to bed on Tuesday last of a son, at the Duke of Clarence's house on Richmond Hill. This is her third child by the Duke'*

Little Pickle, of course, was Mrs Jordan's nickname given to her by *The Times* from the part she played in *The Spoiled Child*. Clarence wanted this son to serve in the navy as he had done, and when the boy was just ten years old he approached his old friend Rear-Admiral Richard Keats and requested his help:

> *'I am anxious to send Henry to sea and ultimately he shall go, but mothers must be consulted. Unfortunately I am afraid there is too much reason to believe that I have lost an unfortunate boy on board the Blenheim which naturally enough causes great uneasiness to Mrs Jordan and makes me cautious as to my method of proceeding relative to Henry … The boy himself is delighted with the idea and talks of you and the Navy with rapture'.*

At the tender age of twelve, his father's wish was eventually granted when he purchased a commission in the Navy for him and young Henry became a volunteer on the ship *Mars*, Admiral Keats's flagship. Despite her misgivings Mrs Jordan was pleased that her son was in the Admiral's care for

> *'the attention and kindness of Admiral Keats to all the boys is more like the affectionate care of a father than master'.*

Henry's first stint of duty was in the Baltic whence Admiral Keats had been sent to rescue 9,000 stranded Spanish troops in Denmark with their artillery and baggage. He followed this up, after just ten days leave, with another in the ill-fated Walcheren expedition lead by the Earl of Chatham, with Keats as second in command of the Fleet under Admiral Strachan. On his return in November 1809 he was granted six months leave before returning to serve on the *Warspite* in the Mediterranean. The next five months were spent blockading Toulon but despite his commanding officer's high regard for him, the latter's reputation for flogging his midshipmen prayed on the young boy's mind and he asked to be transferred. '*I wish he was with Keats,*' wrote his mother, '*before anything unpleasant happens, for he declared in his letter to Sophy (his elder sister) that if they attempted to flog him he would run away, and you know how violent he is*'.

Henry later transferred to the Army where he served in the 10th Hussars, the same regiment as his elder brother George, and there are a number of letters in the Royal Archives which their father wrote to them jointly. Henry appears frequently in his mother's letters to other members of the family. He was constantly in néed of money and often wrote asking her to send some '*Henry is in great want of money, and concludes his catalogue with 'send plenty of money'. Poor fellow-he does not seem to know that it is rather an expensive article and not always to be found. However he shall (have) some*'. In 1813 she duly noted that Henry was about to go abroad again '*Henry goes to Lisbon with Lord Beresford, a very good thing for him*'

His next military expedition was with the army which invaded Southern France. When his regiment returned, he, together with a number of his fellow officers, accused their colonel, George Quentin, of professional incapacity claiming that he '*did not make necessary and proper arrangements to ensure success.*' When the Colonel was found guilty, Henry's uncle, the Duke of York was furious that junior officers should accuse their superior officer and saw to it that all twenty-five officers were dismissed from their regiments including Henry, the latter being ordered to India. To add insult to injury the Prince Regent's private secretary penned a letter to his new commanding officer '*begging that the strictest discipline, not to say severity, should be exercised towards them in consequence of their share in the business of the 10th Hussars*'. To his credit the commanding officer rejected such a proposal replying that he '*had received the Colonel's letter, and that he should have returned it with the contempt it deserved, but that he chose to retain it, that he might have it in his power to expose him, should such unfair and offensive conduct be repeated*'.

Fortunately none of these proceedings affected the small annuity of £200 that Henry received from his uncle the Prince Regent. Sadly, however, young Henry died of a fever in 1817 aged just twenty and unmarried, and just one year after his mother. At the time of his death, he was an ADC to the Governor-General, the Marquess of Hastings, who wrote of his own feelings for the young man: '*I have been pained by the death of Lieutenant Henry FitzClarence … He was a mild, amiable young man, earnest in seeking information, and in improving himself by study*'.

Lady Mary Fox (*née* FitzClarence) (1798–1864)

The second daughter of Mrs. Jordan, by the Duke of Clarence, later King William IV, Mary was born on 19 December 1798 at Bushey House, Bushey Park, where her parents had set up home when her father was appointed Ranger of Bushey Park in January 1797. As with her siblings, she was granted by Royal Warrant in 1831 the precedence of a younger child of a Marquess and in 1818 all five sisters were granted a pension of £500. She was also granted a differenced version of the Royal Arms *charged with a baton sinister azure charged with an anchor between two roses or.*

Like her eldest brother, in 1824 she too married a bastard, General Charles Richard Fox, MP, Colonel of the 57th Foot, Receiver General of the Duchy of Lancaster, and a well known archaeologist, who died in 1873. He was the natural son of Henry Richard (Fox), third Baron Holland, who was an old friend of her father's and who had married in 1797 the divorced wife of Sir Godfrey Webster, 4th Bt. Prior to this, Sir Godfrey had been awarded £6,000 in damages against Lord Holland, because of the son Charles that he had had by Sir Godfrey's wife. It was reported that '*Sir Godfrey Webster with difficulty, and after some time was bribed to divorce her by the surrender of her fortune*'. The Third Baron was also a great-grandson of the 2nd Duke of Richmond, a grandson of King Charles II.

There are a few mentions of the Foxs in Queen Victoria's diaries. Like her siblings, Mary and her husband dined at Windsor from time to time and on 16 February 1839 The Queen described her as '*poor Lady Mary Fox*' and as being '*very much affected but very kind; she is a very nice person*' and '*her voice being like her sisters. Lord M* (Melbourne) *knows her the best of any and says she is the cleverest of them*' (RA-VIC/QVJ 1839 16 February)

On 23 June 1839 there are references to Mary having abused The Queen Dowager and Lady Holland too and being described as '*a very eager person*'. She died aged 66, some nine years before her husband and relatively little seems to have been recorded about her.

Lieutenant-General Lord Frederick FitzClarence, GCH (1799–1854)

Frederick FitzClarence was born 9 December 1799 at Bushey House, the third, but second surviving son of Mrs. Jordan (1761-1816), the well known comic actress, by her Royal lover the Duke of Clarence, later King William IV.

Like his elder brothers, he was destined for a career in the Army and first appears on the pages of history when he was drafted to serve in the Waterloo campaign. The resumption of the war was obviously of some concern to his mother who wrote to her younger son Adolphus: '*Dear Frederick has joined his regiment at Brussels in consequence of the renewal of this cruel war*'. However, she need not have worried as Frederick remained safe and his conduct was exemplary:

> '*Frederick's Col. Had written a very handsome letter to your father, relative to Frederick's conduct on the march to Ramsgate of the Guards, who behaved very ill, got drunk and were near mutiny. Frederick stayed behind and by his zeal and activity prevented much disorder and confusion*'.

After Napoleon's defeat, young Frederick entered Paris with his regiment, only to discover that his mother had fled England to avoid her creditors. Concerned he discovered her whereabouts and wrote to her

> *'Tell all about the Marchs. If you want money for them don't ask me for it, but take my allowance for them; because, with a little care I could live on my father's till their business is a little settled. Now do as I ask you mind you do; for they have always been so kind to us all; and if I can make any return, I should be a devil if I did not. So take my next quarter and, as you may not want to give them some, do that for my sake'.*

Eventually Frederick rose to the rank of Lieutenant General. At one time he had commanded the forces of Bombay and was Colonel of the 36th Foot. Although he was appointed GCH (Knight Grand Cross of the Royal Hanoverian Guelphic Order), he bombarded his father with requests that he should be made a Hanoverian general as well. But Melbourne was not impressed by him, describing him as *'very foolish'*.

As with his siblings, he was granted by Royal Warrant in 1831 the precedence of a younger child of a Marquess and with a special remainder to the Earldom of Munster, failing the heirs male of his eldest brother. He was also granted a differenced version of the Royal Arms *charged with a baton sinister azure charged with two anchors or.* He and his siblings do appear to have had some contact with Queen Victoria, in that there is an entry in her diary dated 22 February 1838 recording the fact that he had dined with her. He married in 1821 Lady Augusta Boyle (who died on 28 July 1876), daughter of the 4th Earl of Glasgow and he died aged fifty-five on 30 October 1854, leaving a daughter who died unmarried.

Elizabeth, Countess of Erroll,
(*née* FitzClarence) (1801–56)

The third daughter of Mrs. Jordan (1761–1816), the well known comic actress, by the Duke of Clarence, later King William IV, was Elizabeth FitzClarence, who was born on 17 January 1801 at Bushey House. As with her siblings, she was granted by Royal warrant in 1831 the precedence of a younger child of a Marquess, although her subsequent marriage gave her a higher precedence. In 1818 all five sisters were granted a pension of £500. She was also granted a differenced version of the Royal Arms *charged with a baton sinister azure charged with an anchor between two roses or.*

Elizabeth married in 1820 William George (Hay), eighteenth Earl of Erroll, KT, GCH, Hereditary High Constable of Scotland, who later served as Lord of the Bedchamber to her uncle King George IV and Master of the Horse to the Queen Consort and Lord Steward of the Household. He was created Baron Kilmarnock and appointed KT and PC among many other honours. Like her siblings, Elizabeth features in Queen Victoria's diaries when she dined or stayed at Windsor. For instance on 7 December 1838 the entry reads:

> *'Saw Lady Erroll who had not yet seen me since the King's death, and seemed much affected but conqured herself; she was very kind and kissed and pressed my hand and said she could not express all she felt; she is grown enormously large. At 10m to 8 we dined …I sat between Lord Albemarle and Lord Erroll and we talked literally of nothing but racing, hunting, horses, breeding horses etc, etc' (RA-VIC/AVJ/1838 7 December).*

On 4 January 1840 they were dining again when The Queen described her as *'such a nice, natural person'*.

Six years later in 1846, Lord Erroll died of diabetes leaving a son and two daughters, one of whom married Charles Edward Allen, the self styled Count d'Albanie, who claimed to be the legitimate grandson of Bonnie Prince Charlie, but was in fact an imposter, another was a bridesmaid to Queen Victoria. Elizabeth survived her husband for nine years, dying in 1856 and for some of this period she was living at one of the lodges in Richmond Park.

The present representative of this illustrious and ancient family is her great-great-great-great-grandson, Sir Merlin Sereld Victor Gilbert (Hay), 24th Earl and Hereditary High Constable of Scotland, (born 1948) who is also the grandson of the Lord Erroll of '*White Mischief*' fame. Another descendant, through their daughter Agnes who married 5th Earl of Fife, is the leader of the Conservative Party, David Cameron.

Rear Admiral Lord Adolphus FitzClarence, GCH (1802–56)

The fourth son of Mrs. Jordan (1761–1816), the well known comic actress, by the Duke of Clarence, later King William IV, was Adolphus, who was born on 17 February 1802 at Bushey House and named after his uncle the Duke of Cambridge. In 1808, his mother describes him as '*really the very finest child I ever saw and certainly the handsomest of all mine*' (*GEO/Add/40/19a*). Indeed, of all her children Adolphus was the one she loved the most, and surviving letters at Wemyss Castle testify to their closeness. The first, dated 1813, was written from Margate:

> '*I trust and believe my dear and darling boy will not impute to neglect or want of affection my silence. I waited till I could see dear Henry to learn from him how and when I could best write to my dear affectionate Lolly [Adolphus]. All the children I saw and dined with at Lloyd's on Friday last, except George, who is gone to Brighton to join his regiment, but he is to be on duty immediately at Hampton Court. The dear children are all well. Henry made me very happy by giving me hopes that the war with America will soon be over, in which case I shall soon see you.*'

The following year, however, aged only twelve, Adolphus joined the Royal Navy and served on board the *Impregnable,* the *Newcastle,* the North American Station as a Midshipman, in the *Tagus,* and the

Rochfort, Flagship of Sir Thomas Fremantle, and the *Glasgow*, all in the Mediterranean.

The fact that he saw soo much service in the Mediterranean gave him little practice in coastal navigation. To remedy the situation his then commanding officer Admiral Fremantle arranged that he be transferred to the sloop *Aid* under the watchful eye of Captain Smyth '*a remarkably good astronomer, draughtsman and surveyor*'; the sloop was to be employed off the Ionian Islands and the Adriatic. In the Admiral's opinion

> '*if these young men [his own son Charles included] are disposed to learn, they can never have a more favourable opportunity. Indeed it is on the score of navigation they are both deficient which is to be accounted for by their serving so much in the Mediterranean out of sight of land*'.

His interest in Adolphus was amply rewarded and in a letter to his brother in October 1818, Fremantle wrote: '*If you should see the Duke of Clarence you may mention that I am quite satisfied with his son(s) who are improving daily*'.

The anxiety of Adolphus joining the Navy at such a tender age was compounded when Mrs Jordan received news that her eldest son had been wounded in action. '*I have been quite ill, but thank God, all my anxiety about dear George has this moment been removed by a letter from the dear fellow wherein he says he is pronounced out of all danger*'. Apparently the wound was received during the capture of Toulouse ' *I lose not a moment in relieving your anxiety about dear George, who tho' he has been severely wounded in the thigh is, thank God, in a fair way of being well*'.

Adolphus's first commission as Lieutenant was dated April 1821 following which he joined the *Euryalus* and then the *Brisk* sloop and *Redwing* on the North Sea Station before being promoted to the rank of Commander. In 1824 he achieved the rank of Captain and was given command of the *Ariadne* in the Mediterranean, the *Challenger* and the *Pallas* and from 1830 the *Royal George* and *Victoria & Albert* yachts. There are a number of references to Lord Adolphus in Queen Victoria's diaries including an entry for 1 Spetember 1842 in which she says '*how highly satisfied we both were with extreme attention and assiduity of Lord Adolphus and all the officers*'. But another entry for 29 August 1838 records that Melbourne thought him '*mad*'.

He eventually rose to the rank of Rear Admiral of the White, being appointed in 1853, some twenty-nine years after first being promoted Captain. He had also been appointed Groom of the Robes and a Lord of the Bedchamber to his father, King William IV, GCH, ADC to Queen Victoria and Ranger of Windsor Home Park. Like his siblings, he had, on his father's accession to the Throne in 1831, been granted by Royal Warrant the precedence of a younger child of a Marquess and with a special remainder to the Earldom of Munster, failing the heirs male of his eldest brother. Like his siblings, he was also granted an annuity by his uncle King George IV and this was continued by both his father as well as by Queen Victoria. He was also granted a differenced version of the Royal Arms *charged with a baton sinister azure charged with two anchors or.*

Nevertheless money always remained a problem for him, especially as he was perhaps the least acquisitive of his siblings. Indeed Queen Victoria notes in her diary on 23 January 1838 *'I told Lord Melbourne that Lord Adolphus FitzClarence on being told that I would continue to him and his brothers and sisters the same annual allowance they enjoyed from the late King, burst into tears and said that it was unexpected, for they did not dare to hope for anything'*. However upon the suicide of his eldest brother in 1842, it fell to Adolphus to have to deliver his brother's letter to the Queen asking that she might extend his pensions to his children, something she did not feel inclined to do, and supported in her decision by Melbourne and Sir Robert Peel. As a sop, however, she did offer to do what she could for them in their respective professions, although she clearly thought that it was remarkable of Lord Munster *'going and premeditatingly shooting himself and then asking me to take care of his children'*.

Yet sadly, when Adolphus died, unmarried, on 18 May 1856, his assets proved insufficient to pay his debts, funeral expenses and legacies. (RA-GEO/Add 39/668). Meanwhile, Queen Victoria's diary entry for the following day (page 218) provides a suitable epitaph in which she says

'Poor Ld Adolphus FitzClarence, of whose paralytic seizure we heard on the 17th, died yesterday evening. We are truly sorry as he was very good natured and kind hearted, but he positively killed himself by living too well. He was only 54, though he looked quite 10 or 12 years older'.

Lady Augusta Kennedy, later Hallyburton, *(née* FitzClarence) (1803–65)

The fourth daughter of Mrs. Jordan (1761–1816), the well known comic actress, by the Duke of Clarence, later King William IV, was Augusta FitzClarence, who was born on 17 November 1803 at Bushey House. As with her siblings, she was granted by Royal warrant in 1831 the precedence of a younger child of a Marquess and in 1818 all five sisters were granted a pension of £500. She was also granted a differenced version of the Royal Arms *charged with a baton sinister azure charged with an anchor between two roses or.*

Very little seems to be known about Augusta and there were no references to her in Quen Victoria's Diaries. Augusta married twice, firstly in 1827 to the Hon. John Kennedy-Erskine, 2nd son of Archibald (Kennedy), KT, FRS, 1st Marquess of Ailsa and 12th Earl of Cassilis. Her husband, who had inherited his maternal grandfather's estate of Dun in Forfarshire when he added the name and arms of Erskine of Dun, died four years later, leaving a son and a daughter, Wilhelmina (who was to marry in 1855 her first cousin the 2nd Earl of Munster). As chatelaine of the House of Dun in Angus, Augusta became a passionate botanist and needlewoman and features in *Great Houses of Scotland* by Hugh Massingberd.

She married secondly on 24 August 1836 a professional sailor with service in the Home, South American and Mediterranean Stations, who saw action with the Toulon fleet in 1814. He was Captain, later Admiral, Lord John Frederick Gordon, who in 1843 changed his name to Hallyburton. He was the 3rd son of the 9th Marquess of Huntly and 5th Earl of Aboyne and he later served as an MP for Forfar in Angus. Three weeks before their marriage, he went on half pay, having paid off the sloop *Pandora*, and just a week before he was appointed GCH. Nevertheless his half pay did not prevent him being promoted successively Rear Admiral in 1857, Vice Admiral in 1863 and full Admiral in 1868. Augusta died in 1865 without any further children but he survived her for another twelve years thereafter.

The Rev Lord Augustus FitzClarence (1805–54)

The fifth and youngest son of Mrs. Jordan (1761–1816) and the Duke of Clarence, later King William IV, was Lord Augustus FitzClarence, who was born in London on 1 March 1805. He was educated firstly at Wimbledon and then went up to Braesnose College, Oxford where he matriculated in 1824, moving on to Trinity College, Cambridge two years later. There he was awarded an LLB in 1832 and an honorary LLD in 1835.

It was William IV's intention '*to make five sons of mine fight for their King and Country*'. However fate decreed otherwise and in the event two sons served in the army, four in the navy and one the church. From the moment of his birth William was particularly anxious that Augustus should serve in the Navy, and he was just twelve years old when he joined the frigate *Spartan* as a volunteer first class on 13 February 1818. Within the year William was writing to Admiral Fremantle requesting that he take on Adolphus and Augustus as midshipmen:

> '*Captain Green having assured me you are kind enough to keep the situation of rated Midshipman on board your Flagship for my son Adolphus who is now with Dundas in the Tagus and has already served four years of his time, I have only to thank you for this act of friendship. But I must request your attention to my other son Augustus who has just entered into our service … I am anxious that he should have the advantage of education under Captain Green and the Chaplain, and to participate in the various branches of foreign languages which will be pursued on board your Flagship*'.

Augustus joined the *Rochfort*, Fremantle's flagship, as a Midshipman on 29 October 1818 and his brother Adolphus followed early in 1819. Unfortunately Augustus's naval career was cut short and he left the service in 1821. The reason he gave was that:

> '*he had been trained as a sailor, the navy being the career that he preferred above all others, but that in consequence of the death of a brother he had been literally taken from on board ship and, in spite of the utmost reluctance on his part,*

compelled to go into the church ... He had not been bred to the church and had
the greatest disinclination to taking orders'

Another variation of this theme is found in *Alumni Cantabrigienses* which states:

[He also] had a great devotion for celebrated actresses, including Fanny Kemble
(1763–1841), who 'he had asked to write a sermon for him, which she indignantly
declined to do. He made a successful and very generous parish priest'. If Fanny
Kemble is to be believed, he also 'had a charming voice that, my father said, came to
him from his mother' and he was 'pleasant looking, though not handsome… '

As his half brother, William Courtenay had died 1807 aged nineteen, when Augustus was only two, the death of his brother to whom he must have been referring was Henry FitzClarence who died unmarried in 1817 aged twenty, when Augustus would have been only twelve, and a year before he himself joined the Navy. This was some four years before Augustus left the Navy and seven years before he went up to Oxford, so his reasoning did not ring true.

After his time at both Oxford and Cambridge, Augustus was indeed ordained a priest and *The Clergy List* records that he became Vicar of Maple Durham, Oxford in 1829 (aged only twenty-four). This parish (value £878 with a population of 481), was in the gift of Eton College, and there he remained for the next twenty-five years until his death.

Despite having been granted by Royal Warrant the precedence of a younger child of a Marquess upon his father's accession to the Throne in 1831 as his siblings had been, and a differenced version of the Royal Arms *charged with a baton sinister azure charged with two anchors or,* he too was dissatisfied and lacking in humility, for he demanded promotion and was then apt to be insulted by what was offered to him, having indignantly rejected offers at Worcester Cathedral and the post of Canon of Windsor. However, he did accept the appointments as Chaplain to his father and thereafter to Queen Victoria from 1840–52.

Some four years before he eventually married, Macready, the actor, says in his Diaries that, in 1841, the Reverend Augustus made a declaration of love to Miss P. Horton, an actress; that he was far more familiar with the stage than the pulpit – and that he made up for the paucity of his sermons by the eloquence of his '*billets doux*' (part of which are cited in GEO/Add/40/255). He was married later in life, aged forty, on 2 January 1845 to Sarah Elizabeth Catherine (who died 1901), eldest daughter of Lord Henry Gordon, the fourth son of the 9th Marquess of Huntly, and he died nine years later on 14 June 1854, aged only forty-nine, leaving issue of two sons (neither of whom had any surviving male issue) and four daughters. Of the latter, only Dorothea, who married in 1863 Captain Thomas William Goff, DL, (1829–76) of Roscommon, left issue and living descendants.

Amelia, Viscountess Falkland, (*née* FitzClarence) (1807–58)

The fifth and youngest daughter and the tenth and youngest child of Mrs. Jordan (1761–1816), the well known comic actress, by the Duke of Clarence, later King William IV was Amelia, who was born 21 March 1807 at Bushey House. As with her siblings, she was granted by Royal Warrant in 1831 the precedence of a younger child of a Marquess and in 1818 all five sisters were granted a pension of £500. She was also granted a differenced version of the Royal Arms *charged with a baton sinister azure charged with an anchor between two roses or.*

Amelia, who was given away by her father, married in 1830 at the Royal Pavilion, Brighton as his first wife Lucius Bentinck (Cary) 10th Viscount of Falkland, PC, GCH, head of an old family dating back to the fourteenth century. He had succeeded his father, who had been killed in a duel, and later served as a Lord of the Bedchamber to his father-in-law, as well as Governor of Bombay. He was also created Baron Hundson of Scutterskelfe in 1832.

There are a number of references to the Falklands in Queen Victoria's diaries when staying or dining with her. Clearly the Queen had a soft spot for Amelia, whom she described as '*such a nice unaffected person*'. When dining with The Queen on 14 April 1838 at Windsor, Queen Victoria was concerned to find Amelia '*very much overcome indeed at dinner, poor thing, not having been here since she left Windsor after the poor King's funeral. She cried, I observed, but really behaved very well and unaffectedly and tried to conquer her feelings which must have been very painful and acute.'*

Amelia died in 1858 aged fifty-one, leaving an only son, Lucius, who himself was to die without issue. However as a small boy he captured the heart of the new Queen Victoria who described him variously as '*a dear boy*', '*a beautiful child*', '*a remarkably nice boy, so natural and not at all shy*'. Lord Falkland, who was much in demand as a family trustee and executor, then went on to marry Elizabeth, widow of the 9th Duke of St Albans *(see page 75)*.

SECTION IV

ROYAL LOOSE ENDS

Chapter XII
Tudor Loose Ends

King Edward IV (1442–83):
Elizabeth, Lady Lumley

In Sections 1, 2 and 3 we have only included those who have been officially recognised as royal bastards, or those about whom there is no doubt. All others are included in this Section 4, *Royal Loose Ends*.

For instance, in this section we have included a number of Royal fables, which although believed firmly by many people at the time, have since been disproved. These include the Mylius Affair (*see* page 240) and George Rex (*see* page 209). With regard to King Edward VII (*see* page 219), there seems to be much gossip and very little substance and the same applies to his grandson, the Duke of Windsor (*see* page 242).

Edward IV's licentiousness was a byword in contemporary chronicles. He is alleged to have had five illegitimate children, but the only one about whom there is no doubt is Arthur (Plantagenet), created Viscount Lisle, whose biography is included in Section 1 (*see* page 18). There is, however, much less information available about the other contenders.

In 1483, the year of Edward's death, Mancini, the Italian chronicler recorded that the king was notorious in his pursuit of the fair sex but '*as soon as he grew weary of dalliance, gave up the ladies much against their will to other courtiers*'. Polydore Vergil also recorded that he '*loved them inordinately*' and even Sir Thomas More, forty years later, recorded that at one time he had three concubines whom he described as '*the merriest, wiliest and holiest in his realm*'. Indeed it was said by More that one of these, Elizabeth Lucy '*a proud high-minded woman*' had pre-contracted to marry the king and was the mother of a child by him. When an investigating tribunal interviewed her, however, she admitted that this was not the case and no promise to marry had been made.

More's statements, however, make it quite clear that she bore Edward a child before his marriage in 1464. The sex of this child is not given in More's manuscript but the surviving evidence suggests strongly that it was most probably a daughter. Near contemporary sources, ie the Lumley Monument at Chester-le-Street, Durham, the Neville pedigree of *circa* 1505 and Tonge's 1530 *Visitation of the Northern Counties* name her as Elizabeth, the wife of Sir Thomas Lumley.

Historian Michael Hicks, however, suggests in his book *Edward V 'The Prince in the Tower'* that she was named Margaret and not Elizabeth. He bases this on a document in the National Archives where it is recorded that *'our most excellent and dread prince and lord King EdwardIV'* requested Bishop Dudley to grant Thomas & Margaret a licence. (reference PRO DURH 3/54/22 m.8). Hicks does not state what the licence was for, but it could have been for permission to marry or to have a mobile altar. This document, however, could equally refer to Sir Thomas's grandparents who bore the same names. Alternatively Sir Thomas may have married twice, firstly to Elizabeth who died pre 1480, possibly in childbirth and then to Margaret.

Sir Thomas's marriage to Elizabeth is alleged to have taken place *pre* 1478, as Richard Lumley, his son and heir, was aged thirty and more when he succeeded his grandfather George, Lord Lumley in 1508; Sir Thomas had died the previous year. As Sir Thomas is alleged to have been born in 1462, he would have been just sixteen years old in 1478 and his wife was probably about the same age.

When Richard, Sir Thomas's eldest son, was granted a dispensation to marry Anne Conyers in 1489, because they were related in the fourth degree, one modern source claimed that this was proof that the degree of kinship was via Ralph Neville, 1st Earl of Westmorland, the great-grandfather of Edward IV's bastard daughter and Anne Conyers. It is equally possible, however, that the degree of kinship was calculated via Ralph's father, John Nevill, Lord Nevill, the great-great-great-grandfather of Richard Lumley and great-grand-father of Anne Conyers. When the dispensation was issued in 1489,

Richard was only eleven or twelve years old whereas his wife Anne, was considerably older, probably twenty or more (her father died in 1469). Their eldest known child, John, was born in 1493, thus making Richard about fifteen or sixteen at his birth and his wife Anne not less than twenty four!

Against the theory of two wives for Sir Thomas, is the fact that the Lumley Monument mentions only one, Elizabeth. In addition she appears to have been granted the Royal Arms: 1. *France and England*, 2. *a plain cross of Ulster,* 3. *as* 2, 4. *barry of siz, on a chief three pallets, between two esquires bastions, dexter and sinister, an inescutcheon Argent, Mortimer, over all a bar sinister,* which are also displayed on the monument. The monument was erected during the lifetime of John Lumley, fist & last Lord Lumley of the 1547 creation, who was born about 1530 and died in 1609. John was the grandson of John, 5th Lord Lumley, born 1493, who in turn was the grandson of Sir Thomas Lumley, mentioned above. If there was a second wife surely she would have been mentioned on the monument?

There is no reference to Elizabeth or her Lumley descendants in the correspondence of her brother Arthur, Lord Lisle. The earliest extant letter in the Lisle collection is dated 1523, any earlier correspondence having been lost. Sir Thomas is credited with seven children: four sons, Richard, John, George and Roger plus three daughters Sybil, Elizabeth and Ann. Determining their ages is problematic, especially for the sons, but it is possible to calculate an approximate date of birth for two of the daughters Sybil and Ann. Sybil appears to have been born 1484–88 and Ann 1490–94. The naming of a daughter Elizabeth suggests that she might have been a full sister of Richard but this is mere speculation and unproven. As Sir Thomas and his wife Elizabeth(?) were related within the fourth degree, a dispensation from the Pope would have been required in order for them to marry. However no such document appears to have survived, thus contemporary confirmation that the marriage did take place is sadly lacking.

The mid and late 1470s was a troubled time for Edward and his kingdom but set against this was his successful invasion of France with an army of eleven thousand men in 1475. The result was a pension from the French king Louis of £50,000 per annum for the next nine years and the promise of a marriage alliance between the dauphin and Edward's eldest daughter the Princess Elizabeth. This was followed by his return to England to quell the disturbances in Yorkshire in early 1476 and it might have been on this occasion that he arranged the marriage of his bastard daughter to the grandson of one of the more prominent Yorkshire noble families, the Lumleys. Such an alliance would undoubtedly have helped to restore calm and peace to the area and seems perfectly reasonable under the circumstances. This was followed by the removal of the remains of Richard, Duke of York and his son Edmund, Earl of Rutland, Edward's father and elder brother, from their temporary resting place to be re-interred at Fotheringhay Castle in Northamptonshire.

The Lumleys were a Yorkist family and Thomas, 1st Lord Lumley (1408–85) was created a peer by King Edward IV in his first parliament in 1461 and he was present at the coronation of King Richard III in 1483, dying two years later. His son, George, 2nd Lord Lumley took part in the Scottish expedition of Richard Duke of Gloucester in 1482 which intended to establish the Duke of Albany upon the Scottish throne. When he died in 1507, he was succeeded by his grandson, Richard, indicating that his only son and heir, Thomas, had pre-deceased him.

Sir Thomas appears to have been a good Yorkist but it is not known what if any support he gave to the young Edward V when he succeeded his father in 1483. He was after all a kinsman of Edward IV but this did not prevent him and his father from immediately submitting to Henry Tudor after the Battle of Bosworth. His foresight was duly rewarded by the retention of his lands. The only reminder of his previous Yorkist sympathies was the fact that he named his eldest son Richard, perhaps in honour of Richard, Duke of Gloucester, later Richard III. It has to be said, however, that the name was extremely popular in the north of England.

When Elizabeth died is unknown but if she was the mother of all of Sir Thomas's children, then she was still alive 1490–1494. The 1490s was a decade of particular concern for Henry Tudor's government; in early 1492 we see the appearance of the youth known to history as 'Perkin Warbeck', who claimed to be the younger son of Edward IV. The threat was only removed in 1499 when he was executed, along with the Earl of Warwick. Durng these difficult years Sir Thomas was appointed a Commissioner of Array in County Durham, Constable of Scarborough Castle and MP for Northumberland, despite having no land there. Despite the fact that he was a son-in-law of Edward IV and brother-in-law of Henry Tudor, he was not singled out for preferment. Indeed that would have been very unwise on the part of Henry Tudor. After all there were plenty of the Queen's kinsmen to plague Henry without creating other possibilities.

Grace Plantagenet, Dame Isabel Mylbery or Audley and Mary Harman

There are even fewer references to Elizabeth's sister Grace, than there were to her. Evidence that she was a child of King Edward IV is based solely on a manuscript in a herald's account of the funeral of Elizabeth Woodville in 1492 *(Arundel MS 26, f, 29v Sutton and Visser-Fuchs, Royal Burials at Windsor II)* where she appears as one of the chief mourners. There she is mentioned as *'Maistres Grace, a bastard doughter of Kyng Edwarde, and upon (among) an other gentilwomen'*. It seems that only two other mourners were present, the queen's chaplain and her cousin Edmund Haute, one of her executors. Thus it seems as if Mistress Grace was indeed regarded as of some importance, being a daughter of King Edward IV, and probably having been brought up in the household of the Queen, and presumably recognised by Edward. This is the sole reference to Grace and nothing is known about her dates of birth or death, nor the name of her mother, nor whether she was ever married. As there are no subsequent references to her in contemporary records, she may have ended her days in a nunnery

The next sister is Dame Isabel Mylbery, whose name occurs in another heraldic manuscript of about 1510 where her arms are illustrated. This is an interesting coat of arms, possibly granted by Sir Thomas Wriothesley, Garter King of Arms. They are shown painted on a lozenge (for a woman), being *'per bend Purpure (or murrey) and azure, in fess a rose between two demi lions passant guardant facing sinister, all argent'*. The colours are the livery colours of the house of York; the white rose being the badge of York; and the two demi lions, which unusually are facing to the left, are reminiscent of the lions of England. The inscription above the arms describes Dame Isabel as *'educata ut fert(ur) per Regem E(dwardum) iiij'*, brought up, it is said, by King Edward IV.

Whilst this could mean simply what it says, when taken in conjunction with the arms granted to her, and there being no reference to any family of Mylbery (which could have been her mother's name), it does seem quite possible that she is a child of Edward IV, and possibly recognised as such by him. Next to Isabel's lozenge is a shield with her arms impaled (ie side by side) with the arms of her husband who was of the Audley family, but differenced by a crescent (which usually refers to a second son). Above her part of this shield is the inscription *'Dame Isabelle uxor eius'* meaning Lady Isabel his wife and above the other half of the shield was the inscription *'Johannes Awdeley, frater Jacobi domini de Awdeley'* meaning John Audley, brother of James Lord Audley.

John seems to have been rather an obscure member of the Audley family which had supported the Yorkists and came from Heleigh. He was mentioned in the will of his mother, Anne Lady Audley; he took part in the Cornish rising of 1497 with his brother James (who was beheaded and forfeited his title), and he was indicted for a part in the Warbeck Conspiracy in 1499, eventually being pardoned in 1504. Their father, John Lord Audley, was present at the coronation of King Richard III in 1483 and was made Lord Treasurer the following year. So they were indeed just the sort of family into which an illegitimate daughter of the King might marry, although nothing more is known about them or any family they may have had.

The fifth and final claimant to be a child of King Edward IV was mentioned in the Kent Visitation of 1574 in the pedigree of Harman. This states that Henry Harman was married to a daughter of King Edward IV, although again, the daughter is not named. It also stated that his crest, but not arms, had been given to him by King Henry VII *'after he had married with E:4 daughter'*. This crest was described as 'out of a ducal coronet an arm erect azure, the hand proper grasping two roses gules and argent, stalked and leaved vert'. As with Dame Isabel, this again sounds like a grant that could have been made to a scion of royalty, with the white rose of York and the red rose of Lancaster and the purple (or murrey) of the chevron in the arms might also be part of the grant. The arms of Harman are described in the Visitation as '*a chevron purple between three periwigs sable*' which presumably reflects Harman's appointments as Clerk of the Crown in the court of the King's bench ('*coroner and attorney in the bench before the king*' – as one of his patents described him) from 1480-1502 when he died. His will shows that his widow's name was Mary and that they had eleven children, but their names gave no clue to any royal ancestry.

King Richard III (1452–85):
Richard Plantagenet (1469-1550)

Anne Smith of the Richard III Society published the following account of Richard Plantagenet, or Richard of Eastwell, in Kent, whom many believe could well have been Richard III's illegitimate son, but the evidence is circumstantial.

On the eve of the Battle of Bosworth, King Richard III is said to have acknowledged a third bastard. The other two, about whom there was little doubt, were Katherine Plantagenet (*see* page 26) and John of Gloucester (*see* page 24). This story was documented in a letter by a Dr. Brett to the 5th Earl of Winchelsea dated 1733 and reprinted in *Desiderata Curiosa*, Vol. 2, by Francis Peck in 1735.

The death of a Richard Plantagenet was certainly registered in the Eastwell Church registry in 1550. He was eighty-one and was therefore born around 1469. Although his name is inscribed on one of the tombs, the grave is considered by some to be more likely that of Sir Walter Moyle, who died in 1480.

Arthur Mee, a noted travel writer in the first half of the twentieth century, wrote about '*The Very Strange Story of Richard Plantagenet*' under Kent (published 1936), which was part of *The King's England, County by County, Covering 10,000 Towns, Villages and Hamlets of the English Counties*. His account is similar to the story published in the Eastwell Manor visitor's guide today.

This relates that Sir Thomas Moyle, building his great house at Easton, was much struck by a white-bearded man his mates called Richard. There was a mystery about him. In the rest hour, whilst the other workmen talked and threw dice, this old man would sit apart and read a book. This was unusual because there were very few working men who could read in 1545. On this particular morning Sir Thomas could not rest until he had won the confidence of the man

It is said the book that Richard was reading was in Latin, which was, of course, a language reserved for the highborn. The mason told Sir Thomas that he was brought up by a schoolmaster. '*From time to time, a gentleman came who paid for his food and school, and asked many questions to discover if he were well cared for,*' wrote Mee. Richard went on to describe having been taken to Bosworth Field and meeting his father there for the first time. The king said: '*I am your father, and if I prevail in tomorrow's battle, I will provide for you as befits your blood. But it may be that I shall be defeated, killed, and that I shall not see you again ... Tell no one who you are unless I am victorious.*' The battle was lost, and Richard Plantagenet then chose a simple trade in which to lose his identity and had thus come to work at Eastwell Manor. According to Mee: '*Sir Thomas Moyle, listening to this wonderful story, determined that the last Plantagenet should not want in his old age. He had a little house built for him in the Park (which is still standing) and instructed his steward to provide for it every day.*'

King Henry VII (1457–1509):
Sir Roland de Velville (1474–1535)

For the last four hundred years or more, no one has doubted that Sir Roland de Velville (also spelt Vielleville, Veleville or Vieilleville), Constable of Beaumaris Castle from 1509–35 was a natural son of Henry VII and he would therefore have been included in Section 1 of this book. Allegedly he was born in 1474 to an unknown Breton woman, while Henry was in exile in Brittany between 1471–85. All those historians who have mentioned de Velville, seem either to have accepted him as such, or have referred to him as a *'reputed natural son'* of Henry VII, and even today, he is included as such in Alison Weir's book '*Britain's Royal Families*' (1996). Indeed, such an authoritative source as the *Dictionary of Welsh Biography* refers to de Velville as *'a natural son of Henry VII'* (under the entry for Katheryn of Berain – de Velville's grand-daughter).

However, in 1967, the late Professor S B Chrimes of Cardiff University, author of the major biography 'Henry VII', (1972), published a short paper in *Welsh Historical Review* in which he put forward the opinion that de Velville was not a natural son of Henry VII after all. This was echoed in 1985 by Professor R A Griffiths of University College, Swansea, in his book '*The Making of the Tudor Dynasty'* and in 1991 a further, much longer paper on the subject, by W R B. Robinson, was published in *Welsh Historical Review*. Whilst Robinson identified a number of significant errors and omissions in Chrimes' earlier paper, he stated that '*the review of available evidence tends to support Professor Chrimes scepticism about Velville's supposed Tudor origins'*. This statement meant, of course, that although Robinson agreed that the available evidence was insufficient to establish de Velville's paternity beyond doubt, he was not suggesting that the evidence established beyond doubt that de Velville was not a son of Henry VII, – which it does not do.

To summarise the position as objectively as we can, we do know or can reasonably assume, that there was this young boy, Roland de Velville, of unknown parentage, who, aged eleven, accompanied King Henry VII to England from Brittany in 1485. He was less than half Henry's age (Henry being twenty-eight in 1485) and the boy was therefore not of 'military age' or a mercenary and he was far too young to be Henry's 'friend'. The earliest reference to him appears to be a grant to 'Roland de Vielle' in Michaelmas term 1488 (ref: *Materials for the Reign of Henry VII (Rolls Series,* 1873–77*)*, vol. II, p. 394, edited by W. Campbell). Nevertheless, for the next twenty-five years, the boy lived at Court, but unusually and perhaps uniquely, he was not given any official position or office. However, clearly he was a favourite of the king, participating in numerous jousts and accompanying the king out hunting. He became a courtier and a member of the Royal Household but not a 'servant', and he mixed on equal terms with the highest members of the aristocracy, including the Duke of Buckingham.

De Velville served in Sir John Cheyne's retinue in the expedition to Brittany in 1489, commanded by Sir Robert Willoughby, and is probably to be identified with the 'Roland de Bella Vill' who served as an esquire in the army which Henry VII took to France in the autumn of 1492. After the Battle of Blackheath, he was knighted on 17 June 1497 and was one of a small group of knights individually rewarded by the king in the course of the military operations in the West Country which led to the capture of Perkin Warbeck in September. As Sir Roland, he was summoned to attend upon the king during the prolonged reception of the Archduke Philip in 1500.

There are also a number of references recording de Velville's participation in tournaments in 1494; in April and in November 1501 (to welcome Katherine of Aragon); in January 1502 (to mark the proxy marriage of Princess Margaret to James IV of Scotland); in February 1506 (in honour of Archduke Philip); and in May and June 1507 (in honour of the Queen of May). Participation in royal tournaments was carefully restricted to noblemen and gentlemen entitled to bear coats of arms and tended to be expensive. Somehow de Velville maintained his life-style by living in the royal household, receiving occasional gifts from the king and drawing an income from the royal revenues. In 1493 the king granted him an annuity of £20 and in 1496 a further annuity of forty marks (£26 13s. 4d.) for life.

In view of the favour in which Henry VII held him, it was wholly appropriate that de Velville was one of the knights of the Royal Household appointed to attend the king's funeral in May 1509. He also participated in the jousts celebrating Henry VIII's coronation on 24 June 1509 and all this might have suggested that his life at Court was to continue unaffected by the young king's accession. However, a fundamental change in his life was imminent, for only days after the king's death, he was appointed Constable of Beaumaris Castle in Anglesey, the ancient seat of the Tudor family, where he is said to have been the last resident constable.

There is nothing to indicate that de Velville had had any previous connection with Anglesey. Until 4 December 1512, when he received a grant of denization, he could not as a Breton own any lands in England or Wales. Having lived at Court throughout his years in England, it is difficult to imagine why he should decide to abandon his privileged way of life to take up residence in a small

and distant Welsh provincial town. This prompts further speculation about Henry VIII's motives in authorizing the appointment and
the question of de Velville's paternity. If rumours about his reputed
royal parentage were current in Court circles in Henry VII's reign,
Henry VIII, or his new queen and her advisers, may have had a
strong motive for wishing to remove him from constant attendance
at Court, as his presence there might encourage speculation that in
the event of the new king's death without issue, de Velville could
have some contingent claim to be regarded as Henry VII's heir. On
this basis, his Tudor paternity remains a possibility.

The royal letters patent dated 3 July 1509 were issued by the chancery of the principality of North Wales at Caernarfon and recorded
the grant to de Velville of the offices of Constable of Beaumaris
Castle and Captain of Beaumaris Castle and town, with all fees,
rewards and profits. Full payment of all sums due was ensured by
a warrant issued at Greenwich on 29 October 1509 instructing the
chamberlain of North Wales to pay de Velville the first half-yearly
instalment due at Michaelmas 1509 of his annual fee of £40 as constable, his wages of 8d. per day as captain, and the wages of twenty-
four soldiers at 4d. a day. On 6 December 1509, a further warrant
was issued at Greenwich ordering the chamberlain to pay de Velville
wages for himself and his soldiers and a priest totalling £350 5s. 0d.
per year. Royal letters patent under the great seal were issued on 1
August 1509 making de Velville a fresh grant of the annuity of £20
first granted in 1493, while the life annuity of forty marks (£26 13s.
4d.) granted in 1496 continued to be paid.

Soon after his appointment as Constable, de Velville moved to
Beaumaris and began to live openly with Agnes Griffith, whom
he was eventually to marry. Agnes was a widow; her first husband
was Robert Dowdyng, a burgess of Beaumaris, who appears with
her as a joint grantor in a deed of 1508 but was dead by 1516 when
she was described both as a widow as well as living with de Velville
in Beaumaris Castle. He may have died before de Velville look up
residence in Beaumaris, because complaints were made against de
Velville by members of the Bulkeley family (one of whom he had
supplanted as Constable) early in Henry VIII's reign, referring to
Agnes as his concubine or paramour. They probably did not marry

until after 18 June 1521, when Agnes granted de Velville a close of land, which would have had no effect if they had been married. The earliest reference to Agnes as de Velville's wife is in deeds of 6 July 1528, and although the pedigrees do not cast doubt on the legitimacy of their children, Grace and Jane, it seems clear that they were born well before this date.

So it was between 1521–28 that de Velville married Agnes, the daughter of William (Gwilym) Griffith Fychan (*d.* 1483) of Penrhyn, (the father of Sir William Griffith (*d.* 1505) and grandfather of Sir William Griffith (*d.* 1531), both of whom held office as Chamberlain of North Wales). She must therefore have been at least in her late twenties at the time of Henry VIII's accession, and their two daughters were born probably in the early years of his reign. The Griffiths were one of the most powerful families in North Wales at the time, being a branch of the Tudor family descended from Ednyfed Fychan and the royal and princely houses of Wales and a distant cousin of the king. Thereafter de Velville was both granted and acquired land in the ancient estates of the Tudor family at Penmynydd. Six acquisitions by him are recorded in documents surviving in the Lleweni papers, and four of these are grants by Owen ap John ap Owen ap Tudor Fychan, a member of the senior branch of the Tudor family. But there is little evidence to indicate what effect de Velville's association with, and later marriage to, a member of the most powerful family in Gwynedd may have had on his relations with the local gentry.

No references have been found to de Velville having married before the 1520s when he would have been in his mid forties, and it is uncertain whether he had remained unmarried, or whether as a young man he had married a wife who had predeceased him. At that time it was unusual for a man to have reached middle age without marrying, although it is possible that de Velville's lack of any assured income before 1509, might have prevented him from marrying someone suitable.

Rumours concerning de Velville's royal parentage were certainly circulating in North Wales during his own lifetime, and many appeared to believe that he was indeed Henry VII's son. This extended to his own family and immediate circle, as well as to his descendants and during the last four hundred and fifty years, no evidence has come to light suggesting any other parentage. Certainly his favoured position and lifestyle would be expained perfectly if he was to have been a natural son of King Henry VII as most people have always believed, but the fraught political situation and the tussle for the Throne, would have called for much discretion at the time.

If then we accept that de Velville was an illegitimate child, as would seem likely, then whose child was he? If not Henry VII's, then his treatment by the King can only mean that he was the child of someone very close to the king or of someone to whom he owed a considerable debt of gratitude, but there is no mention of this. The answer seems clear, in spite of the recent doubts that have surfaced, that Roland de Velville was indeed Henry's illegitimate son and the very secrecy surrounding him supports this conclusion.

Strangely, as Robinson points out, there is one piece of contemporary documentary evidence relating to de Velville's paternity, in the form of an elegy composed before 25 June 1535, the time of de Velville's death, by the bard Daffyd Alaw. For de Velville's Breton origins seem to have made an impression upon some of his contemporaries, in that an elegy (in Welsh) was composed to 'Sr rolant brytaen', but with the telling reference to him being 'a man of kingly line' and 'of earl's blood' (no doubt a reference to Henry VII's father, Edmund Tudor (*d.* 1456), Earl of Richmond). These Welsh bards were the recognised Welsh genealogical authorities of the time and the elegy therefore amounted to a statement by an authoritative contemporary source that de Velville was of royal blood. Whilst elegies may often have exaggerated the good and glossed over the bad, they tended not to make up important assertions of fact. The elegy allows us, therefore, to conclude with reasonable certainty that de Velville was believed to be an illegitimate son of Henry VII in his own lifetime, at least by his immediate circle. This circle included many members of the extended Tudor family, into which de Velville had married, the very people who would have been least likely to accept such a statement as true had it actually been false.

Of course, any form of recognition or legitimization of a bastard son was the very last thing that Henry VII would have done in the circumstances. Not only was Henry an intensely secretive and cautious man, but his claim to the throne was tenuous and his power base was to remain doubtful for some time. However, we know that his marriage to Elizabeth of York was critical in gaining the loyalty of the Yorkist cause and that he was therefore unlikely to take any steps that might be seen as threatening the claim to the throne of any children of that marriage. We know, above all, that the country had just emerged from a ruinous and bloody civil war that had been caused largely by the legitimization of the bastard children of John of Gaunt. Henry was hardly likely to risk his throne and to create a potential future threat to his own legitimate children by recognising an illegitmate child. De Velville's treatment was therefore precisely what we would have expected it to be if he had been Henry's illegitimate child.

However, these doubts have given rise to a number of interesting questions about de Velville. Why, for instance, was de Velville attributed with a quartered coat of arms, which might have indicated that both his father and mother were known? Can his arms be traced in French sources and what link is there, if any, between de Velville and the de Vieilleville family, Counts of Durtal? (Durtal is near Angers in France.) Might de Velville's mother have been a daughter of this family? Again, might Henry have actually married de Velville's mother (who may perhaps have died shortly after the marriage or in childbirth)? After all, Henry VII was twenty-eight in 1485 and it was very unusual then for a man of that age to remain unmarried. Moreover, prior to 1483, Henry had little prospect of succeeding to the throne of England, since there were several legitimate heirs living at that time, and even very little prospect of ever returning to that country – at least alive. Thus he had no incentive to remain unmarried and could have considered himself, as a penniless and untitled exile (he was plain 'Henry Tudor' at that stage) with a price on his head, quite lucky to marry into a good French family. The possibility should not be excluded.

Dr. M. P. Siddons, Wales Herald Extraordinary, author of *'The Development of Welsh Heraldry'*, has confirmed that he was *'unable to find De Velville or his arms in Breton sources'*. Although there was a family of *'de Vieilleville'* (Counts of Durtal, near Angers) living in Maine (not Brittany) at that time, no link to Sir Roland had been forged although it is just possible that de Velville's mother might have been a daughter of this family.

De Velville was attributed with two different coats of arms. The first, *Argent, a Lion rampant Gules charged on the shoulder with a bezant* may have been the coat of arms granted to de Velville upon his being knighted in 1497, although it seems odd that he should be granted new arms when he already had a coat of arms. In the British Library (MS Add. 46354, fo.21, 104v) there is a quarterly coat with these arms on an inescutcheon. The crest is a lion's head issuing from a coronet, but the supporters are bizarre. The second coat, *Argent* (sometimes shown *or), a boar passant* (sometimes shown *statant) sable',* possibly *'armed or, langued gules* may represent his 'proper' coat of arms, being those he inherited at birth i.e. his father's unquartered arms.

It is, of course, intriguing that de Velville should have been attributed these arms for it would seem to imply that the identity of both his father and mother was known. According to Dr. Siddons, John Writhe, Garter King of Arms (*d.* 1505), would have actually known de Velville. On the other hand, Simwnt Fychan refers to a manuscript prepared for Katherine of Berain, de Velville's grand-daughter, who married John Salusbury (*d.* 1566). Kathryn was the daughter of Jane de Velville and her husband Robert Thomas ap Robert of Berain. Cecil Humphery-Smith believes that the arms are suspect like so many Welsh coats (including some even composed by Writhe himself). Certainly, there is no sign of such arms in French sources.

In 1512 Henry VIII granted Letters of Denization for de Velville and the heir of his body. These conferred on him, as 'a native of Brittany', all the rights and privileges of an Englishman - in effect, naturalization, which importantly also entitled him to acquire lands, although none of the surviving grants in his favour is dated earlier than 1519. Two deeds of 1526 show de Velville to have taken steps to improve his two shops in the High Street in Beaumaris, which he had only recently built.

Much of the evidence for his activities as constable of Beaumaris is provided by legal records concerning his disputes with the Bulkeley family, which have been described by Mr. D C Jones and by Dr. Steven Gunn. However, de Velville's duties at Beaumaris did not preclude him from frequenting London and Westminster. In February 1511 he took part in the Westminster tournament to celebrate the birth of the infant Prince Henry, and later that month he attended

the prince's interment. On 2 January 1512 he was one of the mourners at the funeral in London of the French ambassador, Anthoine de
Pierrepont dit d'Arizoles. He took part in the French campaign of
1513 and in November conducted his retinue of three demi-lances,
a mounted archer and seven foot-soldiers from Dover to Anglesey.
His involvement in legal proceedings also involved his attendance at
Westminster. In January 1517 he appeared before the king's council, where he was bound under heavy penalties to keep the peace,
ordered to attend on the king and not depart without licence and
to give Beaumaris Castle to a deputy appointed by the king. He
evidently spent much time in 1517 in and around London, as in July
he was sent to the Fleet for slandering the Council and in October
a recognizance was drawn up, presumably on the Council's orders,
for his good behaviour towards the king's tenants of Beaumaris. In a
letter of 26 June 1535, Sir Richard Bulkeley stated that de Velville had
murdered a man in the Lord Cardinal's (i.e. Wolsey's) time and had
forfeited all his goods, but no indication of the date of the alleged
murder is cited.

Despite his unruly behaviour at this time, he was one of the
knights included in the great retinue summoned to attend the king
and queen at Canterbury in May 1520 and to accompany the royal
party to Calais for the meeting with Francis I at the Field of the Cloth
of Gold. During the same year, he was summoned to attend on the
king during his meeting with Charles V at Gravelines. In the 1520s,
de Velville continued to spend much time at Westminster. On 10
July 1522 he attended requiem masses in St Margaret's, Westminster,
and in the Abbey, following the burial of Lady Anne Hungerford,
the wife of Sir Hugh Vaughan, and a pardon granted to him in 1527
or 1528 described him as 'of Westminster' as well as 'of Beaumaris'.
The offences for which he was pardoned may have included those
making false allegations against the Bulkeleys, for which he had again
been imprisoned in the Fleet in 1522. In a long list of the king's
sworn servants compiled between 1522–26, he was included under
Middlesex, and not among the knights of north Wales. Presumably
during these years he divided his time between Westminster and
Beaumaris. It is perhaps not surprising that he did not participate
in the French campaign of 1523, as he was by then middle aged,

although his diligence in performing his military duties in Anglesey was later authoritatively commended.

However, after Easter 1515 many of the fees and allowances due to him were suddenly disallowed as a result of the Act of Resumption passed early in April 1515. This was designed to reduce royal expenditure by annulling certain categories of grants and fees made since the beginning of Henry VIII's reign, including all constableships in north Wales. In the event, de Velville apparently was to have received the sum of £175 2s. 6d. due to him for the half-year ending at Michaelmas 1515, but the sum was held 'in respite' in the chamberlain's account, and it was only resolved when new letters patent, dated 6 March 1516, were issued by the chancery at Caernarfon including reduced rates of pay. The letters patent went on to authorize the payment to de Velville of the sum held 'in respite'. This was the last payment to de Velville for soldiers' wages, but the substantial loss of income which that represented was offset by a further provision in the letters patent of 6 March 1516 granting de Velville a life annuity of £173 6s. 8d. This certainly confirms the exceptionally favourable terms he had been able to negotiate. Thereafter de Velville received no further royal grants, but given the generous provision made for him then, he could hardly have claimed any further support from the Crown, particularly in view of his unruly behaviour which had led to his imprisonment in the Fleet in 1517 and 1522.

Nevertheless, his appointment as Constable made him one of the richest men in north Wales. Even after his allowance of nearly £300 a year for soldiers' wages was discontinued in 1516, his income from his annuities and constable's fee was over £240 a year. Altogether during Henry VIII's reign, he received £6,176 13s. 4d. from the chamberlain of north Wales and a further £1,236 13s. 4d. from Exchequer revenues. The size of his income raises the question of how he spent his money. The wages of household servants and of soldiers or guards for the safe keeping of Beaumaris Castle would have represented a substantial item of expenditure, but it seems unlikely that he maintained a regular garrison there. During his early years, he must have incurred substantial legal costs arising from his disputes with neighbouring families and forfeiture of bonds to the crown and, of course, his time at Westminster and occasional attendance at Court must also have involved considerable expense.

In his will, made a few days before his death in 1535 at Beaumaris, de Velville made modest bequests to several churches, but left to his wife all his lands within the town and liberty of Beaumaris and the county of Anglesey (making no reference to lands elsewhere) and all his chattels for disposal. He also expressed a wish to be buried in Llanfaes Priory, the Franciscan house about a mile to the north of Beaumaris. Llanfaes was the burial place of Goronwy ap Tudor (*d.* 1382), one of the ancestors of the Tudors. However, when his widow made her will on 16 December 1542, she directed that she be buried in the chapel of the Blessed Virgin Mary in Beaumaris where her husband was buried, and she bequeathed £4 for the repair and building of the chapel and a further £4 for a priest to sing for a whole year for the health of her husband's soul and her own, so that it appears that de Velville's wishes were not complied with and it is regrettable that no monument to him survives.

De Velville also undertook that Robert Thomas ap Robert of Berain should have £20 on the day of his marriage to his daughter, Jane, and the reversion to himself and Jane of the moiety of all lands, to be of annual value of at least £10, in the possession of the survivor of himself or his wife. Jane's endowment was more modest than might have been expected in view of the size of de Velville's income, and suggests that perhaps he had not established himself as a large landowner. Building up an estate through piecemeal acquisitions was often a slow process and the record of de Velville's early years in Beaumaris suggests that he may have been too headstrong to be a good man of business. Long years at Court without the responsibilities of maintaining an estate or household may indeed have accustomed him to spending rather than saving or investing.

King Henry VIII (1491–1547):
Henry Carey, Baron Hunsdon (1525/6–1596)

Henry Carey, subsequently Lord Hunsdon, was born 4 March 1525/6 to Mary Boleyn, the sister of Queen Anne Boleyn, second wife of King Henry VIII. Mary's husband, William Carey, a Gentleman of the Privy Chamber and Esquire of the Body to Henry VIII, was the son of Thomas Carey, of Chilton Folliott in Wiltshire by his wife Margaret, daughter of Sir Robert Spencer and his wife Eleanor Beaufort, daughter of Edmund (Beaufort), Duke of Somerset. William Carey was therefore of royal descent, the Duke of Somerset being a grandson of John of Gaunt, Duke of Lancaster, 3rd surviving son of King Edward III.

The claim that Henry Carey was the illegitimate son of Henry VIII and Mary Boleyn is based on the following second hand statement made by John Hale, Vicar of Isleworth to the Privy Council that:

'… Mr Skydmore dyd show to me yongge Master Care, saying that he was our suffren Lord the Kynge's son by our suffren Lady the Qwyen's syster, whom the Qwyen's grace might not suffer to be yn the Cowrte' (20 April 1535).

Two weeks later Master Hale was executed at Tyburn '*for denying the King's supremacy*'.

But Mary Carey was indeed Henry's mistress before he transferred his attention to her sister Anne, and it is generally accepted that the affair probably lasted from 1520 until 1526. Mary had married William Carey on 4 February 1519/20 and the King was present at the ceremony.

In retrospect the affair did the King little credit and when he sought to marry her sister Anne, his kinsman Cardinal Pole reminded him of the predicament he had put himself in:

'At your age in life, and with all your experience of the world, you were enslaved by your passion for a girl. But she would not give you your will unless you rejected your wife, whose place she longed to take. The modest woman would not be your mistress; no, but she would be your wife. She had learned, I think, if nothing else, at least from the example of her sister, how

soon you got tired of your mistresses; and she resolved to surpass her sister in retaining you as her lover …'

Now what sort of person is it whom you have put in place of your divorced wife? Is she not the sister of her whom first you violated and for a long time after kept as your concubine? She certainly is. How is it, then, that you now tell us of the horror you have of illicit marriage? Are you ignorant of the law which certainly no less prohibits marriage with a sister of one with whom you have become one flesh, than with one with whom your brother was one flesh? If one kind of marriage is detestable, so is the other. Were you ignorant of the law? Nay, you knew it better than others. How did I prove it? Because, at the very time you were rejecting your brother's widow, you were doing your very utmost to get leave from the Pope to marry the sister of your former concubine.

Although written from afar in Rome, the Cardinal was singularly well informed. The reference in his letter to the fact that Henry was the first to spoil Mary Carey is interesting, and could possibly indicate that their relationship began before her marriage. However, it could equally refer to just her reputation rather than anything else more explicit. Either way Mary's relationship with Henry was clearly over by the time her son was born.

Some historians believe that Mary was the elder and Anne the younger sister. The evidence to support this comes from a letter written by Mary's grandson, the 2nd Lord Hunsdon, to Lord Burghley 6 Oct 1597, in which in support of his claim to the Earldom of Wiltshire, he stated that Mary was the elder of the two sisters.

The four year gap between Mary's marriage and the birth of her first known child is interesting. It could indicate that she was very young when she married William Carey in 1520, perhaps just fourteen years old, and the marriage was not consummated until she was more mature. Alternatively she may have had other children prior to her daughter Catherine, who did not survive infancy. Another possibility is that her marriage was never consummated and during the whole period of her marriage she was Henry's mistress. Six years is a long time to retain the affections of a monarch as wayward as Henry VIII, but Cardinal Pole suggests that the relationship was of some length.

Despite contemporary gossip we shall never know for certain if young Master Carey was indeed the King's son. A DNA test might provide the answer but the chances of that happening are very slim. What is known for certain is that royal grants to Mary and her husband were spread over a number of years: 1522 to 1526, with the major grants of manors and royal estates occuring in 1524 when Catherine Carey was born and 1526 when Henry was born. However if evidence of paternity was based solely on a family resemblance, then in the case of Master Carey, not so his sister, it would not be possible to come to a firm conclusion. Portraits of the two children, as adults, have survived as indeed has one of William Carey but Master Carey does not show a marked resemblence to Henry VIII. Indeed his Boleyn ancestry is very predominant. However, it should be said that bearing a resemblance to your parents is not a pre-requisite for proof of paternity. Many children resemble their grandparents.

Of Master Carey's character we are told that he was:

'a fast man to his Prince, and firm to his friends and servants, downright honest and stout hearted … His custom of swearing and obscenity in speaking made him seem a worse Christian than he was, and a better knight of the carpet than he should be'.

Qualities he shared with Sir John Perrott, who is also believed to have been an illegitimate son of Henry VIII.

Master Carey was clearly named after his sovereign lord and master; indeed the latter may have been his godfather. William Carey's duties as a gentleman of the privy chamber to the king and also esquire of the body required his presence at court for a number of months during the year. However in 1528 he fell a victim to the sweating sickness that ravaged London in that year and he died on 22 June without making a will. The event was duly communicated to Cardinal Wolsey by Thomas Heneage in a letter written from Hunsdon House, where the King was then residing in order to escape the sickness: *'This night, as the King went to bed, word came of the death of William Carey'.*

Young Carey's appearance in the world occurred just nine months after the investiture of Henry FitzRoy, Henry VIII's only recognized bastard son, as Duke of Richmond & Somerset at the royal palace of Bridewell on 18 June 1525. Henry's decision to recognize the boy understandably caused his wife some anguish, coming as it did, just as his plans to marry the Princess Mary to her cousin the Emperor Charles V collapsed, the latter having suddenly declared his intention to marry the princess of Portugal instead. Henry's humiliation was only partly redeemed by a subsequent treaty with the French king, Francois I, and a promise that the princess would marry the dauphin. Why he chose to acknowledge the boy at that point is unclear but many years later, in 1538, he declared to the Emperor that Richmond was 'our only bastard son'. A statement that should, perhaps, be qualified by adding our only *acknowledged* bastard son.

If young Carey was indeed the King's son, Henry's reason for never acknowledging him as his child is obvious. Mary Carey was a married woman and Henry a married man, therefore their child would have been born as a result of double adultery. In addition Henry's subsequent passion for Anne Boleyn and his determination to marry her, made his desire to divorce his wife Catherine on the grounds of his tender conscience at having married his brother's widow a farce. As Cardinal Pole so clearly pointed out to him, he would simply be repeating the same mistake again with the sister of his former mistress. Undaunted Henry made certain that the dispensation to marry Anne in 1533 enabled him to marry in the first degree of affinity. This was then followed by an Act of Parliament in the same year permitting marriage with the sister of a discarded mistress. However, the Act was revoked in 1536, after Anne's death.

A few years after William Carey's death, the wardship of young Master Carey was granted to his aunt Anne Boleyn but after her death, it probably returned to the King. The death of William Carey at such a young age and the subsequent death of his aunt Anne Boleyn in 1536 had an unfortunate effect on Master Carey's position. To the King's credit he realized that the young man's mother, Mary, was not the most suitable person to take charge of his education and upbringing – her reputation as a loose woman saw to that – therefore he arranged for him to become a member of his own household. The result was that the young man *'was not badly educated: he wrote fluently, in a simple expressive style, full of proverbs and homely sayings much to the point'*.

Young Carey's choice of wife, Anne, the daughter of Sir Thomas Morgan, of Arkstone, Herefordshire, brought no major benefits to his purse and lifestyle. She did not come from one of the grander aristocratic families of the land, as one might have expected, but her antecedents were distinguished enough and she was also a member of the King's household. Together they had twelve children and fifty years later, he died and was buried in St John the Baptist's Chapel in Westminster Abbey in July 1596.

However, two years after their marriage, which took place in 1545, he inherited his father's lands in Buckinghamshire, Essex, Hampshire and Wiltshire. At the end of that same year he took his seat in Parliament as MP for Buckingham, the first of four occasions in which he did so. During his lifetime, the King did not bestow upon him any special gifts or favours, as a result his situation and income were quite modest and entirely in keeping with that of a typical country gentleman.

On the accession of Queen Elizabeth in 1558 young Carey's position changed dramatically. On 13 January 1558/9 Elizabeth created him Baron Hunsdon of Hunsdon, Co. Hertford and settled an income of £4,000 per annum on him. It was not the title he wanted. All his life he yearned to be given the earldom of Wiltshire but the Queen ignored his pleas. Unfortunately the fecundity of his wife, she bore him nine sons and three daughters, and the burdens of office ensured that he never became a rich man, indeed quite the opposite.

Nevertheless he made his mark in the world and was appointed governor of Berwick-upon-Tweed in 1568, a post he held for nearly twenty years and one to which he was eminently suited. His appointment was an opportune one for the Queen, as he proved to be a reliable lieutenant during the rebellion of the northern earls a short time afterwards. Indeed with a force of only 1,500 men he defeated a much larger rebel force under the command of Sir Leonard Dacre. His reward, many years later, was to be placed in charge of the army of 36,000 men at Tilbury Fort during the Armada scare in 1588.

Despite the attentions to his wife, Carey still managed to enjoy the pleasure of keeping at least two mistresses – not at the same time, of course. The first was during his governorship of Berwick with a lady who was subsequently to become Mrs Hodson. The result was a son Valentine, who later went onto become Bishop of Exeter. In the latter's will – he died in 1626 – he left bequests to several of Lord Hunsdon's grandchildren and his own half brother and sisters. His second mistress was infinitely more attractive and interesting.

In his capacity as Lord Chamberlain, Hunsdon was placed in charge of the Queen's players and it was amongst these individuals that he met Emilia Bassano – according to A.L.Rowse, the dark lady of Shakespeare's sonnets – daughter of Baptista Bassano, Royal Musician to Henry VIII and Elizabeth I. This remarkable lady appears in the notebooks of Dr Simon Forman, the self educated doctor, astrologer and philanderer and it is from these that we learn of her affair with Hunsdon. Her first meeting with Forman was in May 1597 and from her he learnt that *'she was paramour to old Lord Hunsdon .... and was maintained in great pride; being with child she was for colour married to a minstrel'* – the child was a boy named Henry and Hunsdon gave her an annuity of forty pounds for life.

Despite being a co-heir to the Earldoms of Wiltshire and Ormonde, Hunsdon never managed to persuade Queen Elizabeth to grant him either title. It was only on his death bed that she relented and offered to remedy the situation. During his last illness she paid him a visit, bringing with her the letters patent granting him the titles and also the robes of an earl but he declined the honour with the words: *'Madam, seeing you counted me not worthy of this honour while I was living, I count myself unworthy of it now I am dying'*.

Catherine, Lady Knollys (*née* Carey) (*ca* 1524–1568/9)

Catherine Carey, the only daughter of Mary Carey (*née* Boleyn) was born about 1524. She was almost certainly named in honour of Henry VIII's first wife Catherine of Aragon, but whether the latter was her godmother is unknown. The only known portrait of Mistress Carey, painted in 1562 at the age of thirty-eight, shows her heavily pregnant with one of her younger children, either her

daughter Elizabeth or daughter Catherine. Just 4 years old at the
death of her legal father William Carey, little is known of her early
life. Her mother's affair with Henry VIII cast a long shadow over
the question of her paternity but like her brother only a DNA test
would resolve the issue.

Within a few years of her husband's death Mary Carey had taken
another husband, William Stafford, of Grafton and Chebsey, Co
Stafford and by him had a son who died young. Mary died suddenly
in 1543 and William, who went on to become a distinguished diplomat and was knighted, married a second time to Dorothy Stafford,
the daughter of Henry, Baron Stafford and Ursula Pole.

Young Catherine Carey remained for better or worse in the care
of her mother and at the age of fifteen was appointed a maid of
honour to Anne of Cleves during the short time that she was Henry
VIII's fourth wife. Catherine's future husband Sir Francis Knollys, a
gentleman pensioner to the King, also attended Anne of Cleves on
her arrival in England. Within a short time of their first meeting,
in April/May 1540, Catherine and Francis were married but again
the event appears to have passed relatively unnoticed. There were
no major grants of land from the King to support them, although
there was an Act of Parliament in 1540 assuring them of the Manor
of Rotherfield Grey in Oxfordshire, previously held by Catherine's
father-in-law.

In the years that followed Catherine performed her wifely
duties by producing children on an almost annual basis. In all she
had eleven surviving children but the strain of childbearing clearly
diminished her health and she died suddenly at the age of forty-
three whilst in attendance on the Queen on 15 January 1568/9,
although she was not buried in St Edmund's Chapel, Westminster
Abbey until the following April. The Queen of Scots laid the
blame for her early demise squarely on the shoulders of Queen
Elizabeth because of her husband's enforced absence in the north
of England on state affairs. Unfortunately her husband did not
achieve the same prominence in public affairs as his brother-in-
law, Lord Hunsdon. Nevertheless, he earned the Queen's trust
and was used by her on numerous occasions in matters of state.
He first entered the House of Commons in 1542, as a member

for Horsham. This was followed five years later by a knighthood from the Duke of Somerset for his services during the Scottish War of 1547.

On the accession of Queen Elizabeth in 1558, Knollys was admitted to her Privy Council and made Vice-Chamberlain of her Household, whilst his wife was made a woman of the Queen's Privy Chamber. Unlike his brother-in-law however, he was not offered a peerage but he was made Governor of Portsmouth and employed on numerous diplomatic missions. However, his chief claim to fame came when he was asked to take charge of Mary, Queen of Scots when she fled to England in May 1568. She remained in his charge for just one year but during that time his attempts to instruct her in the tenets and doctrines of Geneva aroused the suspicions of Queen Elizabeth and he was ordered to desist Another reason why the Queen wished to remove Mary from his care was his proposal that young George Carey, Lord Hunsdon's eldest son, would be a suitable husband for the Queen of Scots. Such a proposal was almost as ridiculous as the one that she should marry Lord Robert Dudley or one of the sons of Sir Geoffrey Poole, although the latter was at least of royal blood, being a grandson of George, Duke of Clarence.

His position as husband of the Queen's cousin/half sister enabled him to voice his views on matters of religion with some freedom. A situation that was not always to Elizabeth's liking. Nevertheless they were generally on good terms but that never stopped him from concealing his distrust for her lack of statesmanship on occasions. The situation was complicated further by the relationship that developed between his daughter Lettice and the Queen's favourite Lord Robert Dudley, which resulted in their eventual marriage. By his daughter's first marriage to Walter Devereux, Earl of Essex, he became the grandfather of Robert, Earl of Essex, Queen Elizabeth's last favourite.

Sir John Perrott, PC (*ca* 1528–1592)

By his own admission, at his trial for High Treason in 1592, Sir John Perrott '*boasted that he was King Henry's son and has great alliance in*

Wales'. True or false, the statement deserves to be examined in detail
in order to determine if there is any merit to his assertion. In order
to do this we must first establish the basic facts surrounding his birth
and then explore the truth or otherwise of his claim.

According to Thomas Perrott's inquisition post mortem dated 26
September 1531, his son and heir (*sic*) John was two years old on *'the
morrow of the feast of St Leonard'* ie 7 November 1531, thus giving him
a birthdate of 7 November 1529. However, additional documentation
points to an alternative date of birth. An inquisition held on 14 April
1549 terminating the young man's minority, claimed that Sir John
had attained his majority at the Feast of St Martin, 10/11 November
previous, thus giving him a birthdate of 10/11 November 1528. In
support of this alternative date was the award of a knighthood on
17 November 1549, which could only happen on reaching ones
majority. Such inconsistencies in the recording of ages in inquisitions
post mortem were not uncommon. Nevertheless the inclination to
accept the evidence given in contemporary documents is still strong.
However, the argument and documentation supporting a birthdate
of November 1528, is clearly superior to a date of November 1529.
As a result it is possible to postulate that he was conceived around
the end of January/beginning of February 1528.

Thomas Perrott, John's putative father, was the son of Sir Owen
Perrott upon whose death he became a ward of the Crown. However
shortly before September 1523, Thomas's wardship and marriage was
purchased from the Crown by Maurice, 14th Lord Berkeley, the uncle
of Mary Berkeley, his future bride and fellow ward; Mary's wardship
and marriage was purchased in 1521 by Lord Berkeley following the
death of Mary's mother. Mary, was the daughter of James Berkeley,
of Thornbury, Gloucestershire, the 14th Lord Berkeley's younger
brother, and Susan Veill and she appears to have been born about 1510.
As Thomas Perrott did not come of age until August 1526, we can
safely assume that his marriage to Mary probably took place after that
date. As wards of Lord Berkeley, Thomas and Mary must have lived in
his household until their marriage, but subsequent to that, they lived
at Haroldston in Pembrokeshire, Thomas's ancestral home.

In addition to John, Mary Perrott, bore two daughters Elizabeth
and Jane. Which was the elder is unknown as is the sequence of their

births; Elizabeth married John Price, of Cogerthan, Cardiganshire and Jane married William Philips, of Pilston, Pembrokeshire. However, they were both clearly born between August 1526 and 1532, when their widowed mother married in the latter year (Sir) Thomas Jones, of Abermarlais, Carmarthenshire. The first thing that Thomas did on marrying Mary was to purchase the wardship and marriage of her son, John, in September 1533 thereby acquiring the yearly value of all the Manors, Lands and hereditiaments of her late husband until John's majority. Either in consequence of his marriage or shortly afterwards, Thomas Jones was appointed a Gentleman Usher to King Henry VIII, which honour was followed by a knighthood in 1542. Interestingly Sir Thomas was well past his majority at the time. On his death in 1558/9 his widow Mary married again to Sir Robert Whitney, who died in 1567, and she was still known to be alive in 1586, when her son Sir John was Deputy Lieutenant of Ireland. Among her descendants was the infamous Lucy Walters, mistress of King Charles II and mother of the unfortunate Duke of Monmouth.

Sir John's belief that he was a bastard son of Henry VIII is difficult to prove because, apart from his own declaration, there appears to be no other contemporary evidence. Henry certainly did not shower gifts and lands upon Mary Berkeley or her husbands but that does not appear to have been his style. One historian claims that Sir Robert Naunton, who married Penelope Perrott, Sir John's granddaughter, was the author of the rumour that Sir John was King Henry's son. However, Sir John's own statement made at his trial in 1592 would seem to be the correct source. Although there is no record of Mary Berkeley/Perrott ever having been a Lady of the Bedchamber to Catherine of Aragon, that does not rule out the possibility of her appearing at court as a ward of Lord Berkeley. On the latter's death in 1523, Mary and her future husband may have been returned to the custody of the Crown until her marriage in or shortly after 1526, but positive proof is lacking on this point. If his mother was indeed briefly a mistress of the King, we have established that it would have been around the end of 1527 or beginning of 1528.

Sir John's conception and birth occurred at a very important time in the life of Henry VIII. 1528 was the year in which the 'King's Great Matter', his divorce from his Queen Catherine of

Aragon, was finally to be resolved. The King's infatuation with Anne Boleyn had begun in the spring/summer of 1526 shortly before, it is assumed, Mary's marriage and about the time that he ceased intimate relations with his wife. It was not the best of times to begin another affair but if Henry was frustrated in his pursuit of Mistress Boleyn, it would not be beyond the realms of disbelief for him to turn to more willing prey. If he did, there is no obvious proof that either Mary or her first two husbands benefited. All we know is that Sir Thomas Jones, Mary's 2nd husband, was made Constable of Emlyn Castle in 1532 and also Steward of Haverfordwest and Laugharne in the same year. Thereafter there was a gap of 7–8 years before he received any major preferment, becoming Sheriff of Pembroke in 1540/1 followed by a knighthood in 1542. Would he have received these honours automatically anyway, or were they a belated reward for his wife's affair with the King? If Sir John was the King's son, public recognition would have been the most obvious course of action, but this did not happen. To flaunt the result of any indiscretion on his part before Mistress Boleyn would have been unwise. Of his supposed likeness to the King we can only quote the words of Sir Robert Naunton:

> '...compare his picture, his qualities, gesture and yoyce, with that of the King's, which memory retains yet amongst us, they will plead strongly, that he was a subrepticious child of the bloud Royall.'

In the words of his 18th century biographer he:

> 'was a man in stature very tall and bigg, exceeding the ordinary stature of men by much, and almost equal to the mightiest men that lived in his time ... so did he in strength of body'. His hair was alborne ... His countenance full of majestie, his eye marvelous percing and carrying a commanding aspect.'

The same source tells us that he had a very sharp wit and a good understanding of French, Spanish and Italian, but that his greatest defect was that by nature he was hot tempered and could not abide being contradicted. His great height and hot temper were characteristics he shared with King Henry and the latter's grandfather King

Edward IV. But is this conclusive proof that he was King Henry's son? As we have argued elsewhere, many royal bastards bore no discernable resemblance to their either of their parents. The transmission of family characteristics is a lottery where heredity is concerned therefore the knowledge that Sir John bore a passing resemblance to King Henry must count in his favour.

Master Perrott's introduction to the Court appears to have been as a direct result of his placement in the household of Sir William Paulet, Baron St John, subsequently Earl of Wiltshire and Marquess of Winchester. This gentleman, for that is what he was until he won the favour and trust of King Henry, was appointed Comptroller of the Royal Household in 1532, Treasurer of the Royal Household in 1537 and Master of the Court of Wards in 1542 before becoming in succession Lord Chamberlain in 1543 and Lord Treasurer in 1550, a post he held for more than twenty years. His uncle (?), Robert Perrott, reader in Greek to the young King Edward, may also have been instrumental in bringing him to the attention of the young King. He cannot have joined the household of Sir William prior to his eighth birthday ie 1536, when the former was Comptroller of the Royal Household. Short of an appointment as one of the King's pages, Master Perrott could not get a better placement at Court.

Why Sir Thomas Jones decided that his stepson should be placed in the household of Sir William and not remain in Pembrokeshire to live the life of a country gentleman, is unclear. But he certainly benefited from the arrangement. Whilst there, he made the acquaintance of the young Princess Elizabeth and her brother Prince Edward, thus laying the foundations of his later career. By Edward he was knighted at his Coronation in 1547, whilst Elizabeth appointed him one of the gentlemen to carry the Canopy of State at her Coronation. Small marks of favour admittedly, but in the latter case proof surely of Elizabeth's regard for him.

Master Perrott began his political career in 1547, before reaching his majority, when he became a Member of Parliament for Carmarthenshire in the first Parliament of King Edward. The opportunity arose as a result of the sudden death of Sir Richard Devereux and his candidacy was almost certainly supported by his patron Sir

William Paulet, as President of the Council of Wales. He also became Sheriff of Pembrokeshire in 1552 and MP for Sandwich in 1553, whilst his half brother Henry Jones became MP for Carmarthenshire. But it was Queen Elizabeth who gave Perrott the opportunity to display his political and administrative skills by appointing him President of Munster in 1570 and then Lord Deputy of Ireland in 1584.

His first foray into Irish politics was not an unqualified success, and he returned to England without the Queen's permission on the grounds of ill health. However, his plan *'for the suppressing of rebellion and the well-governing of Ireland'* submitted to the Queen in 1581, impressed the latter sufficiently for him to be appointed as Lord Deputy. However, Perrott's language towards his Council and his treatment of them ensured that within four years he was recalled by the Queen. As he departed, one of his sternest critics, Sir Henry Wallop, remarked that he left behind him *'a memory of so hard usage and haughty demeanour amongst his associates, especially of the English nation, as I think never any before him in this place have done'*.

Despite this, Elizabeth saw fit to make him a Privy Councillor on his return, but within a few years he was charged with treasonable correspondence with the King of Spain and and Prince of Parma and amongst other things making disparaging remarks about the Queen. Lord Burghley, Elizabeth's chief minister, was sympathetic to Perrott's situation, but he was eventually brought to trial mainly due to the efforts of Sir Christopher Hatton, one of the Queen's favourites, whose daughter Perrott had seduced. At his trial he was found guilty, despite boasting of the fact that he was King Henry's son and exclaiming *'God's death! Will the Queen suffer her brother to be offered up a sacrifice to the envy of his frisking adversary?'* Fortunately, Elizabeth never signed the death warrant and Perrott died suddenly in the Tower from the effects of his confinement and his continual ill health.

Chapter XIII
Stuart Loose Ends

King Charles II (1630–85):
Mary Walter, later Sarsfield and Fanshaw
(1655–1693)

According to the *Dictionary of National Biography,* Mary Walter, the illegitimate daughter of Lucy Walter, and sister of James Duke of Monmouth (*see* page 36), was born 6 May 1651 at The Hague. However, when the authors checked the sources quoted in the article on Lucy Walter, none contained any record of Mary's date of birth.

As her date of birth is such a vital factor in determining if she was indeed a royal bastard, fresh research was carried out by the authors to discover, if possible, exactly when and where she was born. The result was very interesting and revealed that she was in fact born 1655/6 and not 1651. The documentary evidence in support of this revised date of birth came from two sources; firstly, a *Chancery Proceeding* of 1684 in the Public Record Office at Kew; and secondly, a contemporary letter/ deposition in the Vesey/Sarsfield collection in the National Archives in Dublin. The first established that Mary had married for the first time in the year 1670 and the second that she was just fifteen years old when William Sarsfield '*privately stole her away*' and married her '*without the consent of her guardian*'.

With the knowledge that Mary was fifteen years old in 1670, it is clear that she must have been born between 1 January 1654/5 and 31 Dec 1655. As a result it is possible to calculate that she almost certainly conceived between 1 April 1654 and 1 April 1655. In view of the uncertainty about her parentage it is worth examining the itineraries of the principal characters in the life of her mother Lucy Walters in the 1650's: Charles II, Lord Taaffe, Tom Howard (all alleged lovers of Lucy) and Sir Henry de Vic.

Charles II's itinerary at that time is fairly well documented; until 18 July 1654 he was based in Paris. If he was Mary's father, then she must have been conceived between 1 April 1654 and 18 July 1654, whilst he was still based there, unless, of course, Lucy accompanied him to Germany; for in August 1654 she was reported to be in Leige. On 5 November 1654 Charles arrived at Cologne in Germany, where he remained until February 1655/6.

Lucy Walter's movements are much less well documented. However, we do know that in August 1654 she was at Leige, but from November 1654, after Charles had arrived at Cologne, she was living at the Hague. In December 1654 she suddenly arrived in Cologne, with Sir Henry de Vic, seeking Charles's permission to marry Sir Henry, after which she returned once more to the Hague. Prior to that, in October 1654, Lord Hatton reported to Sir Edward Nicholas from Paris that he had heard of '*scurrilous stuff about Lord Taff and Mrs Barlow*'. However, her alleged presence at The Hague at the end of 1654 and throughout 1655 is seemingly attested by letters written by Mary, the Princess Royal, to her brother Charles where she is intriguingly referred to as '*your wife*'; she was probably using this term as a code name for Lucy.

The itineraries of the other parties involved – Lord Taaffe, a good friend of the King's, and Colonel Tom Howard – can be documented as follows: in October 1654 Lord Taaffe was probably in Paris when Lucy was almost certainly living in The Hague. At the end of the year he was at Cologne, as indeed were Charles and Lucy, but was in Paris again at the beginning of 1654/5. In April and July of 1655 he and Lucy were at The Hague; at the end of March 1655 he was at Dort and then Gertrudenberge. Tom Howard, who was a brother of the Earl of Suffolk and Master of the Horse to Princess Mary, Charles's sister, was also at Dort in March 1655, but before that, he was at The Hague, to which he had returned by August 1655 and was frequently seen in Lucy's company.

In summary it would seem that from November 1654 and throughout the whole of 1655 Charles II was based at Cologne. However, this did not prevent him from making impromptu visits to other cities; in October 1654 he was at Dusseldorf, in March 1655 Middleburg and September the Frankfurt Fair. Lucy Walter appears to have visited Paris at the end of 1654 and possibly the beginning of 1655, before settling at

The Hague for the rest of 1655, as did Lord Taaffe and Tom Howard.

As previously mentioned, in December 1654 Lucy with Sir Henry Vic, Charles's representative at Brussels, suddenly arrived in Cologne to seek, it is alleged, his permission for their marriage. This totally unexpected event caused considerable concern to Charles, who refused to countenance such a union, and poor Sir Henry was reprimanded for leaving his post. The sudden appearance of Sir Henry in Lucy's life is curious and can best be explained as perhaps the infatuation of an older man for a younger woman. Such an act on her part illustrates perhaps that she was to all intents and purposes no longer Charles's mistress and she was attempting to stablize her financial situation by an advantageous marriage. What is unclear at this juncture is whether she was carrying the King's child. No mention is made in surviving contemporary letters of her being in an advanced state of pregnancy; therefore an approximate conception date of April–July 1654, with Charles the father, is highly unlikely. An advanced state of pregnancy – ie nine months – would also have made travelling very difficult and indeed dangerous for her. If with child, she is more likely to have been in the early stages of pregnancy perhaps three to four months, thus making a conception date of August 1654 or even October 1654 more probable. If this was indeed the case, it raises the question of whether Sir Henry was aware of her condition and whether Charles was indeed the father of her child.

Another possibility is that Lucy accompanied Charles during his journey from Paris into the Spanish Netherlands post July 1654. His first port of call was Cambrai, followed by Mons, Namur and then by water to Leige before moving on to Spa where he was joined by his sister Mary; from there he visited Aachen on 7 September 1654 and then Aix-la-Chapelle. If so, Mary could have been conceived between 18 July 1654 and November 1654. However, Lucy's movements are unknown during this period and her sudden appearance in Cologne in December of that year, with Sir Henry de Vic, suggests that she was not in close contact with the King.

Curiously the author of the DNB article on Lucy Walter, despite his unreliability, is quite specific about the alleged day, month and place of Mary's birth. In the light of subsequent research it is just possible that he was right on those points – 6 May at The Hague. If she was indeed born on 6 May 1655 then she was clearly conceived at the beginning of August 1654 when Lucy was briefly at Leige. However, Daniel O'Neill's reference to '*your wife and children*' in his letter to Charles II from London dated 8 March 1654/5, could perhaps be used to discredit a birth date of May 1655, assuming of course that he is alluding to Lucy and her children and that he was not writing in code.

Contemporary opinion about Mary's parentage was also divided – one source, Anthony à Wood, stating

> '*You are to know that the said Mrs Walters gave out that the said King (Charles II) did begat on her body a daughter, but because he would not own her, I shall not number her among the children*'.

However, another source, Michael Deane, a Cromwellian spy who used the pseudonym B. Marshall, reported that '*Madam Barlow … bore Charles Stuart two children*'. Ann Hill, Lucy Walter's maid, who had entered her service in August 1655 at The Hague, also stated that '*those children she had were begotten by Charles Stuart*'.

Why Lucy chose to summon her maid at that particular point is intriguing. Had Lucy just given birth? If that was indeed the case then we are looking at a conception date of around the beginning of November 1654, when Sir Henry de Vic was in tow. In January 1655/6 Charles finally pensioned Lucy off with the promise of a yearly sum of 5,000 livres, the occasion for doing this being presumably the knowledge that she may have been pregnant with another man's child. Tom Howard does not come into the picture until after the birth of Mary, when Daniel O'Neile reported on 14 February 1656/7 that '*the infamous manner of hir living with Mr Howard and of her miscarrying of two children by phissick*'.

The belief that Mary's father was the Earl of Carlingford, comes from the Carte Mss:

> '… *she [Lucy Walter] had at same time a child by E. Carlingson (sic) who grew up to be a woman and owned by the mother to be her's and as like the E.C as possible*'.

The brief reference to '*scurrilous stuff about Lord Taff and Mrs Barlow*' in the correspondence of Lord Hatton is intriguing but hardly evidence of a physical relationship. Undoubtedly the Earl was Mary's guardian, for there is contemporary evidence to support the fact (*see* Calendar of State Papers 1680).

James II's assertion that she was the Earl's child was probably politically motivated and intended to discredit the rumour that Lucy had been married to King Charles and that her children were therefore legitimate. How important it was for him to do so can be appreciated by the fact there were at least two contemporary references to the Duke of Monmouth and his sister touching for the King's Evil (*see* Luttrell's Diary 21 Jan 1680) for only legitimate members of the royal family could do this.

Whilst it is true that Charles II did not publicly acknowledge Mary, he did provide her with a pension. Later she would complain that the pension was '*not ner so much as he was pleased to alowe me when I was but a child*'. Is she perhaps referring to the pension of 5,000 livres (£400) granted to her mother on 21 January 1655/6 or a separate pension granted after her mother's death? Of course, another child that Charles did not publicly recognise, but who also received a modest pension was Charlotte, the Countess of Yarmouth (*see* page 44). But if the Earl of Carlingford really was Mary's father, why then did he not provide her with a pension? As there is evidence illustrating Carlingford's role as an intermediary between Charles and Lucy Walter during the years immediately prior to Mary's birth, it is unsurprising to find him taking on the role of guardian, presumably on Charles's instructions, for Mary after her mother's death. Charles's reason for not acknowledging either child is curious, but in Mary's case may perhaps have been due to the possible political repercussions.

The contemporary documentation recording Mary's life gives some indication of her character and a surviving portrait shows that she had fine black eyes, regular and pleasing features and black hair. In many respects you can see the strong resemblance to her brother the Duke of Monmouth (*see* page 36). By all accounts she was a placid and long suffering woman, who was ill used by both her husbands, with none of the fire and determination of her mother and brother. Indeed Monmouth did not think much of his sister at

all and refused to acknowledge her second marriage for a number
of years after the event.

Mary's first marriage to William Sarsfield, was motivated purely by
financial gain. Sarsfield was anxious to regain possession of his Irish
estates which had been confiscated during the Civil War and he proposed to King Charles that if he granted him the quit rents of his estates
to the value of £160, he would settle on his wife a jointure of £800.
The King duly obliged, but he made it abundantly clear that it

> *'was solely and absolutely done by us for the benefit of the said Mary and her*
> *children by the said Mr Sarsfield'.*

Unfortunately Sarsfield did not keep to his part of the bargain, and
when he died, he only left his wife an allowance of £200 per annum.
When Charles realised how ill used she had been, he promised her
a pension of £600 per annum, but this was stopped by the Earl of
Danby during one of the Government's recurrent financial crises. To
add insult to injury, Sarsfield's will directed that his infant children were
to be placed in the charge of his mother, she being a Protestant, and
not his widow.

Within five months of her husband's death, Mary had married her
second husband, William Fanshaw, who was a great crony of the Earl
of Rochester. Again the motive appears to have been for financial gain.
They had a least five children and at the birth of the eldest, Henry
Savile wrote:

> *'I thought there could be but one lame thing upon this earth in perfect happiness*
> *and that is Fanshaw for his having a daughter, a princesse, who yet remains in*
> *paganisme for want of baptism, which the fond father delayes to take some prudent*
> *resolution concerning the godfather. He thinks the King ought to be kept for a*
> *sonn & the D of Monmouth does not yet owne the alliance enough to hold his*
> *néece at the font etc '.*

However, despite Mary's royal connections, her pension was never paid
regularly with the result that Fanshaw had to petition the Treasury
repeatedly for assistance; but between 1680–84 he received £1,400 in
bounty payments from the King.

Until 1686, Mary remained a Catholic, but when her second husband persuaded her to become a Protestant, King James stopped his pension of £400 a year. For reasons unknown, King Charles had dismissed him from his post of Master of the Revels and Commissioner of the Alienation Office. For the most part, Mary remained in the background, but her husband always took every opportunity he could to advance himself and was often seen at Nell Gwyn's house. He also gained a reputation as a ladies man and was reported to have passed on the result of his infidelities to his poor wife. A contemporary Henry Saville reported that

> 'The other day Mr Fanshaw came & made a third with us, but will have his worse pox then ours passe for the scury out of civilty to his lady though the rogue bee a filthyer leaper than ever was cured in the gospell & without another pool of Bethesda or another Saviour hee is the most incurable animall that now crawles upon the earth.'

However, in 1681 Mary burst into the public eye, when it was claimed that the previous year she had cured one Jonathan Trott, a poor man, of the King's Evil. Trott, it is claimed,

> 'went to Mrs Fanshaw's house near St James's ' and as soon as ever Mrs Fanshaw appear'd 'falling on his knées, he begged her to pardon him. 'Then, grasping her hands with all the violence and passion imaginable, kissed them a thousand times, and directed 'em to his neck, and this throat and all other parts of his body wherein he was afflicted ' etc, within 3 days he was cured.'

The witnesses to this were Lord Gerard, Sir Gilbert Gerard, Col. Langley, Thomas Vernon, Mr Rowe and Mrs Néedham and the incident produced at least one satirical verse:

> 'Fanshawe's Princes posted after
> to take the place of ye Kings Daughter
> Which Royal Priviledge she gott
> By gently stroaking Mr Trot'

The declaration cannot have pleased King Charles, regardless of whether Mary was an innocent party in the affair. It was to all intents and purposes a declaration of her legitimacy and must have caused him grave embarrassment. He had already made three public declarations in 1679 and 1680 that he was never married to Lucy, but still the rumour persisted.

Sadly, Mary's life was cut short when she died suddenly in April 1693 aged only 38. When Will Fanshaw died in 1707, he sought to atone for some of his past behaviour by requesting that he be buried beside '*his dearly beloved wife*' in Barking Church.

Chapter XIV
Hanoverian Loose Ends

Frederick, Prince of Wales (son of King George II) (1707–51): Mary Allbeary (or Aubury)(*d.* 1787)

Little is known about Mary Allbeary (also known as Aubury), but what information there is, came originally from the late Sir Robert Mackworth-Young, KCVO, Librarian of Windsor Castle Library who corresponded with Cecil Humphery-Smith.

Mary was alleged to be a daughter of Frederick, Prince of Wales, born of an undisclosed mother. She was married on 25 August 1764 at Fort St George, Madras to Henry Brooke (1725–86) and she died twenty-three years later on 12 August 1787 at Dublin, leaving a daughter, Catherine. It is said that Catherine married in 1776 Richard FitzGerald, although this would suggest that if Catherine herself was legitimate, she can only have been eleven years of age at most upon marriage.

Frederick was the eldest son of George II but died during his father's lifetime. He was the father of King George III and of four additional sons and four daughters, by his wife Princess Augusta youngest daughter of Frederick II, Duke of Saxe-Gotha-Altenburg.

Prince George of Hanover, later Prince of Wales, later King George III (1763) (1738-1820): George Rex (1765-1839)

For the last two hundred years or more, there has been a continuing and widespread belief that George Rex, of Knynsa, in Cape Province, South Africa, the first owner and settler of Knysna and sometime a Marshal and Sergeant-at-Mace of the Vice Admiralty Court at the Cape of Good Hope, was the son, legitimate or illegitimate, of Prince George of Wales, who later became King George III, by *The Fair Quaker*, Hannah Lightfoot, to whom, some claim, he had been married.

The belief extended to the fact that in 1797 George Rex had been secretly banished to South Africa by a worried king (as he had become thirty-seven years earlier), who by that time had a legitimate brood of his own by his Queen, Princess (Sophia) Charlotte of Mecklenburg-Strelitz, whom he had married on 8 September 1761, a fortnight before his Coronation. It is said that he was keen therefore to remove any possible source of embarrassment and so provided George Rex with a sinecure as a Marshal and Sergeant-at-Mace of the Vice Admiralty Court at the Cape of Good Hope as well as with an estate of some 24,000 acres at Knysna, and various family souvenirs and mementoes, on condition that he destroyed any records of his early life and never spoke of his origins, and that he never married, nor returned to England, dead or alive. Many of his numerous descendants firmly believe all this to be true.

During this period, no less than a dozen books and articles have been written about George Rex as well as a number of television documentaries. Whilst there is no doubt at all that George Rex existed, that he emigrated to South Africa, that he served as Marshal and Sergeant-at-Mace of the Vice Admiralty Court and that he lived and prospered at Knysna, there has been much controversy as to whether or not this belief was true, supported as it was by various circumstantial evidence, but with no hard proof.

However, the most recent and perhaps the most objective and thorough work on the subject is by Patricia Storror, called *George Rex: Death of a Legend*, and published by Macmillan South Africa in 1974. She has come down firmly on the side that George Rex was not the son of Prince George and Hannah Lightfoot, but was the son of George and Sarah Rex, of London. Nevertheless as there has been so much controversy and speculation over the last two hundred and forty years, it seems right to include him under *Royal Loose Ends*, if only to set the record straight once and for all.

A certain amount of circumstantial evidence, when taken together, had suggested that George Rex might have been born prior to

1760 and that he was the son of Prince George of Wales who was shortly to succeed his grandfather as King George III. The mother was said to have been Hannah Lightfoot, known as *The Fair Quaker*, who was born in 1730 and whom some claim had married George on 17 April 1759 in Kew Chapel when he would only have been fifteen years old. However, this seems unlikely, for Hannah herself is now known to have married Isaac Axford on 11 December 1753 in Keith's Chapel, Curzon Street, in London, whereupon she appears to have been abducted, never to be seen again. It is likely that she died between 1758–59, but had she married George and had she survived, the effect of such a marriage, if it had taken place, would have been to render illegitimate all fifteen of George's children by his official wife, Queen Charlotte. Moreover, *The Oxford Dictionary of National Biography* demolishes the idea that Hannah had had any issue by King George III and indeed questions whether they had ever met.

So quite simply, the dates do not add up. Nor indeed do the various fragments of circumstantial evidence, when examined individually, especially in the light of the recent discovery of George Rex's parentage and legal career, by which the whole legend has been comprehensively rebutted. For in her book, Patricia Storror outlines the research conducted by Professor Ian Christie who established that George Rex was born on 29 August 1765, was baptised at Whitechapel on 2 September 1765 and was the eldest son of John Rex (1725–92), a distiller of Whitechapel who was sometime Master of the Distillers' Company, and of his wife Sarah (1730–1803), a widow twice over, who had married in Whitechapel on 17 November 1764.

George went on to become a Notary Public, being admitted in 1786, and practising in London, thereby becoming an ideally qualified candidate to apply for the post of Marshal and Sergeant-at-Mace of the Vice Admiralty Court at the Cape of Good Hope to which he was appointed on 27 January 1797. George Rex also had a younger brother John and a sister Sarah, whose lives are well chronicled.

George Rex served as Marshal and Sergeant-at-Mace of the Vice Admiralty Court from 1798 to 1802 when South Africa was handed back to the Dutch. Thereafter he purchased the estate at Knysna piecemeal between 1804-30 where he prospered exceedingly, largely from the extensive sale of timber, in a country where timber was in short supply. Indeed in 1867, his eldest son, George Rex, junior, as a large landowner and leading citizen, was among a number of people to have entertained HRH Prince Alfred, Duke of Edinburgh during his visit to the Cape Colony, although subsequent research has shown that no special significance should be attached to this, as had been claimed.

Although George Rex never married, he lived successively with two common-law wives (who were mother and daughter to eachother) by whom he had a total of thirteen children (six boys and seven girls). It is probable that the reason that he did not marry, was that he had already been married in London before he came out to South Africa, and could not afford a divorce (which were impossibly expensive), but neither did he want to become a bigamist, having regard to the legal appointment he held. However this has not been substantiated.

The Rev. Frederick William Blomberg, DD, or Count Blomberg (1761–1847)

There is evidence in the Royal Archives to suggest that Blomberg was a Royal Bastard, although probably not of King George III, but rather of one of his brothers.

In its edition of 24 April 1964, *Country Life* published an article *The Lake that became a Valley,* in which it was claimed that the Manor of Kirkby Misperton in Yorkshire had been given in 1812 by the Prince Regent to Count Blomberg, a natural son of George III. This information had come from *Alumni Cantabrigienses* as well as a brochure issued by the Estate Company and it gave rise to various correspondence, including an article on 27 August 1964 entitled *Who was Count Blomberg?*

Certainly the manor had been in the Blomberg family since 1687 when Charles John, Baron Blomberg (1658–1745), Envoy of the Duke of Courland, had married a seventeen year old widow Elizabeth, Lady Shiers. The manor passed to their eldest son, Edmund Charles (1690–1757) – whose arms are on record at the College of Arms - and thence to his nephew, William (1736–74) and to his widow Anne, upon whose death in 1798 it became escheated to the King in right of the Duchy of Lancaster.

According to the Bigland Collection of the College of Arms (XIII, 81), it appears that Frederick Blomberg was the son of a Frederick Blomberg who was the son of a George Diederic Blomberg who was the grandson of Nicholas de Blomberg, of Courland. This Nicholas was the father of Charles John, Baron Blomberg, mentioned above, who came over with King George I. Thus Nicholas was the great-grandfather of William Blomberg, the testator of Kirby over Car, who was in turn a second cousin once removed to Frederick. However, Frederick would only have been entitled to the arms of Blomberg and/or in remainder to the title of Count, providing that his great-great grandfather Nicholas was a Count (as was his son Edmund) and/or armigerous.

However, it has also been suggested that Frederick was a natural son of King George III and took his mother's married name but his baptismal entry of 22 September 1761 in St Margaret's Rochester shows him to be the son of Lieutenant (later Captain) Frederick B. Blomberg and Melissa *(née* Layng) his wife. It so happens that he was baptised two weeks after King George III's marriage and the day after his Coronation. The last owner of the manor seems to have considered Blomberg to be the 'heir-general', and as a second cousin once removed, he could well have been the heir to his cousin.

But in 1801, the Rev. F.W. Blomberg, who by then was Chaplain and Private Secretary to the Prince of Wales, successfully claimed the property, although without any mention of his own alleged parentage. If his claim had been by right of descent (paternal or maternal), he would surely have mentioned his connection and it is perhaps significant that he did not. He did, however, build a large obelisk in the grounds of Kirkby Misperton in 1812 to commemorate the grant of this property to him by George, Prince of Wales, the Regent.

Alumni Cantabrigienses states that the Rev. F.W. Blomberg, DD, was a constant companion of George III's children and that he resembled some of them. It records that Blomberg was admitted to St John's College Cambridge on 7 October 1777 and a Fellow-Com on 18 January 1782, BA 1782, MA 1785 and a DD in 1822. He was ordained Deacon at Ely on 6 June 1784 and a priest the following year. He became Chaplain to

George, Prince of Wales in 1787 and in the same year was appointed rector of Shepton Mallet, Somerset 1787–1833, Prebendary of Bristol 1790–1828, Chaplain to George, Prince of Wales 1793, Vicar of Bradford, Wiltshire 1793–99 and 1808–33, Vicar of Banwell, Somerset 1799–1808, Prebendary of Westminster 1808–22, and of St Pauls 1822–47, Vicar of St Giles, Cripplegate 1833–47, Prebendary of Bath and Wells until 1833, Canon Residentiary of St Pauls and Chaplain to Queen Victoria. He married Maria Floyer, of Bath on 29 May 1787.

The *Gentleman's Magazine* of 1847 carried an obituary for him in which it was stated: *'his family had been long attached to the Court'* and that he was educated *'in intimate association with the children of King George III who always retained great affection for him.'*

In a letter from Christopher Dobson, Librarian of the House of Lords, to Robert (later Sir) Mackworth Young, Librarian of Windsor Castle and Assistant Keeper of the Queen's Archives, dated 8 June 1964, he stated that

> *'as a young man George III had a number of 'flirtations' – innocent no doubt – with various young ladies including Lady Sarah Lennox. No doubt, if there was a child the circumstances and the parentage were rigorously concealed. The only thing that could not be hidden was the striking resemblance to the Royal family.'*

What seems certain is that Blomberg was brought up as a child in company with the children of George III and that he is said to have had a striking likeness to the Royal family. As George III was passionately in love with Lady Sarah Lennox for two years or more before his marriage in 1761, it is perhaps unlikely that he would have been the father.

Nevertheless, there are a few references to Blomberg in the Royal Archives. In the Diary of Lady Charlotte Finch *(GEO/ADDL 21/181)* dated 4 January 1765, it is recorded: *'The Queen determined to take Master Blomberg* [aged only four] *and allow him 50 pds a year and put him under Mrs. Cotesworth's care.'* (sub-governess to the Royal children).

There are later references to payments made to him from 1784 until 1793 as Private Secretary to the Prince of Wales and to an

annuity he received from 1805. There are references to his many
Court appointments as Chaplain to POW (1787) and as Clerk of
the Closet to POW (1808), as Chaplain to the Household at Carlton
House (1821-37), as Deputy Clerk of the Closet and Chaplain in
Ordinary (1827-37) and as Chaplain in Ordinary to Kings George IV
and William IV (1827–37), but none as to his paternity. In Mackworth
Young's letter to Dobson, dated 6 June 1964, he also said:

> 'There is no evidence here to show that he [Blomberg] was an illegitimate son
> of King George III. This does not of course disprove the story since it is quite
> likely that if there had been any such evidence, it would have been removed.
> On the other hand, I am personally doubtful about the traditions that George
> III had illegitimate children. There is one such tradition about the Rex family
> in South Africa which has proved to be false [see page 209]. In general the
> fathering of illegitimate children seems out of keeping with the King's character.
> Unlike his father and sons, he was by no means a bounder, but had, on the
> contrary, an exaggerated sense of duty. He had several illegitimate half brothers
> (including curiously one of my predecessors), but I should be surprised to see
> proof that he ever had an illegitimate child of his own.'

He later wrote on 10 August:

> 'There is no evidence of George III being Blomberg's father. There seems no
> reason in principle why William Augustus, Duke of Cumberland or Edward
> Duke of York should not have been Blomberg's father. In the latter case, the
> dates would fit in particularly well, as the D. of York died in 1767. In 1760
> he was a dashing young naval officer with a reputation for success among the
> ladies, and could well have been the father of an infant born in Rochester in
> 1761. But there is no evidence here to support this speculation.'

However, after Blomberg's death on 23 March 1847 aged eighty-five,
two books entitled *The Unseen World* (1847) as well as *The Journal
and Memories of Thomas Whalley* (1863) were published, attempting to
explain Blomberg's close associations with the Royal Family. They
both claimed that Blomberg's father, a British Officer, who had been
serving in the West Indes, appeared as a ghost to two other officers
serving there, asking them to go to a certain house in Scotland where

in a chest certain documents would be found so as to enable his son to claim his property from Queen Charlotte. This they did and his son apparently came into his inheritance, besides also being brought up with the Royal Family. However, far fetched though it sounds, there is a reference in the Army List to a Captain Blomberg serving in the West Indes in 1765 as Captain in the 62nd American regiment, quartered in the 'Charibbee Islands', but there was no reference to him in the 1767 edition, so Blomberg's father may have died there in 1767 after all. Now, the only thing that remains to remind us of this enigma is his portrait by Richard Brampton, sold at Christies on 16 April 1982.

George, Prince of Wales, later King George IV (1762–1830): William Francis (*b ca.* 1806)

Among the royal papers, those preceding George Crole (*see* page 126), relate to a William Francis who was also in receipt of payments from the Privy Purse for six years. The papers date from 1806, the probable year of his birth, and the payments began in 1817, when his mother or so-called mother, Mrs. Davies died, and were extended until 1823.

However, the impression one gains from the limited correspondence is that Mrs. Davies was troublesome, for on 29 August 1806, three days after her son had been handed over to her, against a receipt, there is a letter from Mr. Anstey to the Prince's Private Secretary, saying

> 'the same gentleman that Mrs. Davies cald her Counsel the day she made the Disturbance came and Produced the Order for the child, which I delivered. I have a recpt from him Acknowledging the same; would you Please to have it Sent to you, or remain with me until I See you; if you think it Proper to have it sent to you, Please to inform me in what manner I am to convey it.' (RA 29958)

The various payments and receipts relate to William's annual allowance of £200 and the payment of his school fees to a Mrs.

Frances Stockdale, of Parson's Green amounting to about another £100 per year and were payable at least from 1819–23.

The papers show that William was born prior to August 1806, being aged about eleven at the time of his mother's death on 29 May 1817, and that he was destined for an army career, with funds available for the purchase of a commission. There is mention too of tentative travel plans for William in 1822, possibly involving friends in Madras. There is correspondence between Mr. M. Anstey (who appears to act as a go-between), Mr. Geldard of Grays Inn Square, seemingly a lawyer, and with Mr. Charles Bicknell, of Charing Cross, solicitor and attorney to the Prince of Wales and sometime a Clerk in his Household, Mr. C. F. Du Pasquier, for many years Groom of the Chamber to the Prince of Wales and Colonel the Rt. Hon. Sir John McMahon, 1st Bt, Private Secretary to the Prince of Wales / Prince Regent and Keeper of the Privy Purse (1805–17).

Moreover on 18 July 1820, suspicions were aroused as we see in the letter from R. Birnie of Bow Street to Charles Bicknall dated 18 July 1820, when he says:

> *'I am still pestered by that woman named Walker who had brought a host of witnesses again, all of which state, and I must say plausibly enough, that the child was not <u>borrowed</u> to impose upon Du Pasquier but on a person of much higher rank; for the Lady who she judges to be the pretended Mother was of a very superior appearance, always came in her Carriage, was very particular in enquiring if the child was fair (this could not apply to Du Pasquier) and that he, Du P, always attended on her as a servant. There is an immense quantity of evidence from various persons, very well dove-tailed I assure you, but this is a Case you well know, wherein a Justice of the peace has no jurisdiction. I apprehend however that they may get into the hands of those who <u>at this time</u> (George IV had been crowned eight days earlier) will make a fine handle of it. It would be well if that could be prevented' (RA 29959)*

So whilst there is no conclusive proof that William Francis is another Royal Bastard, the circumstantial evidence is certainly very strong with his Private Secretary and Groom of the Chamber to the Prince of Wales arranging for the funding and welfare of a William Francis for at least six years. In all probability, William's so-called mother was probably a paid foster mother, rather than his actual mother.

Unfortunately a search of *Alumni Cantabrigienses, Alumni Oxonienses, The Army Lists, The Navy Lists, Clerical Directories, India Office Lists* and others yielded not a single reference to the name. Although a search of the *International Genealogical Index* produced a number of entries for births or baptisms of William Francis, nothing relevant could be identified.

Chapter XV
Victorian Loose Ends

Edward, Prince of Wales, later King Edward VII (1901) (1841–1910)

During Queen Victoria's reign, there are no references to any Royal Bastards stemming from the Queen, although the same cannot be said for her eldest son, Edward, Prince of Wales, later King Edward VII.

The late Theo Aronsen in his book *'The King in Love – Edward VII's Mistresses'* delved most assiduously into any offspring that the King may have had as did Raymond Lamont-Brown in his book *Edward VII's Last Loves – Alice Keppel & Agnes Keyser* (1998).

As was fashionable at the time, most of his lovers were respectably married women, who, rightly or wrongly, passed off their offspring, by whomsoever begotten, as the children of their husband. It is therefore very difficult for us to determine paternity with any certainty, as there is often nothing other than circumstantial evidence to rely upon for DNA had not then been discovered.

The King's three official mistresses, all married, were in chronological order, Lillie Langtry, Daisy, Countess of Warwick and Alice Keppel, but whereas there were undoubtedly many Royal 'flings', we cannot be certain that any of these have led to any further Royal Bastards, possibly as a result of a bout of syphilis he is alleged to have had. Nevertheless, there are a number of claimants.

In his book *The Fox Hunters of Vanity Fair,* Gordon Fergusson states that Edward's mistresses were innumerable and included among their number Patsy Cornwallis-West, whose son George Frederick Myddelton Cornwallis-West (who later married the widowed Lady Randolph Churchill) was born on 14 November 1874. He was a godson of the Prince and was grandson of the Marquess of Headford. Patsy was a court favourite and it is said that George had been

fathered by the Prince in the woods at Eaton whilst staying with the
Duke of Westminster. An estate worker's little girl had *'seen the Prince
on top of her'*. However as might be expected, there is no reference to
this Royal paternity in *Burke's Peerage* (*see* de la Warr, E).

Then there was the child of the 5th Duke of Newcastle's daughter,
Lady Susan Vane Tempest, *née* Pelham-Clinton, born in 1871, for whose
upbringing the Prince was asked to contribute. Others mentioned were
the son of Princesse Jeanne de Sagan, later Duchesse de Talleyrand-
Perigord, who may have had a Royal father, after a dalliance in 1873
when the Prince visited the Chateau de Mello, south of Paris.

Olga, later Baroness de Mayer, the daughter of Blanche, Duchess
di Caracciola, is said to have been the Prince's favourite illegitimate
child and that she was conceived on one of the Prince's visits to
Dieppe, where she was brought up discreetly. It is further said that
Olga went on to become one of Winnarata, Princesse de Polignac's
lovers, long before Violet Keppel/Trefusis shared her bed. Some claim
that Roderick Ross, the Chief Constable of Edinburgh and Sir Stewart
Graham Menzies, head of the Secret Intelligence Service, upon whom
'C' of James Bond fame was modelled, were both sons of the Prince.

Then there was Sophie, wife of Colonel W. Hall Walker who
used to receive the King ingognito as The Duke of Lancaster, even
though he was thirty-five years her senior; and also Grace Forster, *née*
Blomfield, of Co. Fermanagh who had a son Stewart Arthur Forster
(who was born 30 August 1899) and thought by some to be the
Prince's son. Apparently Stewart was teased a lot at Winchester about
his paternity and the fact that his father appeared upon so much of
the coinage of the Realm, yet his children now deny knowing anything about it at all! There was also Miss Margot Thorold of Boothby
Hall in Lincolnshire and Cora Pearl who liked to be dished up on a
silver platter *à la nue*. The Duchesse de Mouchy, the sultry divorcee
and Sarah Bernhardt were also paramours and the list goes on.

It has also been suggested that Rosemary Aimee Douglas Erskine
Crum, *née* Dawson, was yet another daughter of King Edward VII.
According to her husband's entry in *Who Was Who*, Rosemary mar-
ried in 1948 Lieutenant-General Vernon Forbes Erskine Crum, CIE,
MC, (1918–71) and was the daughter of Brigadier-General Sir Douglas
(Frederick Rawdon) Dawson, GCVO, KCB, CMG (1854–1933),

who was Comptroller of the Lord Chamberlain's Department from 1907–20. Dawson had married Aimee Evelyn (Evie), GBE, daughter of Gordon Pirie and she was the widow of Herbert Oakley, whom she had married as her first husband in 1889. Oakley died ten years later leaving no issue and in 1903 Evie married Dawson, although strangely no issue is recorded for them in any reference books. Evie is recorded as having been awarded the GBE in 1918 and as having died in 1946 and a check in the indexes of deaths for 1946 shows that she died aged eighty-two and was therefore born ca 1864.

However, the only reference to Rosemary's paternity is given in the entries for her husband in *Who Was Who* and for her son, Douglas Vernon Erskine Crum, CBE who has been the Racecourse Director at Ascot for the last ten years and whose entry appears in the current *Who's Who*. If Rosemary was to have been the daughter of the King (who died in May 1910), then she would have been at least eight years older than her husband (who was born 1918) and she would have married him in 1948 aged thirty-eight, if born in the King's last year. More significantly, however, her mother, Aimee, who was born in 1864, would have also been forty-six at the time of the King's death, hardly an ideal age for giving birth to her first and only child. Nevertheless her mother did at least have connections at Court through her second husband, who was Master of Ceremonies to King Edward VII from 1903. If she was to be passed off as the legitimate daughter of the Dawsons, then she must have been born after August 1904.

Like so many of these stories, nothing is conclusive, although it does, at least, indicate a propinquity to the King for Rosemary's mother at about the right time. Nevertheless, the dates are not convincing and leave many questions unanswered.

In a more worthy vein was the unlikely Agnes Keyser who with her sister, Fanny, established the King Edward VII's Hospital for Officers in 1899 which flourishes to this day. Despite being a considerable heiress, Agnes never married which was unusual for the king's paramours, but because she was wealthy, she was never considered a social failure. The King was impressed and interested in her good works which brought them into close contact, which became closer still over the years.

It seems that few of the fairer sex could say no to the Prince, and for many of those who succumbed, it was his custom to give them one of his well-known diamante monkey brooches.

Unlike Royal Bastards of earlier centuries, King Edward never officially recognised any illegitimate offspring. This may of course have been because he did not have any, although, as we have seen, there were many contenders, the most likely of which are listed below. At his Coronation, King Edward VII insisted upon inviting a bevy of his girlfriends, old and new, who were seated in a special pew in Westminster Abbey, which was irreverently referred to as '*the King's loose box.*' According to Raymond Lamont-Brown these included: La Favorita (Alice Keppel), Mrs Ronald Greville, Lady Sarah Wilson, Feo Sturt, Mrs. Arthur Paget, Lady Warwick, Lillie Langtry, Sarah Bernhardt, Jennie Churchill, Leonie Jerome, Countess Torby, Lady Albemarle (Alice Keppel's mother-in-law), Princess Daisy of Pless and Baroness Olga Alberta de Meyer (the King's reputed daughter by the Duchess di Carrachiola). From these the following foals have emerged.

Jeanne-Marie Langtry, MBE, CStJ (1881–1964)

There is no doubt at all that Lillie Langtry, (1853–1929) '*The Jersey Lily,*' the beauty who became the first official mistress of Edward Prince of Wales, gave birth to a daughter, Jeanne-Marie Langtry, in France on 8 March 1881 and that the child was duly handed over to the care of Lillie's mother, Emily le Breton, who brought her up at Lillie's love-nest in Bournemouth, with occasional visits from the child's 'Aunt' Lillie, as her actress mother was known to her.

Lillie, who was born in Jersey as Emily Charlotte, was the daughter of the Very Rev. William Corbet le Breton, Dean of Jersey, whose family had been prominent in Jersey from Norman times. Lillie married firstly in 1874 the ineffectual but compliant Edward Langtry, an Irish widower, but he died of drink in 1897, officially leaving a daughter Jeanne-Marie. Two years later, Lillie married again Hugo Gerald de Bathe, nineteen years her junior, who later succeeded as 5th Baronet and died in 1940, she having died eleven years beforehand in Monte Carlo.

It was not until Jeanne-Marie was fourteen that she learned from Margot Asquith that her so-called 'aunt' was in fact her mother. Mother and daughter had never got on well together and had seen little of each other, and this was the final straw. There was even less contact thereafter. Two years later, a reporter of the *Sketch* described Jeanne-Marie as

> *'a simple well-bred looking girl, strongly recalling one or two of her mother's early portraits – those taken when Mrs. Langtry was just bursting upon the world, the fairest among a world of fair women and a dream of lovliness'.*

However, he seemed to have been more taken with the mother than the daughter!

Two years later, there was the difficulty of launching Jeanne-Marie into polite society by her presentation at Court. But this was achieved with the Prince of Wales's help and the assistance of Gladys Countess de Grey, who presented the daughter-in-law of one of Lillie's brothers, a Mrs. H. Langtry, at a Drawing Room, which would then enable Mrs. H. Langtry to present her cousin by marriage, Miss Jeanne-Marie Langtry.

This was all possible because Jeanne-Marie's father was recorded as Edward Langtry. However Jeanne-Marie's birth took place four years after her mother first met the Prince of Wales and became his regular companion, and the question arose therefore as to whether or not the Prince of Wales might not have been her father. But her conception was at a time when their passions were on the wane and both seem to have been running other lovers in parallel. Theo Aronson in his book *The King in Love,* firmly refutes any suggestion that the child's father was Edward VII, believing Jeanne-Marie's father to have been Prince Louis of Battenberg.

In the spring of 1880 Lillie had embarked upon an affair with Prince Louis, who was later to marry one of Queen Victoria's many granddaughters, Princess Victoria of Hesse. If he was indeed Jeanne-Marie's father, she would in fact have been a half sister to Princess Andrew of Greece (mother of HRH Prince Philip) and to Lord Louis Mountbatten, although Jeanne-Marie did not learn of this suggested relationship until the eve of her marriage in 1902 when she married Ian (later Sir)

Zachary Malcolm, 17th of Portalloch, in Argyllshire, who became the hereditary chief of Clan Malcolm, and of a respected Scottish family dating back to 1562 (*see Burke's Landed Gentry of Scotland,* 2002).

Together they led a busy public life. He was a Conservative MP and had served for a time in the Diplomatic Corps, being awarded KCMG, in 1919 and appointed DL and JP. During his time in Parliament he, together with four others, including Winston Churchill, had founded a mildly rebellious pressure group named 'The Malcomtents.' Meanwhile Jeanne-Marie was appointed MBE in 1920 and CStJ in 1930 for her involvement in the Order of St John and she died in 1964 aged 82, leaving three sons and a daughter from who descend many living descendants.

Thus any claims of the Malcolms of Portalloch to descend from King Edward VII would seem to be rather suspect, although they are probably descended from the Battenbergs and are thus related to Princes Philip, Charles, William and Harry through that line instead.

Alexandra Maud Venetia Fawcus (*née* James) (1896–1981)

Alexandra Maud Venetia James, was born on 26 December 1896, the second daughter of William Dodge James, CVO (1908) of West Dean Park, West Sussex. Her father, William (1854-1912), who had been born in Lancashire and educated at Harrow, was the youngest of three brothers, who had travelled extensively and had returned from the USA where his father had made a fortune in the railroad business.

William bought West Dean Park in 1892, which had formerly been the seat of the Peachey family, built in castellated Gothic style in faced flintwork for Lord Selsey to designs by James Wyatt. He also bought Grey Walls, Gullane, East Lothian, but Sussex was his main base where he owned 9,000 acres, and where he duly served as High Sheriff and as a DL and JP. He married in 1880 a Scottish girl, Evelyn (Evie) Elizabeth, CBE, the eldest daughter of Sir Charles John Forbes of Newe, Bt, in Aberdeenshire. Together they had four daughters and an afterthought son, who later in 1964, established West Dean as The Edward James Foundation, an educational charity. Edward, the surrealist poet and art collector, who himself was a godson of the Prince of Wales, is said to have claimed that his mother, Evie, was the mistress of the Prince of Wales, and that she had left to him a bundle of over one hundred letters from the King to his mother. However, it is with his sister Alexandra that we are dealing.

After William's death in 1912, his widow married Lt. Col. John Chaytor Brinton, CVO, DSO, Life Guards, whom she was to divorce two years before she died in 1929.

This then is the confused setting into which Alexandra was born in 1896. Both Queen Alexandra and Queen Maud of Norway were her godmothers, giving her their names, just as King Edward VII was to become godfather to her baby brother Edward, eleven years later. Clearly Edward often stayed at West Dean as many family photographs testify. Although the sprinkling of CVOs to various members of the family is an added indication of Royal service, it is difficuly to guauge just how far that Royal service went. For it is alleged by a number of people well acquainted with the family, that Alexandra (but not her siblings) was the daughter of the fifty-five year old Edward, Prince of Wales, as he then was, and that she bore a striking resemblance to him. Certainly her rather solid build was quite different from that of her slim siblings. If so, Mrs. William James did indeed entertain the King in the words of the ditty. However, in *Burke's Landed Gentry* 1972 edition, under *James of West Dean*, Alexandra is shown as the daughter of William James, and to date there has been no hard evidence to show that this was not so.

What is certain is that in January 1908, Count Albert Mensdorff, the Austro-Hungarian Ambasssador, records in his diary that the King visited West Dean with a large party including Alice Keppel, and two years later upon the King's death, it was an older brother, Arthur and his wife Venetia, (*née* Cavendish Bentinck), with whom Alice Keppel and her children went to stay in Grafton Street so as to console themselves after the death of King Edward VII. Venetia is also alleged to have been another favourite of Edward VII, just like her sister-in-law, who is recorded on 4 May 1910, two days before the King's death, to have been playing bridge with Alice Keppel in the Chinese Room at Buckingham Palace.

Meanwhile Alexandra married in 1918 Lt Col Arthur Edward Flynn Fawcus, DSO, MC, TD, the second son of James Fawcus of Keswick, Cumberland. He lived in Berkshire as well as in Kenya, but was killed in an aeroplane accident in 1936 leaving two sons and a daughter, Venetia, now Mrs. Michael Worthington, who lives at Hurley, near Maidenhead. In correspondence with her, she stated that her mother

> *'was fully aware that she might possibly have been the daughter of Edward VII, but as she adored Willie James, she liked to think he was her true father … As you see, I am unable to confirm or deny these rumours'. She added 'I too like to think he [Willie James] was [the father of Alexandra], as from everything I have heard and read about him, make him out to be a delightful person and a much nicer character than the King'.*

Alexandra, who was prominent in the British Red Cross Society, of which she was an honorary Vice President, lived at Mapledurwell House, Basingstoke, Hampshire until her death in 1981.

The Hon. Maynard Greville (1898–1960)

The Hon Maynard Greville was born on 21 March 1898, the third but second surviving son of Frances Evelyn (Daisy), Countess of Warwick. She was the elder daughter and co-heir of Colonel the Hon Charles Henry Maynard, who was the son of 3rd and last Viscount Maynard which is where his name came from. From the age of three, Daisy was a significant heiress in her own right.

Seventeen years earlier, in 1881, Daisy had married Francis Richard Charles Guy (Greville), Lord Brooke and later 5th Earl of Warwick (1853–1924), the owner of Warwick Castle, by whom she was officially to have three sons and two daughters. Of these it would seem that Leopold (later 6th Earl) (born 1882), Charles (1885–87) and Marjorie (born 1884) were all born safely before their mother met the Prince of Wales in 1889. Then twelve years after her last confinement, Maynard was born, and perhaps it was significant that he was given no Greville names.

For nine of those years Daisy and her Prince had been inseparable. Before her husband succeeded to the Earldom of Warwick, the Prince used to call her his '*Babbling Brooke*' after her courtesy title, and later on, somewhat rashly, '*His darling Daisy wife*'. But Daisy ended the affair in January 1898 – two months before Maynard's arrival – by writing to Princess Alexandra. In reply the Princess sent her 'a small crucifix wrapt in a piece of paper on which was written these words '*From one who has suffered much and forgives all.*" Thus it is possible, if not probable, that the Prince may have been Maynard's father.

However, the King was not the father of her youngest child, Mercy, born in 1904 to a mother then aged forty-three, with whom he had broken up six years earlier. For Mercy's mother had not broken up with the new '*love of her life,*' Captain Joseph Laycock, who shared her left wing inclinations. They had met in 1899, according to Anita Leslie in *Edwardians in Love,* and it is he who is alleged to have been Mercy's father, despite having married only two years before her birth, Katherine Mary, the recently divorced wife of the 6th Marquess of Downshire. He went on to become Brigadier General Sir Joseph Frederick Laycock, KCMG, DSO, TD (1867–1952), the father of four sons and two daughters. Meanwhile Mercy went on to marry in 1925 as his second wife, Basil Herbert Dean, the film producer, and himself a descendant of Nell Gwyn and Charles II, and they lived at Little Easton Manor, Dunmow, Essex, part of the estate which used to belong to her mother.

Maynard was a particularly beautiful child and Daisy lavished on him the love and attention that had been singularly lacking with her other children. He was the subject of three portraits, one of which was by Rita Martin dated 1909. Maynard later served as a Lieutenant in the Royal Air Force in World War I, and had a short career as a film actor, possibly inspired by his brother-in-law Basil Dean. He was also described as a journalist, although his main expertise was as an aboriculturalist. He married in February 1918 to Dora Pape of Moor Hall, Battle, Sussex, who was the subject of four portraits by Bassano.

The following year, they had an only daughter Felice, now the widow of Eric James Spurrier, who still lives today on part of her grandmother's Easton estate with her son, Neil, and daughter, Caroline. This had been left to her father upon Daisy's death in 1938 aged seventy-six, together with property worth £37,000. But this was all that was left of her vast inheritance and Maynard immediately tried to lease the house and gardens but with no success. Throughout the Second World War and up until 1950, the estate was occupied successively by the British Army, the Home Guard, the US Airforce, the Royal Air Force and then by the British Army again, all of whom wrought much destruction. Most of the house had been demolished and the estate ruined and thereafter, Maynard, who was much respected in arboriculture, started to create an arboretum there. But this was cut short by Dora's death in 1957 followed by his death three years later on 21 February 1960, when much of the property was sold off and the gardens were completely abandoned.

Since then, others have bought different parts of the estate and have worked wonders in clearing and restoring the gardens. In 1995 Felice leased the remainder of the gardens and work began on clearing the overgrown Italian Garden and the Glade and restoring the grandeur of former years.

Sonia Rosemary Cubitt, *née* Keppel, OBE, DStJ (1900–86)

Sonia Rosemary Keppel was born on 24 May 1900 at 30 Portman Square in London. Her mother was Alice Frederica, the Hon Mrs. George Keppel, who was the ninth and last child of Admiral Sir William Edmonstone, 4th Bt, CB, a family of Scottish Baronets, which descended from King Robert the Bruce and still live at Duntreath Castle in Stirlingshire. Her background is set out in Raymond Lamont-Brown's book *Edward VII's Last Loves – Alice Keppel & Agnes Keyser* as well as in her own autobiography.

Sonia's father, according to all the reference books, was Lt. Col. the Hon George Keppel, MVO, (born 1865), 3rd son of the 7th Earl of Albemarle. Alice and he had married on 1 June 1891 and they lived together, more off than on, for the next fifty-six years, until they both died within two months of eachother in 1947 and were buried together in the Protestant cemetery in Florence. They are recorded in the reference books as having had two daughters, although it is alleged that George was the father of neither, having turned a blind eye to his wife's shenanigans and infidelities over many years.

The elder daughter was Violet, best known as the lesbian lover of Vita Sackville-West She was born on 6 June 1894, four years *before* her mother met the Prince of Wales, and it was Vita who told the writer, Philippe Jullian, that Ernest William Beckett, the future Lord Grimthorpe, was Violet's father and that she had been named after his sister, Violet. This is also corroborated by her nephew-in-law, Major Bruce Shand, who stated that

> *'George did not like his elder daughter and made it quite apparent – largely, presumably, because she was a cuckoo in the nest!'*

Nevertheless Alice was to maintain contact with Grimthorpe and his family on and off throughout her life. This is despite the fact that Violet herself later claimed to be of Royal blood and a true 'FitzEdward', yet moments later, she would be resenting the inference that only her half sister was a 'royal brat'. But be that as it may, Violet, described by Major Shand as '*a pretty dreadful character*' married in 1919 Major Denys Robert Trefusis (who died 1929), and she died without issue in 1970 after a very controversial and scandalous life, which has no place here.

Sonia was the younger daughter, who was born six years after her sister, and just two years after her mother, known as *'La Favorita,'* had first met the Prince of Wales with whom she had an affair lasting from 1898 until the King's death in 1910. Speaking later about her position, one of Alice's best known remarks was that '*a Royal Mistress should curtsey first – and then jump into bed*'.   It has been said that Alice turned adultery into an art and that the Prince used to like to visit her at teatime '*for cake, claret and Keppel*'. It is highly plausible therefore that the Prince, known to Sonia after his Coronation as *'Kingy'* and also *'Tum-Tum'*, was in fact her real father, and perhaps this is strengthened by the fact that Sonia, some sixty years later, wrote the memoirs of her first twenty years, entitled *Edwardian Daughter* – a tantalising *double entendre*. However, within its 207 pages, there is no hint at all that her father (and Violet's too) was anyone other than George Keppel, who is referred to throughout as Papa. However, she does concede that Kingy's death in 1910 *'changed all our lives'*. According to her autobiography, Sonia, then aged ten, was very much aware of the sombre change in their home at the King's death. Her mother went into deep mourning and her hair turned white almost overnight. Sonia wrote

> *'A pall of darkness hung over the house. Blinds were drawn, lights were dimmed and black clothes appeared, even for me, with black ribbons threaded through my underclothes.'*

When Edward became King, Sonia was only a toddler, but this did not prevent her from being told by her nanny to curtsey to the bearded king whenever she saw him. This she tried to remember to do, but she often mistook her mother's bearded financier, Sir Ernest Cassel, for the king, curtseying to him too! Her upbringing consisted of a round of visits at home and abroad to many famous people in many big houses. Later on, her sixteenth birthday party was broken up in full swing when it was learned that the Battle of Jutland was raging involving many naval friends of the family. Sonia came out in 1918, introduced by Elinor, Lady Kinloch and chaperoned by Mary, Viscountess Harcourt and Edith, Lady Jessel. Soon afterwards she also obtained a job as a parlour maid to a Russian hospital for officers in South Audley Street, before being presented at Court by her mother in 1919, whose first visit to Buckingham Palace it was since her 'widowhood' as the King's mistress.

Unlike other alleged royal bastards, the Prince was not one of Sonia's godparents. These were the Grand Duke Mikhail Mikhailovich, grandson of Czar Nicholas I of All the Russias and his wife Sophie Nicholaievna Countess of Merenberg (who was created Countess Torby) when he had married her morganatically. Sonia's other god-mother was the Hon Margaret Greville, a controversial figure who later became a millionairess in her own right. She was an illegitimate daughter of the Liberal MP William McEwen by his cook and she later married the Hon Ronald Greville, a friend of George Keppel.

Alice, often described as 'voluptuous', was one of the leading per-sonalities of Edward VII's Court and she survived his accession to the Throne, when many people thought that she would have been discarded.

Although society gossips waited in vain for Alice to be appointed the 1st Lady of the Bedchamber, she was in fact *maitresse en titre,* and much respected and accepted and the King loved her dearly. She handled him well, besides being the soul of discretion, qualities vested also in her great grand-daughter, Camilla, Duchess of Cornwall.

By contrast to her half sister, Sonia led a quiet and respectable life and was appointed an OBE (1959) and a DStJ for good works and services to the community. After a two year unofficial engagement, she married in some splendour in 1920 at the Guards' Chapel the Hon Roland (Rolie) Calvert Cubitt, of the Coldstream Guards and of building fame and fortune, who succeeded in 1947, (just after their divorce), as 3rd Baron Ashcombe. He went on to marry twice more and died in 1962 when he was succeeded by their elder son, Harry, who is the present 4th Baron. Although the Ashcombes were a very formal family which Sonia found difficult, they remained married for twenty-seven years and lived at Hall Place, West Meon, near Petersfield in Hampshire. Sonia stayed on there after their divorce into her old age and was well placed financially having benefited significantly from her mother's English will which was proved at £177,637 in 1947 (excluding American and Italian assets) and divided between her two daughters. Sonia had two sons, Harry and Jeremy and a daughter, Rosalind, of whom more anon. What, if anything, she received from her putative Royal father, is not known.

Sonia, who was a striking looking woman and was photographed by Cecil Beaton, spent much of her later life writing. She published her autobiography in 1958 (which was republished in 1961), covering the first twenty years of her life and *A Sovereign Lady* in 1974 – being the life of Elizabeth Vassall, third Lady Holland and her family. She also wrote *Three Brothers at Havana* 1762, published in 1981, but her first book had been nearly fifty years previously when she wrote a novel, *Sister of the Sun*, published in 1932. This was reviewed as an 'unadmiring' assessment of Victorian and Edwardian society. Following her death in 1986 all her mother's jewellery and *objects de vitrine* were sold by Sothebys at Hotel Beau-Rivage in Geneva. It signalled the end of her mother's era.

Their only daughter Rosalind Maud was born in 1921. Her coming-out dance in 1939 at Holland Park was attended by King

George VI and Queen Elizabeth and led to gossip about how for-bearing the king was in attending a dance given by the daughter of his grandfather's mistress. Others opined that the King was merely attending the dance of his half first cousin.

Seven years later, Rosalind married Major Bruce Shand, MC and bar, late 12th Royal Lancers and a member of the Queen's Body Guard, The Gentlemen at Arms. He was in the wine business and was a very popular man, having served as a joint Master of the Southdown Foxhounds. He also became the literary executor of his mother in law and was thus well versed in family matters. They lived at Plumpton in Sussex, where much time was spent in the saddle, but like her mother, Rosalind died in 1994 of osteoporosis, of which she had done much to raise public awareness. She left a son, Mark, and two daughters, the elder of which is Camilla Rosemary. He died in 2006.

It is Camilla, born on 17 July 1947, who married in 1973 Andrew Parker Bowles (now a retired Brigadier of the Blues and Royals, from whom she is divorced), and who for many years has been the constant companion of the present Prince of Wales, her half second cousin once removed, if her grandmother's father was, as is believed by many, Prince Charles' great-great-grandfather. Camilla, it is said, much enjoyed the idea of history repeating itself. She has now become the Prince of Wales's second wife, and is styled as HRH The Duchess of Cornwall, with the precedence of the fourth most important woman in the land. In due course she will be known as the Princess Consort when her husband succeeds to the Throne. She also descends from Louise de Keroualle, the French mistress of King Charles II, as do her own two children, Tom and Laura Parker Bowles, and her two royal step-sons.

Certainly the late Theo Aronson in his scholarly works *The King in Love* and *Royal Subjects* was in little doubt that Edward VII was Sonia's father, despite him writing *'Alas, despite various pointers, I have never come across any firm evidence of Edward VII's illegitimate offspring'*. At Sonia's birth, not only did the Prince send garlands of Marechal Niel roses, delivered by a liveried coachman, but those who saw Sonia, had no doubt that her face mirrored the baby features of the Prince of Wales as captured by the painter Sir William Ross in 1843. Four years later, when painted by Gertrude Massey, her likeness to the Prince was again noted, as observed by Raymond Lamont-Brown in his book *Edward VII's Last Loves – Alice Keppel & Agnes Keyser.*

Other members of the family, and in particular Bruce Shand, dispute this, but have little firm evidence to offer either. Their conviction is based more upon the obvious devotion that George Keppel had for the younger daughter throughout his life; upon possible family likenesses (and the Keppel hooked nose and eyes in particular) and her size, for Sonia was tall like George Keppel (who was 6'4" tall) in contrast to the King and her mother who were much smaller in size. Moreover there was also the fact that George and his wife Alice were apparently reconciled about the time of Sonia's conception, despite the fact that Alice was still deeply involved with the Prince of Wales at that time. This view is also shared by Diana Southami in her book *Mrs. Keppel and her daughter.* So nothing is certain.

But what is certain is the fact that history has repeated itself again, in that for many years, Alice Keppel's great-granddaughter, Camilla Parker Bowles has been the close companion of King Edward VII's great-great-grandson, the present Prince of Wales and indeed has now become his wife. *Plus ca change!* Whether or not they are also half second cousins once removed to each other has not yet been proved, although perhaps it seems more likely than not.

Prince Albert Victor Christian Edward (Eddy), KG, Duke of Clarence & Avondale (1864–92):
Clarence Guy Gordon Haddon (1890 – ca. 1940)

Much of the information about Clarence Guy Gordon Haddon and his alleged parents comes from the *Sunday Times* in an article published on 27 November 2005 by Peter Day and John Ungoed-Thomas entitled *Royal cover-up of illegitimate son revealed*, supplemented by the television programme on *Channel* 4 about the Duke of Clarence shown on

21 November 2005 which attempted to rehabilitate the Prince's poor reputation.

Until recently, there has been very little information available about the Duke of Clarence. His life has been subject to much speculation and conspiracy theories. His intellect, sexuality and sanity have all been the subject of various alternative theories. He is also alleged to have been Jack the Ripper, a serial killer in nineteenth century London, although there appears to be little hard evidence to support any of these allegations. He has often been dismissed as having been somewhat backward intellectually, whilst exhibiting marked playboy tendancies with a reputation as a womaniser and heavy drinker. Some have claimed that he was homosexual and that he had been involved in the *Cleveland Street Scandal* of 1889, when the Metropolitan Police uncovered a male brothel which was frequented by some high profile members of London's upper classes. Details of the scandal emerged with the release of police papers by the Public Record Office in 1975, and the publication of the letters of one of the other participants in the scandal, but there was no evidence that the Prince was involved. The official biography of Queen Mary by James Pope-Hennessy euphemistically stated that the Prince's private life was '*dissipated*'. However the strict code of public morality at the time meant that even minor transgressions would have been severely censured.

As a result, his early death at Sandringham aged only 28 from influenza must have been regarded as a merciful release for the monarchy, in that it enabled his younger brother George to come to the throne in his place. The official biographer of King George V, Harold Nicolson, stated in his diaries

> '*that it appeared that Prince Albert Victor had been involved in a major scandal and there had been a cover-up at the highest levels. However, the establishment wished to emphasise the relative merits of the stolid George over his brother.*'

Robert Lacey, a royal biographer, commented that the prince

> '*had a reputation as a somewhat debauched character and it's interesting if there is evidence of a royal cover-up. There was always great anxiety among the royal family about protecting his reputation.*'

Moreover, there were many rumours and conspiracy theories surrounding his death for which there would seem to be no evidence at all. One theory states that he actually died of syphilis; another claims that he died of a morphine overdose, deliberately administered to him; yet another claims that he survived until the 1920s in an asylum on the Isle of Wight and that his death was faked to remove him from the line of succession.

Prince Albert Victor Christian Edward, KG, Duke of Clarence and Avondale, known as Prince Eddy, was born at Frogmore House, Windsor, on 8 January 1864, ten months after the marriage of his parents, The Prince and Princess of Wales (later King Edward VII and Queen Alexandra). Queen Victoria was on the throne and he was second in line to it after his father. He was educated at home with his younger brother George, eighteen months his junior, and in due course they both became naval cadets and travelled the world together. After a brief spell at Trinity College, Cambridge, where Eddy became involved in undergraduate rather than academic life, he left in 1885 to join the Army, in the 10th Hussars.

The *Channel* 4 film noted that Eddy was said to have kept a mistress in St John's Wood, and that he shared her with his brother George, which seems to be taking brotherly love a bit far. He was also said to have fallen in love with a commoner, Sybil Erskine. But now that he was twenty-five years old, three women were being lined up as possible brides for him. The first, in 1889, was Princess Alix of Hesse (future Empress of Russia) who did not return his affection; the second, in 1890, was Princess Hélène of Orléans, a staunch Roman Catholic. So he succumbed to the third in the same year, and after a number of years of riotous living, Eddy became engaged to his second cousin once removed HSH Princess (Victoria) Mary (May) Augusta Louisa Olga Pauline Claudine Agnes, LG (1867–1953), only daughter of HH The Duke of Teck, GCB, GCVO, by HRH Princess Mary Adelaide Wilhelmina Elizabeth, younger daughter of HRH 1st Duke of Cambridge (son of King George III). However, Eddy was to die unexpectedly within the next year and before their marriage could take place and his younger brother, George, gallantly stepped in to fill the breach by marrying her instead in 1893.

But the recent release of various documents in the National Archives in Kew, have shed some new light upon Eddy's lifestyle and have revealed that the Police conducted an intensive investigation into an alleged affair between Prince Eddy and a married woman, Margery Haddon, which, it was claimed, had resulted in the birth of an illegitimate son, Clarence Haddon. Their liaison is supposed to have started during a royal tour of India in the late 1880s that Eddy and George were making and it is said that they met in 1889 after a ball in Calcutta, which was the seat of power. Margery, described as 'vivacious', was the daughter of a civil servant who had been born and brought up there, and was by then the wife of Henry Haddon, a civil enginéer.

It is alleged that Margery gave birth the following year in India to Clarence Guy Gordon Haddon and that Eddy was his father after whom the boy had been named, although he was given the surname of his mother's husband. Of course, Eddy himself was to die two years later and so saw little or nothing of his alleged son, although it does seem that he may have been in correspondence with his mother in the interim. However, some twenty years later, when Margery's life was falling apart from two divorces and drink-related problems, she travelled to London to stake her claim that she had conceived Eddy's child. She made such a hullaballoo that she was even arrested outside the gates of Buckingham Palace for shouting out about this. But it is now clear that the Royal Family and Scotland Yard took the matter very seriously and a full report was ordered from Superintendant (later Sir) Patrick Quinn, Head of Special Branch. He is described in *Who Was Who* as attached to the Criminal Investigation Department, Scotland Yard, 1883; to Special Branch 1887 as Superintendent of Special Branch, 1903; and that he had been engaged in the suppression of anarchism and kindred matters, and has been attached for duty to the suite of all foreign Sovereigns visiting this country officially.

In July 1914, there is reference in these papers to a meeting held at Buckingham Palace between Quinn and the Rt. Hon. Sir William Carington, Keeper of the Privy Purse and formerly Controller and Treasurer to the Prince of Wales, in order to discuss the issue. During this meeting Carington invited Quinn's opinion as to the wisdom of making a payment to Margery, for he was afraid that she might have some proof.

There may indeed have been cause for some alarm. For it is said that Eddy's military aide, Lieutenant George Rogers, who, *inter alia* had arranged for Eddy to meet Margery in the first place, was himself implicated in her divorce. The implication too was that he had fathered Clarence, although his family had told Police that he had acted as a royal scapegoat for this royal relationship and that his family had provided maintenance payments for Clarence even though he was not his true father – although whether this was on his own behalf or on behalf of Eddy is not clear. Moreover, an unnamed spokesman from Lewis and Lewis, the Duke's solicitors during the divorce proceedings, agreed that '*certainly there were some relations*' (between Margery and Eddy), although he denied that there was any child from the union.

Documents also show that the Duke had written a number of letters to Margery and the Special Branch report dated July 1914 commented that '*there were grounds for thinking Lewis and Lewis obtained those letters from her upon payment*'.

In the end, it was decided by Scotland Yard and Buckingham Palace that Margery should be removed from the country and a one-way ticket was bought for her back to India, all arranged for her by the political adviser to the Secretary of State for India. Clothes and other provisions were provided for her through a Scotland Yard account and she was also given £5 spending money. A secret account was also set up and a go-between arranged and Margery duly departed for India on 20 February 1915, never to return insofar as is known.

And there the matter might have rested, had it not been for Clarence himself who decided to start a campaign to be recognised as a son of the Duke of Clarence. He wrote a book '*My Uncle, King George V*', published in America in the early 1930s but not available at the British Library, and and he also wrote to King George V complaining of the '*underhand*', '*dirty*', and '*unjust*' treatment that he had received. '*I will not rest until the whole world will see these Royal methods in their true colours*', he wrote. Although officials had hoped that they would be able to deal with Clarence in the same way as with his mother, and duly provided him with a one way ticket to America, paid out of police funds, he later returned to England to pursue his claims. This was to result in his appearance at the Old Bailey in Jauuary 1934 when he was bound over for three years by Mr Justice Charles, on condition that he made no

claim that he was the son of the Duke of Clarence. But he breached
that condition and was jailed the following year for twelve months.

Like his mother, Clarence became an increasingly sad character,
because all evidence relating to his alleged paternity had long since
disappeared. He died a broken man and no one took his oft repeated
claims seriously. Indeed, they were dismissed regularly by the authorities
as '*ridiculous*'. However, virtually nothing is known about Clarence's life,
other than the fact that he spent much of his early life working overseas
and had settled in the USA in the mid 1930s.

However, he may have spent some time in Islington during the mid
1930s, because a Mr. Archibald Scott, a relieving Officer in Islington
during that time, was given the job of arranging Clarence's passage to
America, when he came out of prison, so that he would be out of the
country by the time of the Coronation.

It is not known whether he married, although a photograph in the
Sunday Times shows him with his unnamed fiancée. There is only one
reference on the Internet to the unusual name of Clarence Haddon,
and he is a black gospel singer rejoicing in the title of bishop with many
songs to his name and very much alive!

A brief perusal of the India Office records at the British Library
did provide a few clues. Firstly, a search of the general catalogue of
books produced none written by Clarence, Margery or Henry Haddon,
although there were 955 references to the name. Secondly, in the Index
of Bengal Marriages (including Calcutta), there was one relevant entry
for a Haddon between 1880–92. This was a marriage on 22 December
1883 of Henry Edmund Haddon, an exec-engineer of Indian State
Railways, (of full age and therefore born before 1862), son of Henry
Haddon, to Mary Jane Reid or Reed, (then aged eighteen and therefore
born c. 1865). She was the daughter of Robert Reid/Reed and they
married at St Bartholomew's Church, Barrackpore, Bengal. References
were also found to the births and baptisms of their three children in
the Index of Bengal Baptisms 1885–1948 between the years 1883–93.
Their son, Gerald Philip Haddon, was born on 11 March 1885, when
his father was described as a civil engineer. The elder daughter, Marjory
Katherine Masters Haddon, was born on 5 May 1886 and baptised on
the following 12 August, when her father was described as an executive
engineer in the Department of Public Works. The younger daughter,

Dorothy Mary Kate Haddon, was born on 18 October 1887 and baptised on 10 March 1888.

It later became clear from the English 1901 census, that these children, Gerald (16), was a student at Tonbridge, Kent and that he and his sisters Dorothy (13) and Margaret (*sic*) (14) were living ten miles away in Frant. The Tonbridge Alumni, in which he was described as the only son, show that he was there from 1900-02 and then joined the Royal Navy rising to Paymaster Lieutenant Commander and being seconded to the Royal Canadian Navy, dying in Victoria, BC on 8 August 1926.

There were no references to any Haddons in Indian Biographical Indexes, nor were there any references to these Haddons in the Indexes to the Register of births and of marriages in England & Wales and in the overseas section between the same years. However, in the List of Residents for 1890–93, there was just one reference to an H.E. Haddon, described as an exe.-engr at Bandikui Division of RMS (Rajputasa-Malwa Railway System) responsible for 800 staff, who must have been Henry Edmund Haddon. But in 1913, there was a reference to an H.E. Haddon, who was a Lt, Qr-mr, 119 Infantry (The Moolton Regt) at Ahmednager, who turned out to have been a Harold Esmond Haddon who was born 1895 and was educated at Tonbridge, being killed in action in 1915. It is probable that these two HE Haddons were uncle and nephew.

A further search of the marriage records showed that on 24 February 1909, Henry Gorbold, 27, bachelor, Assistant to Cuthbertson Harper, of Calcutta, son of James Gorbold, married Marjorie Kathleen Haddon, 31, widow, of Calcutta, daughter of Robert Reed. At first sight this might appear to have been the daughter, born in 1886 who would therefore have been aged 23, not 31 and was not the daughter but the grand-daughter of Robert Reed. Her mother, although named Mary Jane, was certainly known as Margery, and was widowed, although we know not when. She was certainly the daughter of Robert Reed, although her age in 1909 would have been 44 and not 31. Was the mother lying about her age when marrying a 27 year old toyboy, as might seem to have been the case?

There were no other relevant references to Haddon or Gorbold births/baptisms, marriages or deaths/burials, although clearly there is scope for further research in India. We have come across no references to Clarence Haddon and we suspect that there will be little evidence to support his claim. Whether or not his mother was attempting to pass off her son Gerald as Clarence is not known, although to date we have seen no firm evidence of his existence.

But be that as it may, Robert Lacey, the biographer, has rightly said that even if Clarence Haddon's claim had been proved, it would have made no difference to the succession of the royal line. Many royals have had illegitimate children over the centuries, as we have seen, but although many of them may have been given money, it was never argued that they had any right to the throne, other than in the case of the Duke of Monmouth. A Buckingham Palace spokeswoman drew a veil over it all by stating *'This is not something we could comment on'*.

Chapter XVI
Windsor Loose Ends

George, Prince of Wales, later King George V (1910) (1865–1936): The Mylius Affair (1911)

George V is alleged to have had a number of liaisons before and after he was married to Queen Mary in 1893 and later (1910) settled down on the Throne. It has even been suggested that he was the father of the notorious Sir Anthony Blunt, although we have seen nothing to substantiate this.

However, in 1892, George's elder brother Albert, Duke of Clarence, known as Eddy, had died unexpectedly aged only twenty-eight, leaving George as heir-in-line to the throne. About this time, an ugly story started circulating widely alleging that whilst serving in Malta as a naval cadet between 1889–91, George had married morganatically Mary Culme Seymour, an Admiral's daughter, and that he had had several children by her. As George had then been about to marry his brother's fiancée, Princess Mary of Teck, which was duly accomplished the following year, it was argued that George had '*foully abandoned*' the woman whom he had married in an earlier year, and the offspring which it was said that she had borne, in order that he might contract this bigamous marriage with the then Queen (Mary) under the Royal Marriages Act.

Shortly after succeeding to the Throne, these allegations appeared in print on 19 November 1910 in the Paris based *The Liberator*, which described itself as '*A Journal devoted to the International Republic*', Edward Frederick Mylius from Notting Hill in London was arrested on 28 December 1910 and charged with seditious libel. It was alleged that he was the person responsible in this country for the publication and distribution of this left wing magazine and certainly 1,000 copies were delivered to his premises on 23 November 1910.

The hearing took place in the King's Bench Division of the High Court before the Lord Chief Justice, on 1 February 1911 and attended by the Home Secretary, Winston Churchill. The Attorney General, who led for the Prosecution, opened, followed by evidence from Detective Inspector James McBrian, Admiral Sir Michael Culme Seymour and from his elder daughter, (Mary) Elizabeth, the alleged bride, by then happily married to a Captain Trevelyan Napier. This was followed by evidence from her two brothers, Captain Michael Culme Seymour, RN and Captain George Culme Seymour, 60th Rifles, from the Crown Advocate of Malta, who had brought with him all the registers of marriages which had taken place in Malta between 1886 and July 1893; and Sir Arthur Bigge, one of the King's Private Secretaries. The defendant did not give evidence or call any witnesses.

The judge's summing up drew attention to the fact that Prince George and Elizabeth Culme Seymour had only met once in 1879 when she was aged seven or eight, that neither of them were in Malta during the years in question and that Mrs. Napier had stated that she had only been married once in 1899 and that was to her husband. After only one minute's deliberation, the jury declared Mylius to be guilty on all three counts. He was sentenced to the maximum penalty of one year's imprisonment, after which the Attorney General read out a statement from the King who denied the allegations.

After serving his year's sentence, Mylius appears to have been unrepentant and in 1912 claimed to produce further evidence in a pamphlet published in New York. However, *John Bull* published an *'unqualified condemnation of Mylius – final and conclusive refutation of a foul slander'* dated 10 February 1912 showing conclusively that the Prince was in Gibraltar between June 9th to 25th, the period during which the alleged marriage took place. But by then Mylius had been discredited and the press and public had lost interest in him. So ended this odd chapter, which, whilst not spawning any Royal Bastards, did give rise to a large volume in the Royal Archives, containing 152 pages of press cuttings from 166 different newspapers, at the end of which is a cartoon of a sovereign piece depicting St George slaying the dragon and entitled '*The Sovereign that rings true*'.

David, Prince of Wales, later King Edward VIII (1936) and Duke of Windsor (1894–1972)

In Philip Ziegler's biography *Edward VIII*, he suggested that in fact the Duke was impotent following a severe bout of mumps. Others have claimed, with what authority we know not, that the Duke *'was not very well endowed in that department'*. Nevertheless it does not seem to have prevented him from consorting with Parisian prostitutes during World War I, nor indulging in a string of affairs afterwards, many arranged by 'Smiler' Harry Tyrwhitt-Wilson. One of his biographers commented: *'Indeed, during the whole of his youth the Prince was criticised for his over indulgence in the sexual act.'* Yet when the Duchess of Windsor was asked why she had no children by her husband, she joked about his disability saying *'The Duke is not heir-conditioned.'*

Among these *affaires de coeur* were those with Lady Rosemary Leveson Gower (born 1893), to whom he proposed, the younger daughter of Cromartie, 4th Duke of Sutherland; and Marion, Viscountess Coke, daughter-in-law of the 3rd Earl of Leicester and fifteen years his senior. As with his grandfather, most of his lovers were respectably married women, who, rightly or wrongly, passed off all their offspring as the children of their husbands. It is therefore very difficult for us to determine paternity as there is nothing other than circumstantial evidence to rely upon. None of the Duke of Windsor's illegitimate issue were officially recognised or remembered in his will, and and in all probability his wife Wallis Simpson, who admitted *'that he had had a lot of girls before me,'* was at pains to play them down.

In some cases, the authorities seem to have been all too keen to remove every trace, as in the strange case of Michael Bower Spencer or Berkeley. In fact the allegation here is so weak and uncorroborated that it would not have been mentioned atall, were it not for the fact that it was told to us by Cecil Humphery-Smith, the well known genealogist, who was directly involved. For on 11 February 1970, an interview was held in Canterbury between Humphery-Smith and

Michael Bower Spencer, who claimed to be a son of David, Prince of Wales (to whom apparently he bore a striking resemblance).

At that time Spencer told Humphery-Smith that he was living at 227 Bloomfield Road, Bath and claimed that he had been educated at Dauntsey's School, near Devizes in Wiltshire (which has not replied to our enquiries). A birth certificate for a Michael Bower Spencer shows that he was born on 1 March 1928, the son of Sidney Harold Spencer, a commercial traveller of Bath, by his wife Dorothy Marion *née* Upward, (born 1896) and they had been married on 21 April 1924.

Later on, Spencer, described as an agriculturalist of Limpley Stoke, was married on 14 February 1957 aged twenty-nine, to Margaret Jill Filer, aged twenty, spinster, of Rosewell Farm, High Littleton, Somerset, the daughter of Leonard Joseph Filer, a farmer, but none of this had any Royal ring to it whatsoever. The following March, at Humphery-Smith's request, Michael dictated more than half a dozen tapes about his life and family background which were duly transcribed on to thirty-three pages of typescript, which in due course were sent to a trustworthy journalist, who appears to have died without trace.

Nevertheless, at 11.45 on 9 April 1971, Special Branch arrived suddenly, with a Sergeant Vicars in charge, demanding that Humphery-Smith should hand over these tapes, which he duly did, and he was warned that he would be in breach of the Official Secrets Act if he were to mention this matter to anyone. For the last thirty-five years he has said nothing.

In these tapes, it was Michael's view that his surname at birth was really Berkeley and that he was the son of Caroline Berkeley (whoever she was) by the Prince of Wales. If true, it is probable that he was farmed out to foster parents – the Spencers – and he alleged that Mrs. Spencer had previously fostered children in 1920s and 1930s but showed no signs of being pregnant herself in 1928. Michael also alleges that he and they had received funding from an unknown source on a regular basis until he became 21 in 1949 (or possibly direct to Coutts Bank 1928-59). However, we lack any corroboration for any of this, even though there are not dissimilar precedents in this book. But above all, the actions of Special Branch do indeed raise a great many questions in themselves.

Nothing seems to be known about the alleged mother, Caroline Berkeley, whom Spencer alleges was confined during the significant months of 1928, having earlier been flirting with the Prince of Wales. Spencer also confirmed that he had been under surveillance by Special Branch from the age of eighteen (1946) and that they even paid off his bills. He also said that following the recommendation of one Bruce Ogilvie, at Danny Park, Hurstpierpoint, he took the transcripts to the Queen Mother's Equerry, one Piers Leigh (presumably 5th Baron Leigh – born 1935). Spencer would now be seventy-eight years of age and if he reads these words, it might perhaps encourage him to come forward and inject some certainty into the situation.

There is also a reference to an Australian half Aboriginal woman named Barbara Chisholm, who claimed that she was a grand–daughter of Edward VIII. Allegedly she was the daughter of Tony Chisholm (1921–87), an Australian grazier, who was the son of Mollie Little, the wife of Roy Chisholm. According to Lord Louis Mountbatten, Mollie was smuggled aboard HMS *Renown* for an afternoon, during the Prince's world tour in 1920. She is alleged to have met the Prince in Sydney Town Hall the day before, when he accidentally stood on her foot. When he apologised profusely, she wittily replied, *'Sire, tread on the other toe, its jealous!'* They talked for a while and got on well. She was good looking, witty and flirtatious and the Prince asked her to visit his ship. Nine months later a son was born, named Tony, who is said to have had an 'uncanny resemblance' to his alleged father, although not so petite. Tony was brought up and educated by the Chisholms, who were a wealthy family, owning a large station near Alice Springs and it is said that later on, he had an illegitimate daughter, Barbara, by an Aboriginal servant, although no evidence for this is forthcoming. Nevertheless, the story does feature in print.

However there are two rather more serious contenders.

(William) Anthony, 2nd Viscount Furness (1929–95)

William Anthony Furness, or Tony as he was known, was born 31 March 1929. His mother was the glamorous socialite, Thelma, who had married in 1926 as his second wife the much older Marmaduke,

2nd Baron Furness, the shipowner and shipbuilder who was created 1st Viscount Furness in 1918. They were divorced in 1933 when Tony was aged only four. Thelma was formerly the wife of James Converse and the twin daughter (along with Gloria Vanderbilt), of Harry Hays Morgan, the US Consul General at Buenos Aires.

Tony's father was officially Marmaduke Furness whom he succeeded as 2nd Viscount on 6 October 1940, aged only eleven. In her book *'A Lion in the Bedroom'*, Pat O'Cavendish O'Neill stated that Tony's father was vile to him and often said that as Tony was the bastard son of the Prince of Wales, he did not want to leave his money to him. In the end Tony and his stepmother did get half each, although Thelma sued her predecessor for some of it too. His elder half brother, Christopher, who won the Victoria Cross, had been killed in action in France five months earlier in May 1940. His father was described as a shadowy figure in Tony's life and Tony always said that he did not feel attached to his comparatively recent titles and took no steps to perpetuate them by marrying and having an heir. Indeed that was the least of his preoccupations.

However, two years after Thelma had married her second husband, she met the Prince of Wales and in 1928 she was accompanying him to Kenya on safari. Nine months later, she gave birth to her only child Tony, whom many people, including Tony himself, considered to be the Prince's son. However, there was never any official acknowledgement of this and Tony, to his chagrin, was left nothing in the Duke of Windsor's will. Moreover when he had visited the Duke of Windsor in New York following his mother's death in 1970 so as to return the letters that the Duke had written to his mother, he was treated very formally and curtly. However, there has been mention of a letter written by Thelma to Queen Mary acknowledging the Prince of Wales's paternity, but the Royal Archives say that they have no record of this. It is hardly surprising that all this uncertainty and rejection left its mark upon Tony, making him rather a sad, lonely and complex figure, psychologically.

By virtue of his official paternity, Tony became heir to the income estimated at over £500,000 per annum from the considerable shipping fortune amassed by his father and grandfather, although much of it was tied up in trusts that he could not break. As Thelma had been baptised a Catholic, Tony was brought up as a Catholic and was educated at Downside and in the United States, being devoted to both his American mother and aunt, Gloria Vanderbilt. However, in later life, and particularly when he had left England to live a reclusive life in Montreux, Switzerland, Tony used to have above his bed, a portrait of his mother, allegedly by Singer Sargent, which he had facing the wall, because, as he said, '*She was an adulteress.*'

Tony Furness took his membership of the House of Lords seriously, playing an active part in the Inter Parliamentary Union and as a member of the Hansard Society. But at heart he was always rather a rebel and refused to conform to rules not of his own making. In any event, his interests were unusual and diverse. For instance, he fostered cultural links with Mongolia, founding the Anglo-Mongolian Society, of which he was chairman, in 1963, and Tibet, being a Vice President of the Tibet Society. He also took an active role in the world of West End theatrical management, backing a number of unsuccessful productions and even forming his own company of theatrical producers, *Furndel*. He also held directorships in a wine shipping business and a pharmaceutical firm.

Perhaps his most enduring interest was in the Sovereign Military Order of Malta, also known as the Knights of Malta – the international Hospitaller order dating back to 1099. This he joined in 1954, becoming Secretary and later Secretary General of the British Association. He gave over much of his office in St James's Street as the headquarters of the Order for almost a generation until 1979 when he became a tax exile. He was promoted many times within the Order finally becoming a Bailiff Grand Cross of Justice in 1988. For this he had taken the monastic vows of poverty, chastity and obedience. Quite how he reconciled his vow of poverty with living the life of a tax exile and of a devoted gourmet is hard to understand. How too he fulfilled the exacting nobiliary requirements of this final promotion within the Order, having regard to his rather short and commercial Furness pedigree, is again hard to explain, unless he was acknowledged by the Order as the son of a Sovereign, as would seem likely, and for which there are special exemptions. Roman society abounded in stories of the affair between his mother and the Prince of Wales long after Tony had succeeded his father. The Chigi family (who had produced a Grand Master) were most certainly aware of it and, for the son of a sovereign, whether officially acknowledged or not, there are special exemptions and precedence for the recognition of inherent noblesse. Tony served as a member of the Sovereign Council of the Order in Rome and as a member of the Board of Auditors there where he was known as Fra' Anthony Furness.

Tony suffered from much ill health during his life, being invalided out of the Welsh Guards after six weeks and later suffering from diabetes. He died unmarried at the Order's hospital, The Hospital of St John and St Elizabeth in London in May 1995, leaving a capital fund of £20 million. London's St James's will never be the same without his stately progresses from Boodles to Overtons in a black suit and a black hat carrying a black walking stick and wearing the blackest of dark glasses. Except for his increasing size, a number people claimed to be able to see in him a distinct resemblance to the Duke of Windsor, although to others it was not at all obvious.

Timothy Ward Seely (*b.* 1935)

Timothy Ward Seely was born on 10 June 1935 and his mother was Vera Lilian Seely, the third and youngest daughter of late Col Charles Wilfred Birkin, CMG (of the family of Baronets of that name). Thus, more notably, he is the second cousin of Jane Birkin, OBE, actress and pop singer, best known for her song *'Je t'aime moi non plus'* which was banned by Pope Paul XII.

However, it has been stated by many different sources, including several from Nottinghamshire (such as the late Stephen Dobson), that Tim (as he is known) is the illegitimate son of Edward, Prince of Wales, later King Edward VIII and later still Duke of Windsor, although his entries in *Burke's* and *Debrett's Peerages* show him to be a member of the family of Seely, Baronets, (whose motto is '*I ripen and die yet live')* and from which the Barons Mottistone and Sherwood also descend. They record that he was the second and middle son of Major (Frank) James Wriothesley Seely, JP, DL, MFH, High Sheriff of Nottinghamshire (who died 1956) by his wife Vera, whom he had married in 1925. Other children born to the marriage were: Michael (1926–93), a racing journalist, Clare (1929–57),

Cherry (1931–92) and James (*b.* 1940), but no aspersions have been cast about their paternity.

There is nothing recorded to suggest Tim's alleged Royal paternity, except for the fact that Vera's eldest sister was Winifred (Freda) May, who was born in 1894, married 1stly in 1913 (divorced 1931) Rt. Hon. William Dudley Ward and had issue of two daughters. She later married again in 1937 (divorced 1954) Peter de Casa Maury who died in 1968. Freda Dudley Ward, as she was known, was indeed closely associated with the Prince of Wales and was well established as his mistress for sixteen years from 1918-34, before being peremptorily dismissed. This was brought about by the Prince's sudden instruction to the telephone operator to refuse all calls from her.

In a telephone conversation with the author on 4 November 2002 about his alleged Royal paternity, Tim did mention that he had contributed towards a biography of the Duke of Windsor by John Parker, entitled *King of Fools* (1988) as well as appearing on *the Terry Wogan Show* and on the front page of the *Daily Express* on 21 and 22 March 1988. Although there is no mention of any Seely in the index of that book, there is an anonymous reference to him in the text which we quote verbatim:-

> *'He [The Prince of Wales] once spoke vaguely of a spot of bother he got into with a Swedish woman around this time but would not be pressed on the 'bother' and in September of 1934, he left Wallis to continue the holiday while he returned to England by plane for a series of public engagements he was committed to. It was towards the end of the month and, with Wallis out of the way, he had a brief encounter with a past friend whom it is said, would be left carrying his child.*
>
> *He had renewed his acquaintance with the beautiful wife of an old friend, a wealthy gentleman with whom he had been on close terms in the twenties. The couple's eldest son (Michael) has memories of those days when the Prince of Wales came to call. Once he came home and found both the Prince of Wales and the Duke of York relaxing in their parlour, two future kings under the same roof at the same time.*
>
> *The children would all become keen horsemen, like their father and one of them was the subject of pointed gossip on the local hunting field. It was said that he was the illegitimate son of the Prince of Wales, the result of a liaison between the mother and the prince on that day in September 1934 when they were reunited*

for such a short time. The story was repeated to the author (Parker) from several different sources during the course of his interviews and eventually, the question had to be put to the family.

The mother and father are now dead but the eldest brother (Michael) said 'Yes, of course I have heard the rumour, though it was never confirmed to me by my mother. She was a very beautiful and very romantic person and dearly loved His Royal Highness in her youth. She used to confide in me a great deal when I was a young man, particularly during the war when my father was serving abroad. Is it possible my brother is his son? It is difficult to say, I can't remember her saying anything about it. I think it is something best left alone; let the dead be buried with their secrets'.

The story of the family's possible links with Royalty have at times been acknowledged by the man who is the alleged illegitimate son (Tim). His sister-in-law said: 'It became a bit of a joke, and he would sometimes laugh about the Royal blood running through his veins.' The man himself is an enigmatic character. He broke the mould of his family's landed, country life and became an actor, though he retained a great passion for horses, hunting and racing. The author (Parker) discovered him at his London flat where he spends a great deal of time seeking work in his chosen profession. Is he the son of the Prince of Wales?

He replied: 'I could not say yes to that question without damaging the memory of my mother and I am not prepared to do anything that would tarnish her name. I agree, however, that I have physical and temperamental likenesses to the Prince of Wales, particularly – I am told – in the way of my short temper and flashes of arrogance.' These were his own words, and descriptions of his own personality. There was a very definite resemblance to the prince, but for reasons of possible libel the author is unable to name him, or publish the pictures he has of the man. These and various documents are lodged with the publishers.

A further interesting fact emerged during the author's interview. When a television series on Edward and Mrs. Simpson was being cast, the alleged son had considered applying for the part of Edward because of his likeness, both facially, and in his general demeanour. So is he the son of a once-King of England? If he is, Edward himself did not want to be reminded of it. In 1955, when the eldest son and his father were sitting on the veranda of the Hotel de Paris in Monte Carlo, the Duke of Windsor appeared with his duchess. He walked over, they shook hands and briefly exchanged greetings. The duchess could be clearly heard in the background remarking, 'Who is that?' and then she called, 'Come on, David.' The duke obeyed and any connection with a past life was severed then and there.'

Tim now dismisses his cooperation with John Parker as no more than '*a publicity stunt by an out-of-work actor*'. Today he claims his Seely ancestry is his true paternal line. Nevertheless the dates correspond exactly and there is an undoubted physical resemblance and a childhood friend attests to his pride in his Royal ancestry.

His mother, Vera, a notable beauty, was born in 1903 and was thus nine years younger than the Prince. Presumably she had been introduced to the Prince by her sister. Certainly she came to know him very well and was given by him a beautiful silver dressing table set and had a sketch of the Prince which hung in her bedroom. However, at the time of Tim's conception, the Prince also had Thelma Furness and Wallis Simpson in tow, having rather cruelly rid himself of Freda just beforehand. It would seem that this affair, if such it was, was very short lived, for there is no suggestion that any other of Tim's siblings have a Royal father. Vera died in 1970.

After being brought up in Nottinghamshire, followed by Eton and RADA, Tim became an actor and was active in theatre as well as films. Certainly, his most memorable part was as Edward Young, alongside Trevor Howard and Marlon Brando in the epic *Mutiny on the Bounty* in 1962, directed by Lewis Milestone. However, his first film, *The Poacher's Daughter,* was made four years earlier, when aged twenty-three, followed in 1960 by *Julius Caesar* and *Please Turn Over.* In 1979, after a gap of seventeen years, he starred in *Agatha,* in 1982 in *Kipperbang,* in 1984 in *Singleton's Pluck,* in 1985 in *Plenty,* in 1990 in *Strike It Rich,* in 1991 in *King Ralph,* as King of England, and finally in 2004, aged nearly seventy in *Vanity Fair,* a total of eleven films.

Spotlight, the Who's Who of the acting profession, records little about Tim or his acting career other than giving us his height of 5'9" with blue eyes and the name of his current agent, Mint Management of London SE22, having earlier been Britt Management of Ramsgate, Kent. It includes a copy of his photograph where the resemblance is striking. Happily, the Internet, was more informative as to his actual career.

Tim has married twice; firstly in 1960 to Anne Henrietta Maria St Paul, formerly wife of James Dugdale Burridge and the only daughter of Horace George St Paul Butler of Wooler, Northumberland. They had a son Hugo, born in 1961, now a wine merchant living in Nottinghamshire, who married in 1991 and has a son Toby born 1996 and a daughter India, born 1992. Later on, Tim was divorced and he married again in 2001, Camilla Cartwright who hails from Ireland, although they now live in Castle Street, Farnham, Surrey. If Tim is the Duke of Windsor's son, as would seem likely, he would be, insofar as we are aware, the only Right Royal Bastard still to be living, besides also being a first cousin to the Queen. But is this a true life story, or a role that he and his mother have been acting? To determine which, a first step might be to see if Tim and his younger and only surviving brother, James, share the same DNA y genetic chromosome as they should do if they are full brothers, sharing the same father.

Happily, Tim has told us that he does not object to anything that we have written, although he says that he would really prefer to lay it all to rest, once and for all. Nevertheless he did agree to participate in Granada Television's programme '*In Search of Lost Royals*', which has been based largely upon this book. We are told, however, that no admissions have been made!

Epilogue

For the sake of completeness and because there has been a good deal of comment and speculation in the tabloid press in recent years, we here comment upon two allegations that have been made, which would either qualify or disqualify those concerned from inclusion in this book. We can state categorically that we have found no evidence whatsoever for these allegations and therefore find that neither HRH Prince Andrew nor his nephew HRH Prince Harry are eligible for inclusion.

HRH Prince Andrew, Duke of York, KG, KCVO

The first allegation is that the father of HRH Prince Andrew Albert Christian Edward, Duke of York (born 1960) was Lord Porchester (1924–2001) and not HRH The Duke of Edinburgh. Lord Porchester, a childhood friend of The Queen who went on to become her Racing Manager from 1969, later succeeded his father in 1987 as Earl of Carnarvon, and was honoured with KCVO, KBE and DL. Although we understand that it is claimed that there are some physical resemblances between the Duke of York and Lord Porchester, these are always subjective and unreliable. Gyles Brandreth, in his recent book, *Philip and Elizabeth: Portrait of a Marriage,* rightly condemned the claim as 'simply preposterous.' He went on to show that the alleged conception dates between 20 January and 30 April 1959 whilst Prince Philip was abroad in *RY Britannia,* simply do not 'stack up' with Andrew's date of birth on 19 February 1960. Whilst the Carnarvons have known of this rumour for many years, they have always been very annoyed and embarrassed by it and no evidence of any kind has ever been forthcoming. Therefore, legally and from every other point of view, the Duke of York remains the second son of HM The Queen and HRH The Duke of Edinburgh.

HRH Prince Henry (Harry) of Wales

The second allegation is that HRH Prince Henry (Harry) Charles Albert David of Wales was the son of Captain James Hewitt, Life Guards, rather than of HRH The Prince of Wales. Again, we have seen no evidence at all to support this allegation. Although much has been made of Harry's red hair, this is, after all, a characteristic of his maternal Spencer family as much as it may be of Hewitt's family. Indeed we have always understood that James Hewitt first met Diana, Princess of Wales in the summer of 1986 at a party given by Hazel West, the Princess's Lady in Waiting, almost two years *after* Harry's birth on 15 September 1984. Moreover, both Hewitt and Diana are on the record in denying that he is the father, as recorded by her bodyguard Inspector Ken Wharfe in his book *Diana – Closely Guarded Secret*. Nor, we believe, should any conclusions be drawn from the fact that Harry has joined the Blues and Royals of the Household Cavalry of which Hewitt's old regiment, the Life Guards, just happens to be a part!

However, recently the waters were muddied following a television interview on *Channel 5* with Rob Butler, broadcast on 22 September 2005, which Hewitt gave whilst hyponotised. It was during which Hewitt made a number of admissions. These included that he had first met Diana at a polo match at Tidworth in 1981 and saw her again a few months later which was when their relationship started, as had also been mentioned by *Private Eye*. This, of course, is three years earlier than all the accounts he had given previously, and if true, it would make the possibility of paternity more likely. However, it seems incredible that Diana would have embarked upon an affair within months of her marriage to the Prince of Wales which took place on 29 July 1981, which, after all, seemed to augur so well. Nor is it credible that it would have taken place during the time leading up to the birth of Prince William Arthur Philip Louis of Wales on 21 June 1982 about whose paternity there never seems to have been any question.

We do not find Hewitt's hypnotic ramblings to be credible and we have heard nothing convincing, legally or otherwise, to indicate that Prince Harry is not the younger son of the Prince and Princess of Wales.

Appendix I
Bastardy

By Cecil Humphery-Smith, OBE, FSA, Principal of the Institute of Heraldic & Genealogical Studies

Children begotten or born out of wedlock were generally regarded as illegitimate, though Statutes of State have, from time to time, interpreted the meaning and, for example, a child born under an annulled marriage is deemed not to be illegitimate and the subsequent marriage of parents usually legitimated those children born before. Most European countries had regarded illegitimate children as virtual outlaws and in those countries where Roman law operated, there were no inheritance rights for the illegitimate child. It is presumed that unless there is any clear evidence to the contrary, a child is born legitimate within a marriage and it is insufficient evidence of another paternity to question the reputation of the mother. While natural parents are usually given custody of their illegitimate offspring, in law the mother would be given priority and while fathers formerly had no legal obligation to support, many laws have been introduced to change this in favour of the child and, ultimately, of the mother. The subsequent marriage of the parents of an illegitimate child may grant him all rights of the legitimate child in law, but in armorial matters he remains a bastard.

> *'I am the son of my father......according to my mother!'*
> *Tristram Shandy in Lawrence Sterne's novel of the name.*

Certainly there was a considerable stigma upon illegitimacy in all classes of the agricultural, trading and labouring classes, but as the Marquis Ruvigny states in his *Plantagenet Roll*, (*Mortimer-Percy* volume), *'with few exceptions, none have descended to or are at least traceable among the trading or labouring classes'.* All that this really means is that Ruvigny did not trace them.

John of Gaunt and Edward I produced enough progeny to bring all their descendants into the lower echelons of English society within a century or two. Anthony Wagner in *English Genealogy* points out that there were nineteen settlers in New England before 1650, with established descents from Edward I, and at the best they were tradesmen. Samuel Pepys suggests that hardly one of them is not already branded on the hand for some criminal offence, and Daniel Defoe went out of his way to denigrate most of them. However, most provide gateway ancestors to royal ancestry, and among them are the illegitimate issue of the several members of the Royal Family of the past

One of the earliest significant marriages to spread the royal blood was that of Sir Roger Kynaston to Elizabeth Grey. She was seventh in descent from Edward I through Edmund of Woodstock and eighth in descent from Edward I through Joan of Acre. Her mother was Antigone, the bastard daughter of Humphrey, Duke of Gloucester, who died in 1447. Humphrey was son of King Henry IV. While the Beauforts were legitimated by Act of Parliament, Joan, who died in 1445 and was the granddaughter of John of Gaunt, married first in 1424 James I of Scotland, and secondly in 1439, Sir James Stewart, the Black Knight of Lorn, thereby carrying the English royal blood into many Scottish families.

Clearly, the larger the families, the less could be done to assist the social progress of the younger children and it has often been said that the fourth child of the fourth child of an Earl is no longer interested in his blood or his armorial bearings, even if he should know that he has any. He would be far more concerned with making a success of a subsistence career, when he is apprenticed to some cum-brother of a craftsman's guild. No doubt, therefore, most bastards of royal and noble blood have remained unknown, but many were acknowledged and provided for, descendants being innumerable. Several scholars have, for example, written about the descents from Henry VII's bastard, Sir Roland de Velville, who died in 1553 (*see* page 177). He was the grandfather of Catherine of Berain, who died in 1591. Her progeny, by her three husbands, was so great in North Wales that she was known as Ma'm Cymru, though perhaps much more infusion of royal blood into the English people came through Robert, Earl of Gloucester, who died in 1147. While Catherine may be called 'mother of Wales', he, one of the many bastards of King Henry I, might be described as 'father of England'.

That the church took a dim view of illegitimacy is obvious from the number of records of penances inflicted by the ecclesiastical courts for the incontinence of parents. This is not the place to go into the nature of the penances and punishments for fornication and adultery which, it is perhaps a relief to know, hard and shaming as they were, do not compare with the one that Christ himself stopped or those inflicted even today in Muslim countries. Judging by parochial records of the sixteenth and seventeenth centuries, the birth of an illegitimate child seems to have been a fairly unusual event. The increase of movement of the populous following the destruction of the social services provided by the several religious orders at the dissolution of the monasteries, led not only to more profligacy but to the propagation of the tenets of the increasing number of Protestant preachers. By the seventeenth century, the occurrence of mention of illegitimacy in parochial records becomes more common, and commoner still by the eighteenth century. From the 1750s onwards there was no great consternation among the local populous in any rural parish to encountering the extent of the occurrence of bastards. Parochial concern seems to have been social, rather than moral, by that time. Before enclosure, which soon followed the dissolution of the monasteries, the general standard of living among the peasantry was relatively high, even by the end of the seventeenth century, some form of housing was readily available for the labourer. Then with the development of mechanical tools to assist farming, squatters were discouraged from the common lands and manorial lords began to destroy the cottages at about the same time as the population was rapidly increasing. No longer could scraps of land be taken to set up small farms, nor was copyhold readily obtained. The moral restraints of the Old Faith had long gone and tenements and cottages were largely destroyed because the poor were a charge upon the parish.

Knobsticks weddings, named after the staves of office carried by the churchwarden, were a means of forcing couples into marriage, whether they had to end up living under sacks in hedgerows or in the homes and beds of their parents. By Acts passed in 1610 'any lude woman having had a bastard chargeable may be sent to the House of Correction for a year'. If she offended again, she had to provide securities for her good behaviour or stay in the House of Correction, which meant being involved in hard labour for the duration of her sentence. These laws, of course, encouraged abortion and infanticide. Such goods as they might have were confiscated from any father or mother of a bastard who ran away from the overseer. The accounts of the overseer often give note of the costs incurred by the constable retrieving putative parents of a foundling bastard, paying for transport, court fees, meals and accommodation at an inn! There is a splendid measure of the consumption of ale in such accounts. When maintenance orders were imposed, they were seldom fulfilled more than once or twice and many questions yet remain to be answered, which will keep social and local historians at bay for many years to come.

Normally, an illegitimate child took the father's or the mother's settlement under the Poor Laws that were introduced in the sixteenth century, and by the Act of 1662. Responsibility for bastards was clearly laid down by the Vagrant Act of 1575/6. Two justices were empowered to make an order against the mother or the father and any offence against performance of the order would result in gaol until the next sessions, though often security was given for appearance. Later Acts dealt with the punishment of unmarried mothers, with incidents of infanticide and, not unnaturally, with the parents absconding. By the Act of 1732/3, it was laid down that a pregnant woman with a bastard child was bound to declare herself and to name the father. Until 1743, bastards had a legal settlement in their father's birthplace but the 1732 Act had prescribed public whipping for the mother and ordained that the child should have the mother's settlement. Of course, parochial records only described bastards who were baptised. The Lancashire Quarter Session records for 1590–1606, for example, record the reputed father of a bastard child being ordered to maintain the child until she is twelve years of age and then that he shall be whipped in the market place at Manchester. This sentence appears to apply to the child!

Often, the putative father was declared to have come from another parish and parish officers were under pressure to persuade the couple to marry, which could secure the ultimate legitimacy of the child, and settlement with the mother in the father's parish, which would result in removal under the Act. Even bribing was used to achieve this, in order to legitimize the child. So the first child born soon after marriage might well be of suspect paternity, since a mother might appear to have had a predisposition for choosing to impute the man she wanted to marry rather than the real father, or, as on a number of proven occasions, the lord of the manor or the vicar or curate! This was not for reason of a 'crush', but for the prospect of a more secure life. By the seventeenth century 'Gossips' were paid to report the indiscretions of women in the parish. Records of archdeacon's visitation and of ecclesiastical courts provide the stuff of evidence.

A somewhat bizarre selection of Latin terms was used to describe the status of illegitimate children in some parish registers up to the third quarter of the seventeenth century, while the English phrases were generally brutally frank. The naming of foundlings has always proved of interest and provided amusement for students of this subject. Mr Bumble in Charles Dickens's *Oliver Twist* will be remembered as having named them by working through the alphabet 'S-Swubble … T-Twist … I named him … next one … comes … Unwin and the next Vilkins… !'

A foundling admitted to Cripplegate Charity School in 1716 by the parish officer of St Olave's is described in the meeting book in the following entry:

'Then by what name th'unwelcome guest to call
Was long a question and is posed them all;
For he who lent it to a babe unknown,
Censorious men might take it for his own:
They look'd about, they gravely spoke to all,
And not one Richard answered to the call.
Next they enquired the day, when, passing by,
Th'unlucky peasant heard the stranger's cry;
This known, – how food and raiment they might give,
Was next debated – for the rogue would live;

At last, with all their words and work content,
Back to their homes the prudent vestry went,
And Richard Monday to the workhouse sent.'

Mr Crabbe's poetic description of the vestry minutes and the fate of the foundling now named Richard Monday, after a name of no-one on the council and the day of the meeting gives some indication of the disdain in which the unfortunate were held.

This writer remembers in childhood a contemporary child found on the parish church porch and named by the vicar at baptism after the then prime minister, a then-famous aircraft company, and the subject matter of the silent film being shown in the parish hall (Ramsay Vickers Todd!). By the eighteenth century, the convenience of disposing of pauper children as apprentices became the lot of many an illegitimate child. The euphemistic description '*to learn the art and the mystery of…*' or '*the art and science of…*' led to the children becoming slaves as farm labourers, domestic servants or whipping boys of tradesmen. Life for most in the workhouses was hardly much better, and for some much worse.

For the earlier period, one has to remember that *hand vesten* was an ancient custom for the legitimisation of a union with a single concubine, that continued under the Danish code of Valdemar II until 1683, and probably survived in English common law down to 1901 and in Scotland, through to 1947. It is probable that royal bastards of the tenth and thirteenth centuries, if not somewhat later, were considered as *nothi* (as they were under Roman law) that is children born in concubinage and thereby entitled to the support of their fathers but with no right of inheritance from him.

Concubines formed part of the royal households of Europe well after the conquest of England; in a historical context, the behaviour of such men as King Henry I (Beauclerk), who is credited with at least nine sons and eleven daughters by some six women, was not then to be regarded as scandalous. Indeed it was part of his grand foreign policy to people the top tables of Europe with his progeny. However, it appears that the reputation of the mistresses suffered somewhat. Perhaps the goings on of more recent times in Paris, the Antibes, Micheldever Woods, SW1 or SW7, can barely be censured when what was accepted in the Middle Ages was made to appear licit. For a decree, or command, or an Act of Parliament, might right the position of royal children from one or more mothers other than the Queen or the legal wife. Kings, as well as commoners, no doubt salved their consciences and reconciled themselves with Holy Church by believing that they were constantly in love with one woman, though not always the same one at the same time.

The monkish historian, William of Malmesbury, in his *De Gestis Regum* was helped by King Henry I to excuse his lust in the great benefactions that he made to the church, though it seems that the Almighty took His vengeance in the end. It was Maud, one of Henry I's illegitimate daughters by Edith, who called William Aetheling, the only legitimate son and heir of Henry I of England and Duke of Normandy back to the white ship that went down on the night of 25 November 1120. Several Earls and Barons and members of the household drowned with him, along with two of the royal bastards.

As already remarked, poorer folk fared less well and were far less protected or respected. The peasantry took their sport and left unfortunate mothers to care for themselves and their offspring, or to abandon themselves to the charity of parish Overseers of the Poor. On the other hand, a Hampshire clergyman, from a landed gentry family, had eleven children by four girls in his parish. In his Will he provided for each one of them and for their mothers. He died a bachelor. Some bastards of royalty were similarly cared for, not by mention in wills, but by regular visits from court officials, even in plain clothes and high collared mackintoshes, arriving with a subsistence stipend at the home of a foster parent.

By the Victorian age, hypocrisy had reached its zenith and this continued well into the late 1940s, when the workhouses were still in action in providing a roof over the heads of the poor and indigent. The mother of an illegitimate child was as much ostracised in her lifetime as the child would be throughout its life. There are still frowns, even into the twenty-first century, when illegitimacy is mentioned. In his now classic *God Stand Up For Bastards* (1973), David Leitch provides a splendid and touching autobiographical account of relationships between his mother, his putative father and his adoptive parents, and many friends, and of course with himself. An experience in the task of tracing the origins of an illegitimate child brought this writer to the end of the quest by identifying the putative mother and the most likely father. The father, eventually cagey, admitted to the possibility of the offence and wanted to meet the son. The mother, however, denied all knowledge and fought off every possible approach that might have given comfort to the disturbed psyche of the son. In another instance, the parentage was traced but the mother had already died. The father refused to see his son but some three years later, when he himself was approaching the end of his life, asked for arrangements to be made for him to meet his only surviving child. In a Sussex village in the 1930s, a girl in trouble was sent to the workhouse for her confinement and released to become a kitchen maid in a local inn. She refused to be parted from her child, the father being a married man living in a neighbouring street, who denied all knowledge or responsibility. The mother took various jobs and cared for that child, working several jobs to have her properly educated. The child went into a career, eventually as a manager of a Cooperative store, but still, by the 1960s, she was stigmatised locally for her origins.

'It's the rich what gets the pleasure …. it's the poor what gets the blame….'

Not so in royal circles. A good deal can be done to discover royal paternity by reference to coats of arms which first appear with the children of King Henry I. While the *lion passant guardant or on Gules* may well indicate royal bastardy, it could also indicate royal patronage. In the early heraldry, those royal children of the Middle Ages who made good in the court were often accorded land holdings and titles, but it was not really until Tudor and Stuart times that both illegitimate issue and concubines (*vel* mistresses) were accorded titles of nobility and peerage. To these were added substantial grants of funding, contrasting violently with the lot of the workhouse poor.

The great Samuel Johnson, who probably made much of his reputation for his substantial contributions to *The Gentleman's Magazine* in the 1740s, collaborated strenuously with William Oldys in cataloguing the great library of the Harley brothers which, ultimately, went to the British Museum Department of Manuscripts. He also helped his old school-fellow from Lichfield, Dr Robert James, in the production of *A Medicinal Dictionary* and set out his plan for the *Dictionary of the English Language*. His splendid work, *An Account of the Life of Mr Richard Savage, Son of the Earl Rivers*, was as Mr Johnson claimed for himself *'the best of biographies written by those who had eaten and drunk and lived in social intercourse with their subjects'*. There was, however, considerable scepticism over his claim that Savage was the bastard son of the nobleman. In such cases as in that, the peer or putative father, while publicly disowning, privately made allowances to the mother and child. Contributing to the association of illegitimacy with poverty was the tendency to exclude the child by law and social circumstances from what the community regarded as customary in the structure of a respectable family.

Often, the identity of the putative father can be discovered from the names given by the mother at baptism or registration. Thus, William Harrison Smith, son of Mary Smith would automatically impute the father believed by the mother to be responsible for the child and somewhere in the community the said William Harrison can be discovered. Dangers for genealogists arise here when later generations hyphenate the 'extra' surname confusing it with those derived from estates and inheritance of blood. More oblique is the habit of naming children after places of birth in royal bastardy. Most scholars are now aware that the Tudors employed Polydore Vergil with a handsome purse to rewrite *The History of England* in their favour and, in the process, he destroyed much of the ancient documentation. His work was plagiarised by Hollingshed and others and these were the sources for Shakespeare's historical plays. In his *King John* he has Philip Faulconbridge, half-brother of Robert Faulconbridge, declared to be Sir Richard Plantagenet, illegitimate son of King Richard the Lionheart.

Post Commonwealth anti-Catholicism brought the several divisions of English Protestants into some form of union against the survivors of the old faith. Anglicans persecuted Quakers and Baptists, and others of the Protestant sects, and when government claimed to have discovered a radical plot, thousands were imprisoned. It was in prison that John Bunyan wrote his *Pilgrims Progress* in 1678, he, amongst his dissenting followers, railed against and ridiculed the

debased and debauched life of the court, actually naming the Duke
of York, Charles I's third son by Henrietta Maria Bourbon, daughter of Henry IV, King of France, and Mary, daughter of Francis I
Medici, Grand Duke of Tuscany. James had been designated Duke
of York from birth. He was made a Knight of the Garter when he
was only eleven and created Duke of York two years later. He succeeded his brother in 1685 and was crowned King by Catholic rites
on 22 April 1685 at Whitehall Palace and by the traditional rite in
Westminster Abbey on the following day by the Anglican Archbishop
of Canterbury, William Sancroft.

It is said that James married at Breda in Holland sometime in
November or on Christmas Eve 1659, but there is much doubt
about this. Certainly, when she was large with child he had a shotgun
wedding at Worcester House in the Strand on 3 September 1660
to Anne, daughter of Edward Hyde, the first Earl of Clarendon.
The child, Charles, died the following May. Anne bore him eight
children in wedlock before dying on 31 March 1671. By proxy in
September 1673 at the ducal palace in Modena, Italy, and at Dover on
21 November that year, James subsequently married Mary Beatrice
Eleanor Anne Margaret Isabella, daughter of Alphonso d'Este, Duke
of Medina. By Mary he had a stillborn child born in the late spring of
the following year and eleven other legitimate children. By Arabella,
daughter of Sir Winston Churchill, and sister of John Churchill, Duke
of Marlborough, James had four illegitimate chiliden and perhaps
others between 1667 and her death. His children by Arabella were
called FitzJames. By Catherine Countess of Dorchester, daughter of
Charles Sedley, James was having children from about 1679. They
were given the name of Darnley. The family were scandalised and
shamed, not least of all by the King himself, the Duke's brother, who
had produced at least fifteen illegitimate children by as many as seven
paramours. His marriage with Catherine Henrietta, the daughter of
John IV, King of Portugal and Duke of Braganza, was not successful,
her four children were stillborn.

In the eighteenth century, the development of the lampooning
satirist, the state of the royal illegitimate progeny and their perpetra-
tors was put into some rational perspective. Perhaps the best example
of this, without having to quote from the many journals and news

sheets available to the frequenters of coffee shops and taverns is heraldic. A book that is rare simply because scholarly armorists have thrown it out as being poor heraldry is a work of social history.

In 1785 there was published, *The Heraldry of Nature; or Instructions for the KING of ARMS: comprising, The Arms, Supporters, Crests, and Mottos [sic] both in Latin and English of the PEERS OF E--L--D. Blazoned from the Authority of Truth, and characteristically descriptive of the several Qualities that distinguish their Possessors. To which is added several Samples, neatly etched by an eminent Engraver.* This was printed for M. Smith and was sold at booksellers in Piccadilly, the Royal Exchange and in Fleet Street. Arms (illustrated) for *'The -----, First, argent, a cradle proper; second, gules a rod, and sceptre, transverse ways; third azure, five cups and balls proper; fourth, gules, the sun eclips'd proper; fifth, argent, a stag's head between three jockey caps; sixth, or, a house in ruins. Supporter. The dexter, Solomon treading on his crown; the sinister, a jack-ass proper. Crest Britannia in despair. Motto: Neque tangunt levia.'* (Translated as 'Little things don't move me'). Another example is B----K, DUKE OF ST A------- *Arms. Quarterly; first and fourth, or, a prison door azure, second and third, sable, a scourge proper. Supporter. Dexter, a joilor, sinister, A Tityrus laboring, both proper. Crest A chain pendant. Motto; Uni lapsa virtus ? ('Where is all my continence departed?')* A variation of the crest for this family was suggested recently, being *'a penis rampant supporting a basket of oranges proper!!'*

The stigma attached to bastardy whereby the child was blamed for the sins of the parents was brought to the fore by the puritanical reaction to the behaviour of the House of Stuart through to the twenty-first century partnership fashions, which produced some 40 per cent or more of children born out of wedlock in the United Kingdom, thus providing a genealogical nightmare for any who are truly interested in tracing their ancestries and discovering their family histories without insulting their true progenitors with false claims to others. Blood tests in the twentieth century assisted in determining who might not be responsible for paternity by excluding fathers. Only the advent of the examination of the DNA patterns has provided a more tenable means of identifying familial origins, for even the mother may not be the mother following IVF!

Appendix II
The Arms of Royal Bastards

By Cecil Humphery Smith, OBE, FSA,
Principal of the Institute of Heraldic &
Genealogical Studies

Somewhere in Edgar Wallace's *Four Just Men* is a remark about the 'bar sinister' being used in the arms of illegitimate children. This expression was erroneous at its concept and has been employed erroneously by journalists ever since. In fact, the expression is a muddle between the French and the English words of blazonry, the language used to describe heraldic displays. The barre is the French term for a bend which is a diagonal band running from the top left hand top corner of the shield to the right hand base side (as you look at it), the left hand side being called the dexter and the right hand the sinister, because it is thought of from the point of view of the knight bearing the shield on his arm. The *bar* in English blazonry is a diagonal strip across the shield having no particular elevation either side. What, in fact, is intended is the bendlet sinister, that is a thin band running from the top right hand side of the shield to the bottom left hand side of the shield, as you look at it.

Among the first dozen examples of coats of arms of illegitimate issue of Kings of England, the *bendlet sinister* is only used once among the first dozen with a total of four times amongst the first twenty five bastards. Indeed, any system of brisures appropriate to bastards was not to be found before the fifteenth century and most writers on the subject had not recognised the importance of studying them among medieval rolls of arms.

While the Baron de la Roche, Mathieu de Bourbon, called 'le Grand Bâtard de Bourbon' bore *Azure, semy de lis Or a bend(let)* (or a *baton* – the shortened bendlet) *Gules*, Louis de Haeze, the illegitimate son of Count Louis de Male, Count of Flanders, bore in the *Armorial de Gelre* (around 1380) *Argent, a canton Or charged with a lion* Sable. A somewhat more complex coat of arms were born by the bâtard Antoine de Bourbon died in 1504.

The chief herald (or king of arms) of the Duke of Burgundy, John de Fever imposed the *baton sinister* on the arms of the father of every illegitimate child. It is likely that the word *sinister* of blazonry cast a pejorative imputation upon the reputation of the individual who bore such arms particularly when the *baton sinister* became more common in use towards the end of the seventeenth century particularly among royal bastards. Not infrequently such *batons* were charged with other insignia to assist in the differencing.

A Uterine bastard was frequently distinguished by the paternal arms of the mother bearing a *canton* of the arms of the putative father. Apart from the *canton* in which the arms representing the maternal origins might also appear, a *chief* has been used in this context and more frequently a *bordure.* The most famous of the *bordures* was that employed by the illegitimate children of John of Gaunt by his mistress Catherine Swinford. He married her in 1397 whereupon by an Act of Parliament the children were made legitimate as the Beauforts, the royal arms appearing within a *bordure* of the livery colours of the house of Lancaster. Wavy borders were introduced by the English Kings of Arms by the end of the eighteenth century as a brisure of bastardy.

The illegitimate children of the royal house of France and its heraldry have been studied in detail by Hervé Pinoteau, *Héraldique Capetienne,* (1954).

A female bastard in whose name arms have been registered, granted or matriculated becomes an heiress, in that the bastardised coat can become *quartered* by her descendants. Often, in Scotland, on account of hand-fast marriages, a bastard is treated more favourably in Scottish heraldic law. On proof of paternity, he may matriculate exactly as any lawful cadet. However, the Lord Lyon King of Arms would impose a difference upon matriculation, usually of a *bordure compony,* although occasionally with a *baton* or *riband sinister,* but these show that the cadet is not of the legal line of succession. He would not be reckoned as '*filius nullius*' as in England, necessitating him to apply for a new grant of arms, but he would be treated as one of his father's clan having hereditary rights to armorial ensigns. With evidence of paternity he could take *quarterings*, a standard and enjoy nobiliary status. A bordure compony counter-compony is not necessarily a mark of illegitimacy, which is as well for the relationship with many police forces.

In 1702 Alexander Nisbit published *An Essay on Additional Figures and Marks of Cadency. Shewing the Ancient and Modern Practice of differencing Descendents in This and other Nations* ... He concentrated on the Scottish systems referring extensively to advice obtained from William Camden as appears in Dugdale's *Ancient Usage of Arms* (1682). Much has been written in the great books of nobility, the best being Nicholas Upton's *De Studio Militari* (Bysshe's edition, 1634) and the essay of John Johan Baptista Christyn who was Chancellor of Brabant. Christyn had given serious attention to the methods of distinguishing one individual of a house from another, including the bastards who came into military and public prominence.

A fascinating example that appears for Sir John de Clarence, *Per chevron two lions in chief and a fleur de lys in base*, representing the royal family and Sir John's descent from Thomas, Duke of Clarence, the second son of Henry IV who bore *France and England quarterly and a label ermine charged with a canton Gules.* Nisbet expands upon his ideas and shares more of his acquired knowledge in *The System of Heraldry* (1722). He suggests that Sir John de Clarence was the first of the bastards in England to carry arms resembling those of his father. This is not so if we can accept that Henry I bore a lion before his son who appears on the Le Mans enamel (See *Family History* 1976). Nisbet goes on to draw attention to Robert, the illegitimate son of William the Lion, who married the heiress of Lundin of that Ilk taking her name and arms but much later taking on the arms of Scotland within a *bordure gobonated Argent and Azure.* It was, of course, not uncommon in the Middle Ages for a husband to take on the name and arms of the wife along with her title, or, rather, the title of her late father or husband.

Charles, the illegitimate son of Henry, Duke of Somerset bore a *baston* or *bendlet sinister* over the legitimated Beaufort coat.

The shortened baton appears in the arms of Arthur Plantagenet, Viscount Lisle the natural son of Edward IV (*see* page 18) and in that of Henry Fitroy, Earl of Nottingham and Duke of Richmond and Somerset, the natural son of King Henry VIII. That is the baton couped sinister. Question, did Humphrey, Duke of Gloucester, the fourth son of Henry IV bear arms of France and England quarterly *within a bordure compony Argent and Sable* as Gayre says? His daughter Antigone bore them with a *baston sinister Azure*.

Arms can also be used to prompt questions rather than resolve them. For in the case of Thomas Dunckerley, the chief evidence that has been advanced in support of his mother's deathbed claim that Thomas was an illegitimate son of the Prince of Wales, later King George II, were the arms that he used. These were the Royal Arms, debruised by a baton sinister argent, which is often used as an indication of illegitimacy. His seal bore a motto *Fato Non Merito* (By Fate Not Desert) and beneath it was his name Thos. Dunckerley Fitz George (the appendage Fitz, often being used to denote illegitimacy. However, no reference to these arms or to any Royal Licence could be found in the records of the College of Arms. There is no doubt, however, that Dunkerley was a close friend of the Duke of Clarence and other sons of King George III and that he used his seal openly in their presence. But without this seal, it is doubtful whether his claim would have been even considered at all and his position therefore remains an enigma.

Bibliograpy

Abdication (1966) by B. Inglis

A Catalogue and Succession of the Kings, Princes (1622) by R.A. Brooke

A Catalogue of English Medieval Rolls of Arms (1950) – ed A.R. Wagner

A Collection of the Wills of the Kings and Queens of England from William the Conqueror to Henry VII (ed. J. Nichols, 1780)

A Crown for Elizabeth (1971) by M.M. Luke

A Genealogical History of the Kings and Queens of England and Monarchs of Great Britain, 1066-1677 (1677), Samuel Stebbings (1707) by Francis Sandford

A General History of the House of Guelph 2 vols. (1821) by A. Halliday

A History of Greenwich (1973) by B. Platts

A House of Kings: The History of Westminster Abbey (1966) ed. E. Carpenter

Albert and Victoria (1977) by D. Duff

All The King's Women (1988) by Derek Wilson

Alumni Cantabrigienses

Alumni Oxonienses

A Matter of Martyrdom (1969) by H.R. Williamson

Ancient Funeral Monuments within the United Monarchy of Great Britain, Ireland, and the Islands adjacent, their Founders, and what Eminent Persons have been in the Same Interred (1631) by John Weever

Ancient Heraldic Manuscript of David Lyndsay of the Mount, 1542 (1822) by D. Laing

Angevin Kingship (1955) by J.E.A. Joliffe

Anglica Historia (ed. D. Hay, 1950) by Polydore Vergil

Anne and the Princesses Royal (1973) by H. Cathcart

Anne Boleyn (2 vols., 1884) by P. Friedmann

Anne Boleyn (1972) by M.L. Bruce

Anne Boleyn (1974) by H.W. Chapman

Anne Boleyn (1979) by N. Lofts

Anne Boleyn (1984) by C. Erickson

Anne of Denmark (1970) by E.C. Williams

Annuaire de la Noblesse de Russie, (1900)

Anominalle Chronicle (ed. V.H. Galbraith, 1967)

Archaeologia (102 vols – Society of Antiquaries of London, 1773-96)

Armorial de Gelre – various volumes

A Rose of Savoy (1909) by H. Noel Williams

A Treatise on Heraldry British and Foreign 2 vols (1896) by J. Woodard & G. Burnett

A Tudor Tragedy: The Life and Times of Catherine Howard (1961) by L.B. Smith

Banners, Standards and Badges, (1904) by J.Foster

Baronagium Genealogicum, (1764) by J. Edmondson

Bastard Prince Henry VIII's Lost Son (Stroud, 2001) by Beverley A. Murphy

Battle Royal (Muller, 1965) by T. Beamish

Blood Red the Roses: The Wars of the Roses (1973) by C.S. Alderman

Bloody Mary (1978) by C. Erickson

Bosworth Field and the Wars of the Roses (1966) by A.L. Rowse

Boutell's Heraldry (1973) by John.P. Brooke-Little

Britain's Royal Brides (1977) by J. Argy, & W. Riches,

Britain's Royal Family – The Complete Genealogy (1989) by Alison Weir

Britannia (1695) by W. Camden

British Kings and Queens by Mike Ashby

Broken Lives (1993) by Lawrence Stone

Burke's Extinct & Dormant Baronetcies (1841) reprinted 1985

Burke's Extinct & Dormant Peerage (1883) reprinted 1978

Burke's Guide to the British Monarchy (1977) by Hugh Montgomery-Massingberd

Burke's Guide to the Royal Family (1973)

Burke's Landed Gentry - various

*Burke's Landed Gentry of Great Britain – The Kingdom in Scotland (*2001*)* ed Peter
Beauclerk-Dewar

Burke's Peerage and Baronetage – various, inc 2003.

By Royal Appointment (1970) by P. Berry

Calendar of Charter Rolls preserved in the Public Record Office (6 vols., 1903)

Calendar of Documents preserved in France, illustrative of the History of Great

Calendar of Letters, Despatches and State Papers relating to Negotiations between
England and Spain (ed. G.A. Bergenroth, 13 vols., 1862-1954)

Calendar of Letters and Papers, Foreign and Domestic, of the Reign of Henry VIII
(ed. J.S. Brewer, J. Gairdner, and R.H. Brodie, 21 vols., 1862-1932)

Calendar of Patent Rolls preserved in the Public Record Office (1906)

Calendar of State Papers: Milan (ed. A.B. Hinds, 1913)

Calendar of State Papers: Venice (ed. R. Brown and A.B. Hinds, 38 vols.,
1864-1937)

Calendar of State Papers Domestic Charles II 1661-62, 1663-4

Calendar of State Papers Domestic Elizabeth 1591-1594, *p* 167

Calendar of Treasury Books 1667-8, 1669-72, 1672-75

Caroline Matilda, Queen of Denmark (1971) by H.W. Chapman

Caroline the Illustrious (1904) by J.H. Wilkins

Caroline, the Unhappy Queen (1967) by Lord Russell of Liverpool

Catalogue of Honour, (1610) by T. Milles

Catherine of Aragon (1942) by G. Mattingley

Catherine of Aragon and her Friends (1966) by J.E. Paul

Catherine of Braganza (1967) by H. Elsna

Catherine the Queen (1967) by M.M. Luke

Chancery Proceedings, Six Clerk Series, C9/131/1

Charles the First (1975) by J. Bowle

Charles – Victim or Villain? (1998) by Penny Junor

Charles I (1968) by Christopher Hibbert

Charles I (1972) by D.R. Watson

Charles II (1972) by Christopher Falkus

Charles II (1973) by Maurice Ashley

Charles II (1989) by Ronald Hutton

Charles II – His Life and Likeness (1961) by Hesketh Pearson

Charles II, the Man and the Statesman (1971) by Maurice Ashley

Charles the Second's French Mistress (1972) by Brian Bevan

Charles, Prince of Wales (1979) by A. Holden

Chronica (ed. H.C. Hamilton, 2 vols., 1848-9) by Walter of Guisborough:

Chronica (ed. H.T. Riley, 1865) by William Rishanger

Chronica (ed. W. Stubbs, 4 vols., 1868-71) by Roger of Hovedon

Chronica (ed. J.R. Lumby, 2 vols., Rolls Series, 1889-95) by Henry Knighton

Chronica Anglicanum (ed. J. Stevenson, 1875) by Ralph of Coggeshall

Chronica Majora (ed. H.R. Luard, 7 vols., Rolls Series, 1872-3) by Matthew Paris

Chronicle (ed. G. Rokewoode, 1840) by Jocelin of Brakelond

Chronicle (ed. W.A. Wright, 2 vols., Rolls Series, 1846-8) by Pierre de Langtoft

Chronicle Containing the History of England, H Ellis (ed.) (1809) by E. Hall

Chronicle of England during the reigns of the Tudors (ed. W. Douglas-Hamilton, 2 vols., 1875)

Chronicles of Engand, France and Spain (ed. J. Jolliffe, 1967) by John Froissart

Chronicles of England, Scotland and Ireland (ed. H. Ellis, 6 vols., 1927) by Raphael Holinshed

Chronicle of the Grey Friars of London (ed. J. Nichols, 1852)

Chronicle of the Kings of England (ed. J.A. Giles, 1866) by William of Malmesbury

Chronicles and Memorials of the Reign of Richard I (ed. W. Stubbs, 2 vols, Rolls Series, 1864-5)

Chronicle of the Kings of England from the Time of the Romans' Government unto the Death of King James (1643) by Richard Baker

Chronicles of the White Rose (ed. J.O. Halliwell, 1835)

Chronicon (ed. E.M. Thompson, 1889) by Geoffrey le Baker

Chronicon Angliae (ed. E.M. Thompson, 1874) by Thomas Walsingham

Chronicon ex Chronicis (ed. B. Thorpe, 1848-9) by Florence of Worcester

Chroniques des Comtes d'Anjou (ed. L. Halphen and R. Poupardin, 1913)

Clarence (1972) by M. Harrison

Cobbett's Complete Collection of State Trials (1809 – 1972)

Collectanea (ed. T. Hearne, 6 vols., 1774) by John Leland

Collins' Peerage - various editions

Constant Delights (2002) by Graham Hopkins

Continuation of Hardyng's Chronicles (ed. Sir H. Nicholas, 1809) by Richard Grafton

Continuato Chronicarum (ed. E.M. Thompson, Rolls Series, 1889) by Adam Murimeth

Correspondence with Robert Innes-Smith

Correspondence with Tim Seely

Correspondence with Major Bruce Shand

Correspondence with Mrs. Michael Worthington

Country Life - The Lake that became a Valley (24 April 1964)

Cupid and the King (1991) by HRH Princess Michael of Kent

Debrett's Peerage and Baronetage – various editions

Debrett's Great British Families, by Hugh Montgomery Massingberd

De Nugis Curialum (ed. T. Wright, 1850) by Walter Map

Devil's Blood: The Angevin Family (1957) by A. Duggan

Diana – Closely Guarded Secret (2002) by Inspector Ken Wharfe

Diana, Princess of Wales (1983) by P. Junor

Diary of Mary, Lady Cowper (1714 – 20) ed by Hon C.S. Spencer Cowper

Dictionary of National Biography (ed. L. Stephen and S. Lee, 63 vols., 1885 – 1900)

Display of Heraldry – various editions – by J. Guillim

Dynasty by Donald Spoto

Edward IV (1974) by C. Ross

Edward V: The Prince in the Tower (2003) by Michael Hicks

Edward VI: The Threshold of Power (1970) by W.K. Jordan

Edward VI: The Young King (1968) by W.K. Jordan

Edward VII (1972) by K. Middlemas

Edward VII (1982) by Christopher Hibbert

Edward VII and his Circle (1956) by Virginia Cowles

Edward VII's Last Loves – Alice Keppel & Agnes Keyser (1998) by Raymond Lamont-Brown

Edward VIII by Philip Ziegler

Edward VIII (1974) by F. Donaldson
Edward of Kent (1938) by D. Duff
Edward The Confessor (1970) by F. Barlow
Edwardian Daughter (1958) by Sonia Keppel
Edwardians in Love by Anita Leslie
Elizabeth I (1963) by B.W. Beckingsale
Elizabeth I (1972) by N. Williams
Elizabeth I, Queen of England (1967) by N. Williams
Elizabeth II (1982) by E. Longford
Elizabeth of Bohemia (1938, 1964) by C. Oman
Elizabeth of York, Tudor Queen (1973) by N. Lenz-Harvey
Elizabeth the Great (1958) by E. Jenkins
Elizabeth, the Winter Queen (1977) by J. Gorst-Williams
Elizabeth Woodville, 1437-1492 (1938) by D. MacGibbon
Eminent Elizabethans (1983 London) A.L.Rowse
Encyclopedia of Mistresses (1993) by Dawn B. Sova
England under the Tudors (1955) by G.R. Elton
England without Richard (1965) by J.T. Appleby
English Court Life from Henry VII to George II (1963) by R. Dutton
Fanfare for Elizabeth (1946) by E. Sitwell
Flores Historiarum (ed. H.R. Luard, 3 vols., Rolls Series, 1890) by Matthew Paris
For My Grandchildren (1966) by HRH Princess Alice, Countess of Athlone
Four Fine Gentlemen (1977), by Hester W Chapman
From Hanover to Windsor (1960) by R. Fulford
Genealogical History of the Kings & Queens of England (London, 1707) by Francis Sandford
Garter Stall Plates illustrated Manuscript from the collections of Naylor and others (15 vols)
     pre 1830
George I (1974) by J. Marlow
George I by R. Hatton
George I, Elector and King (1978) by R. Hatton
George III (1972) by J. Clarke
George III and the Mad Business (1969) by I. Macalpine R. Hunter
George IV (1972) by A. Palmer
George IV: A Portrait (1966) by J. Richardson
George IV, Regent and King (1975) by Christopher Hibbert
George V: His Life and Reign (1952) by Harold Nicolson
George VI (1974) by K. Middlemas
George the Third (1972) by S. Ayling
George Rex: Death of a Legend (Macmillan South Africa 1974) by Patricia Storror
Gesta Henrici Quinti (ed. B. Williams, 1850) by Thomas Elmham
Goodwood (1975) by David Hunn
Grand Armorial de France, 7 vols., (1934-52) by H.J. De Morenas
Great British Families (1988) by Hugh Montgomery-Massingberd
Great Dynasties (Various authors, 1976, 1979)
Great Harry: A Life of King Henry VIII (1980) by C. Erickson
Handbook of British Chronoloty (ed. F.M. Powicke and E.B Fryde, 1961)
Heirs to the Throne (1966) by A. Joelson
Henrietta Maria (1936) by C. Oman
Henrietta Maria (1976) by E. Hamilton
Henrietta Maria, Queen of the Cavaliers (1973) by Q. Bone
Henry V (1967) by H.F. Hutchison
Henry V (1972) by P. Earle
Henry V: The Cautious Conqueror (1975) by M.W. Labargé

Henry VII (1968; revised edition 1983) by R. Lockyer

Henry VII (1972) by S.B. Chrimes

Henry VII (1972) by N. Williams

Henry VIII (1902) by A.F. Pollard

Henry VIII (1962) by J.J. Bagley

Henry VIII (1964) by J. Bowle

Henry VIII (1968) by J. Scarisbrick

Henry VIII (1972) by Robert Lacey

Henry VIII and his Court (1971) by N. Williams

Henry VIII and the Reformation (1962) by D. Maynard-Smith

Henry VIII, the Mask of Royalty (1971) by L.B. Smith

Henry the Eighth (1973) by F. Hackett

Henry the Eighth (1963) by B. Saunders

Heraldic Exhibition Catalogue, Edinburgh, (1891)

Heraldic Exhibition Catalogue, London (1934)

Heraldry of the illegitimate issue of the Blood Royal – articles in various issues of *The Coat of Arms* by C.R. Humphery-Smith

Heraldry in Westminster Abbey (1955) by C.W. Scott-Giles

Heraldry of York Minster, 2 vols (1890-6) by A.P. Purey-Cust

Her Majesty (1962) by H. Cathcart

Hessian Tapestry (1967) by D. Duff

Histoire de Guillaume le Maréchale (ed. P. Meyer, 1891-1901)

Histoire de Roy d'Angleterre, Richard (ed. J.A.C. Buchon, 1826) by Jean Creton

Historia Anglorum (ed. F.H. Madden, 3 vols., Rolls Series, 1866-9) by Matthew Paris

Historia Anglorum (ed. T. Arnold, Rolls Series, 1879) by Henry of Huntingdon

Historia Ecclesiastica (ed. A. le Prèvost, 5 vols., 1838-55) by Ordericus Vitalis

Historia Novorum and *Vita Sancti Anselmi* (ed. M. Rule, 1884) by Eadmer

Historia Regum and Historia Novella (ed. W. Stubbs, 1887-9) by William of Malmesbury

Historia Rerum Angliae (ed. T. Hearne, 1716) by John Rous

Historia Rerum Anglicarum (ed. R. Howlett, 1884-5) by William of Newburgh

Historiae Anglicana (ed. H.T. Riley, 2 vols., 1863-4) by Thomas Walsingham

Historiae Croylandensis Continuato (ed. W. Fulman, 1684; trans. T. Riley)

Historical Works (ed. W. Stubbs, Rolls Series, 1879-80) by Gervase of Canterbury

History and Antiquities of the Tower of London (1830) by J. Bayley

History of the Kings of Britain (ed. S. Evans & C.W. Dunn, 1963) by Geoffrey of Monmouth

History of the Lennards

History of Parliament Trust

HRH The Princess Anne: A Biography (1984) by B. Hoey

Imagines Historiarum (ed. W. Stubbs, 1876) by Ralph de Diceto

Incertie Scriptoris Chronicon Angliae de Regnis Henrici IV, Henrici V et Henrici VI (ed. J.A. Giles, 1848)

In Good King Charles's Golden Days (1939) by Bernard Shaw

Ingulph's Chronicle of the Abbey of Croyland (ed. H.T. Riley, 1854)

Itinerarium et Peregrinorum et Gesta Regis Ricardi (ed. W. Stubbs, Rolls Series, 1864)

I was James the Second's Queen (1963) by Brian Bevan

Jack the Ripper: The Final Solution (1976) by Stephen Knight

Jacobean Pageant, or the Court of King James I (1962) by G.P.V. Akrigg

James (1971) by P. Miller

James I by his Contemporaries (1969) by R. Ashton

James II (1948) by F.C. Turner

James II (1972) by P. Earle

James II (1977) by Maurice Ashley

James V, King of Scots (1971) by C. Bingham

James Duke of Monmouth (1973) by Bryan Bevan

John of Gaunt (1904) by S. Armitage-Smith

Katherine (1954) by A. Seton

King Charles II (1931) by Arthur Bryant

King Charles II (1979) by Antonia Fraser

King Edward VII (1964) by P. Magnus

King George III (1972) by J. Brooke

King Henry V (1934) by P. Lindsay

King James I (1967) by D. Mathew

King James III of England (1962) by Brian Bevan

King without a Crown (1977) by D. Bennett

Kings and Queens (1953, 1983) by E. & H. Farjeon

Kings and Queens of Britain (1977) by J. Marlow & E. Mackay

Kings and Queens of England (1966) by M.C. Scott-Moncrieff

Kings and Queens of England (1976) by A. Palmer

Kings and Queens of England and Great Britain (1966) by E.R. Delderfield

Kings and Queens of Great Britain: A Genealogical Chart Showing their Descent, Relationships and Coats of Arms (1986) by A. Tauté, J. Brooke-Little, & D. Pottinger

Kings in the Making: The Princes of Wales (1931) by E. Thornton-Cook

Kings of Merry England (1936) by P. Lindsay

Ladies in Waiting (1976) by D.M. Ashdown

Lady Jane Grey (1962) by H.W. Chapman

Lady Jane Grey: The Setting of the Reign (1972) by D. Mathew

Lady of the Sun: The Life and Times of Alice Perrers (1966) by F.G. Kay

Lancaster and York (2 vols., 1892) by J.H. Ramsay

Lancastrians, Yorkists, and Henry VII (1964) by S.B. Chrimes

Leopards of England (1913) by E.E. Dorling

Les Souverains du Monde (1718) by F.L. Bresler

L'Estoire des Engles (ed. T. Hardy & C.T. Martin, 1888–9) by Geoffrey Gaimar

Letters and Papers, Henry VIII Vol 4, no 5807

Letters and Papers illustrative of the Reigns of Richard III and Henry VII (ed. J. Gairdner, 2 vols., Rolls Series, 1861, 1863)

Letters and Papers of the Reign of Henry VIII (ed. J.S. Brewer, J. Gairdner and R.H. Brodie, 21 vols., 1862–1932)

Life and Times of Charles II (1972) by Christopher Falkus

Life of King Alfred (ed. W.M. Stevenson, 1904) by Bishop Asser

Life of the Black Prince (ed. M.K. Pope and E.C. Lodge, 1910) by Chandos Herald:

Lines of Succession: Heraldry of the Royal Families of Europe (1981) by J. Louda & M. Maclagan

Lives of the Hanoverian Queens of England 2 vols (1911) by A. Greenwood

Lives of the Princesses of Wales (1983) by M.B. Fryer, A. Bousfield & G. Toffoli

Lives of the Queens of England (8 vols., Henry Colburn, 1851) by A.L. Strickland

Lord Hervey's Memoirs, 3 vols (1931) ed Romney Sedgwick

Lord Rochester's Monkey (1974) by Graham Greene

Louis and Victoria The First Mountbattens (1974) by R. Hough

Love and the Princess (1958) by L. Iremonger

Lucy Walter – Wife or Mistress? (London, 1947) by Lord George Scott

Majesty: Elizabeth II and the House of Windsor (1977) by Robert Lacey

Margaret of Anjou, Queen of England (1948) by J.J. Bagley

Margaret of Anjou, Queen of England (1970) by P. Erlanger

Marie of Roumania (1973) by T. Elsberry

Mary II, Queen of England (1953) by Hester W. Chapman

Mary of Guise (1977) by R.K. Marshall

Mary of Modena (1962) by Carola Oman

Mary, Queen of Scots (1969) by Antonia Fraser

Mary, Queen of Scots (1974) by G. Donaldson

Mary Tudor (1940 & 1953) by H.F.M Prescott

Mary Tudor (1973) by J. Ridley

Mary Tudor, the White Queen (1970) by W.C. Richardson

Materials for a History of the Reign of Henry VII (ed. W. Campbell, 2 vols., Rolls Series, 1873–7)

Matriarch: Queen Mary and the House of Windsor (1984) by Anne Edwards

Mémoires (ed. M. Jones, 1972) by Philippe de Commines

Memoirs of the Beauties of the Court of King Charles the Second (1838) by Anna Jameson

Memoirs of the Comte de Grammont (1930) by Anthony Hamilton

Monarchs Murders Mistresses by David Williams

Monasticon Anglicanum, 6 vols., (1846) by W. Dugdale

Monumenta Westmonasteriensia (1683) by Henry Keepe

Monumental Effigies of Great Britain (1817) by C. Stothard

Mrs Jordan (London, 1965) by Brian Fothergill

Mrs. Jordan's Profession (1994) by Clare Tomalin

My Lord of Bedford (1963) by E.C. Williams

Nell Gwyn (1969) by Brian Bevan

Nell Gwyn (1987) by Roy MacGregor Hastie

Nell Gwyn (2000) by Derek Parker

Nell Gwyn – A Biography (2005) by Charles Beauclerk (Earl of Burford)

Nell Gwyn, Royal Mistress (1952) by John Harold Wilson

Nell Gwyn, The Story of Her Life (1923) by Lewis Melville

Nell Gwynne (1924) by Arthur Dasent

Nell Gwynne – a Passionate Life (2000) by Graham Hopkins

Notes & Queries April 1956, Sidney Lodge (1648-1682) and his pupil Charles FitzCharles,
    Earl of Plymouth (1657–1680), pp 159-197

Notes & Queries, 8th series IV 28 Oct 1893

Now I Remember: A Holiday History of England (Pan, 1964) by R. Hamilton

O'Beirne's Naval Biographies

Old Rowley – A Private Life of Charles II (19334) by Dennis Wheatley

Ordeal by Ambition: An English Family in the Shadow of the Tudors (1972) by William Seymour

Our Sovereigns (1937) by O. Lancaster

Overture to Victoria (1961) by M. Porter

Oxford Dictionary of National Biography (2004)

Painted Ladies, Women at the Court of Charles II by National Portrait Gallery

Papers of the Benedictine Congregation

Philip and Elizabeth: Portrait of a Marriage (2004) by Gyles Brandreth

Polychronicon (ed C. Babington & J.R. Lumby, Rolls Series, 1865–6) by Ranulph Higben

Poor Fred and the Butcher (1970) by M. Marples

Prince Eddy and the Homosexual Underworld, (1994) by Theo Aronson.

Prince Eddy: The King Britain Never Had (2006) by Andrew Cook.

Prince of the Renaissance (1973) by Desmond Seward

Princess Alice: Queen Victoria's Forgotten Daughter (1974) by G. Noel

Princess Margaret (1985) by C.L. Warwick

Princess Marina, Duchess of Kent (1969) by J. Wentworth-Day

Princess Michael of Kent (1985) by P. Lane

Princess of Wales (1979) by D.M. Ashdown

Princesses in Love (1973) by Ursula Bloom

Prinny's Daughter: A Biography of Princess Charlotte of Wales (1976) by T. Holme

Privileged Persons (1966) by H.W. Chapman

Queen Adelaide (1946) by M. Hopkirk

Queen Alexandra (Constable, 1969) by G. Battiscombe

Queen Anne (1970) by D. Green

Queen Anne's Son (1954) by Hester Chapman

Queen Charlotte (1975) by O. Hedley

Queen Elizabeth I (1934) by J.E. Neale

Queen Elizabeth the Queen Mother (1966) by D. Laird

Queen Katherine Parr (1973) by A. Martiensson

Queen Mary (1959) by J. Pope-Hennessey

Queen Victoria: Her Life and Times, Vol. 1 (1972) by C. Woodham-Smith

Queen Victoria's Mother (1974) by D.M. Ashdown

Queens of Britain (1977) by N. Lofts

Regal Heraldry (1821) by T. Willement

Reliquiae Hearnianae by Thomas Hearne

Richard III (1955) by P.M. Kendall

Richard III (1972) by A. Cheetham

Richard III and the Princes in the Tower (1965) ed Langdon-Davies

Richard of Cornwall (1947) by N. Denholm-Young

Richard the Lion Heart (1973) by J. Gillingham

Robert the Bruce and the Community of the Realm of Scotland (1965) by G.W.S. Borrow

Royal Blunders by Geoffrey Regan

Royal Children (1984) by C. Clear

Royal Confinements (1980) by J. Dewhurst

Royal Duke (1976) by M. Gillen

Royal Dukes (1933) by Roger Fulford

Royal Family, Royal Lovers, by David M. Bergenon

Royal Feud: The Queen Mother and the Duchess of Windsor (1985) by M. Thornton

Royal Handbook – Kings and Queens of Britain by Alan Hamilton

Royal Romance (1980) by L. Picknett

Royal Subjects (2000) by Theo Aronson

Royal Survivor – A Life of Charles II (1999) by Stephen Coote

Royal Wives (1967) by H. Jenner

Rule of Three (1967) by I. Butler

Scots Heraldry (1956) by Sir Thomas Innes of Learney

Scottish Kings (1967) by G. Donaldson

Seven Queens of England (1953) by G. Trease

Shakespeare's Heraldry, (1971) by C.W. Scott-Giles

Siebmacher's Wappenbuchen – various editions

Simon de Montfort (1962) by M.W. Labargé

Sir Charles Sedley (London 1927), V de Sola Pinto

Six Royal Sisters: The Daughters of George III (1969) by Morris Marples

Smyth's Lives of the Berkeleys (1821), Thomas D Fosbroke, MA, FSA

Sophia Dorothea (1971) by R. Jordan

Sophie, Electress of Hanover: A Personal Portrait (1973) by Maria Kroll

Sorrowful Captives: The Tudor Earls of Devon (1960) by H. Durant

Sovereign Legacy by William Seymour

Spotlight – Actors – various editions

Story of Nell Gwyn (1852 & 1908) by Peter Cunningham

The Abdication of King Edward VIII (1966) by Lord Beaverbrook

The Age of Chivalry (1963) by Arthur Bryant

The Ancestor, 12 vols, (1904–14) by O. Barron

The Anglo-Saxon Chronicle (ed. G.N. Garmonsway (1954)

The Ardent Queen (1976) by J. Haswell

The Black Prince (1976) by H. Cole

The Black Prince (1976) by B. Emerson

The Book of Burials of True Noble Persons (MS. In the Royal College of Arms)

The Book of the Illustrious Henries (ed. F.C. Hingston, 1858) by John Capgrave

The Brut, or The Chronicles of England (ed. F. Brie, 1908)

The Butt of Malmsey (1967) by H.R. Williamson

The Clergy List – various

The Cleveland Street Affair (ca 1976) by Colin.Simpson, Chester Lewis & David Leitch

The Cleveland Street Scandal (1976) by H. Montgomery Hyde

The Coat of Arms (The Heraldry Society) - various editions

The Coat of Arms, on the heraldry of Royal Bastards (NS Vol III no 112 (1979/80) and NS Vols III–IV (1978–82))

The Complete Baronetage, by G.E. Cokayne

The Complete Guide to Heraldry – various editions by A.C. Fox-Davies,:

The Complete Letters of Lady Mary Wortley Montagu, 3 Vols (Oxford, 1965) by Robert Halsband

The Complete Peerage of England, Scotland, Ireland, Great Britain and the United Kingdom (ed. V.Gibbs, G.E.Cockayne, G.H.White, et al.,13 vols., 1910–94)

The Concordance of Histores: The New Chronicles of England and France (ed. H. Ellis,41811) by Robert Fabyan

The Countess of Warwick by Margaret Blunden

The Country Life Book of the Royal Silver Jubilee (1977) by Patrick Montague-Smith

The Court of St James by Christopher Hibbert

The Court at Windsor (1964) by Christopher Hibbert

The Court Wits of the Restoration (1967) by John H. Wilson

The Courtiers of Henry VIII (1970) by D. Mathew

The Crime of Mary Stuart (1967) by G.M. Thomson

The Diary of Samuel Pepys, 11 vols, ed. by R.C. Latham & W. Matthews (1970–83)

The Disastrous Marriage (1960) by J. Richardson

The Divorce (1965) by M.A. Albert

The Duchess of Kent (1971) by H. Cathcart

The Dukes (1975) by Brian Masters

The Dukes of Britain (1986) by Arthur Foss

The Early Elizabethan Succession Question (Stanford UP1966), Mortimer Levine

The Earlier Tudors, 1485-1558 (1952) by .J.D. Mackie

The Early Life of Anne Boleyn (1886) by J.H. Round

The Elizabethan Epic (1966) by L.B. Smith

The Elusive Mistress: Elizabeth Lucy and her family (1997-9) by J. Ashdown-Hill

The Empress Brown (1969) by T. Cullen

The End of the House of Lancaster (1966) by R.L. Storey

The England of Charles II (1934) by Arthur Bryant

The Enigma of Mary Stuart (1971) by I.B. Cowan

The Enigmatic Edwardian: The Life of Reginald, 2nd Viscount Esher (1986) by James Lees-Milne

The Feudal Kingdom of England (1961) by F. Barlow

The Fifteenth Century Chronicles (ed. J. Gairdner, 1880)

The Fifteenth Century, 1399–1485 (1961) by E.F. Jacob

The First English Life of Henry V (ed. C.L. Kingsford, 1911)

The First Four Georges (1956) by J.H. Plumb

The Fox-Hunters of Vanity Fair, by Gordon Fergusson

The Genealogists' Magazine, Vol 20, No 1, March 1980 – letter re Nell Gwynne

The Genealogists' Magazine, Vol 20, No 5, March 1981 – article by G.W. Iredell

The Genealogists' Magazine, Vol 20, No 6, June 1981 – article by David Williamson

The Genealogists' Magazine, Vol 21, No 7, September 1984 – article by Lydia Collins

The Genealogists' Magazine, Vol 22, No 7, September 1987 – article by Philip Hall

The Glorious Revolution of 1688 (1966) by Maurice Ashley

The Golden Longing (1959) by F. Leary

The Great Chronicle of London (ed. A.H. Thomas and I.D. Thornley, 1983)

The Great Seals of England (n.d.) by A.B. & A. Wyon

*The Heraldry of Canterbury Cathedral (*1947) by A.W.B. Messenger

The History & Antiquities of the Abbey Church of Westminster (1723) by John Dart

The History of That Most Eminent Statesman, Sir John Perrott etc (1728), Richard Rawlinson

The Hollow Crown: A Life of Richard II (1961) by H.F. Hutchison

The Holy Roman Empire, (1956) by J.V. Bryce

The House of Hanover (1960) by Alvin Redman

The House of Kent (1969) by Ursula Bloom

The House of Nell Gwyn 1670-1974 by Donald Adamson & Peter Beauclerk-Dewar

The House of Tudor (1967) by R. Strong

The House of Windsor (1973) by D. Judd

The Illegitimate Children of Richard III, by Peter W Hammond, Richard III: Crown & People, ed. J. Petre 1985.

The Killing of William Rufus (1968) by D. Grinnell-Milne

The King in Love (1988) by Theo Aronson

*The King of Fools (*1988*) by John Parker*

The Kings and Queens of England by W.M. Ormerod

The Kings and Queens of Scotland (1976) by C. Bingham

The King's Lieutenant: Henry of Grosmont, First Duke of Lancaster, 1300-1361 (1969) by K.A. Fowler

The King's Great Matter (1967) by G. de C. Parmiter

The Kings' Mistresses, (1980) by Alan Hardy

The King's Peace, 1637–41 (1955) by C.V. Wedgewood

The King's War, 1641–47 (1958) by C.V. Wedgewood

The Last Tudor King (1958) by Hester W. Chapman

The Later Middle Ages in England (1977) by B. Wilkinson

The Later Plantagenets (1955) by V.H.H Green

The Letters of King Henry VIII (1936) by M. St Clair Byrne

The Life and Reign of Edward IV (2 vols., 1923, 1967) by C.L. Scofield

The Life and Reign of George VI (1958) by J. Wheeler-Bennett

The Life and Times of King James (1974) by A. Fraser

The Life and Times of Victoria (1972) by D. Marshall

The Life of Anne Boleyn (1923) by P. Sergeant

The Life of James, Third Earl of Derwentwater etc (1929), by Major F. J. A Skeet

The Life of Henry VII (1622; ed. J.R. Lumby, 1902) by Francis Bacon

The Lion and the Lilies: The Stuarts and France (1977) by E. Cassavetti

The Lion in the North (1973) by J. Prebble

The Lisle Letters, Vol 1 & 6 (Chicago, 1981), by M St Clair Byrne

The Lives of the Kings and Queens of England (1977) ed. Antonia Fraser

The Lives of the Princesses of England (6 vols., London, 1849-55) by M.A.E. Green

The Making of Henry VIII (1977), by Marie Louise Bruce

The Mariner's Mirror by Roger Powell

The Marriage made in Blood (1968) by H.R. Williamson

The Marshal Duke of Berwick (London, 1953) by Sir Charles Petrie

The Metrical Chronicle of Robert of Gloucester (ed. W.A. Wright, 1887)

The Mistresses of Charles II (1979) by Brian Masters

The Monarchy in Britain (1977)

*The National Library of Wales Journal (*1993*/*4*), 'A Note on the Date of Birth of Sir John Perrott',* by R.K. Turvey

The Naval Sons of William IV and Mrs. Jordan by Captain Hugh Owen, RN

The Norman Conquest (1966) by D.J.A. Mathew

The Normans (1966) by T. Baker

The Outrageous Queens (1977) by Marc Alexander

The Plantagenet Ancestry of Elizabeth of York (1928) by W.H. Turton

The Plantagenets (1948) by J. Harvey

The Prince and his Lady (1970) by M. Gillen

The Prince of Pleasure and his Regency, 1811–20 (1969) by J.B. Priestley

The Princes and Principality of Wales (1969) by F. Jones

The Princes in the Tower (1978) by E. Jenkins

The Princesses Royal (1973) by G. Wakeford

The Private Life of Henry VIII (1964) by N. Brysson-Morrison

The Queen (1983) by A. Morrow

The Queen Mother (1984) by A. Morrow

The Queen over the Water (London, 1953) by Mary Hopkirk

The Queen's House by Edna Healey

The Queen's Lineage (1977) by G.S.P. Freeman-Grenville

The Queens and the Hive (1962) by E. Sitwell

The Queens of England (1976) by B. Softly

The Reign of Elizabeth (1959) by J.B. Black

The Reign of Henry VII from Contemporary Sources (ed. A.F. Pollard, 3 vols., 1913–14)

The Reign of Stephen, 1135–1154: Anarchy in England (1970) by H.A. Cronne

The Restoration Land Settlement in County Dublin 1660-1688 by L.J. Arnold

The Ricardian, Vol. 13 (2003,

The Right to be King (London 1995), Howard Nenner

The Royal Archives, Windsor Castle - Press Cuttings of the Mylius Case 1911

The Royal Archives, Windsor Castle – extracts from HM Queen Victoria's Diaries relating to the FitzClarences

The Royal Baby Album (1984) by D. Thomas

The Royal Bastards of Medieval England 1066–1486 (1984) by Chris Given Wilson & Alice Curteis

The Royal Daughters of England (2 vols., 1910) by H.M. Lane

The Royal FitzRoys (London, 1950) by Bernard Falk

The Royal George (1963) by G. St Aubyn

The Royal Heraldry of England – various issues of *The Coat of Arms* by C.R. Humphery Smith & M. Heenan

The Royal House of Scotland (1970) by Eric Linklater

The Royal House of Tudor (1974) by M. Roulstone

The Royal House of Windsor (1974) by E. Longford

The Royal Line of Succession (1967) by Patrick Montague-Smith

The Royal Malady (1964) by C. Chevenix-Trench

The Royal Palaces (1970) by P. Howard

The Royal Whore (London, 1971) by Allen Andrews

The Royals (1997) by Kitty Kelley

The Saxon and Norman Kings (1963) by C. Brooke

The Scots Peerage – 9 vols (1904–14) by Sir J. Balfour Paul

The Secret of Henry VIII (1953) by P. Lindsay

The Sisters of Henry VIII (1969) by H.W. Chapman

The Six Wives of Henry VIII (1937) by P. Rival

The Six Wives of Henry VIII (1968) by M. Cowan

The Shy Princess (1958) by D. Duff

The Stall Plates of the Knights of the Garter (1870) by W.H. St J.Hope

The Stewart Kingdom of Scotland (1974) by C. Bingham

The Story of Nell Gwyn (1911) by Cecil Chesterton

The Stuarts (1958) by Charles Petrie

The Stuarts: A Study in English Kingship (1958) by F.P. Kenyon

The Stuarts in Love (1963) by Maurice Ashley

The Survey of London (1598; 1956) by John Stow

The Tower and the Traitors (1961) by B.L. Picard

The Tower of London: Official Guide (1966)

The Tower of London in the History of the Nation (1972) by A.L. Rowse

The Tragedy of Charles II (1964), by Hester W. Chapman

The Transactions of the Hon Soc of Cymmrodorian (1992), 'Sir John Perrott, Henry VIII's Bastard ?', by R. K. Turvey

The Trial of Charles I (1964) by C.V. Wedgewood

The Trial of Queen Caroline (1968) by Roger Fulford

The Triumphant Reign of King Henry the Eighth (ed. C. Whibley, 1904) by Edward Hall

The Troubled Reign of King Stephen (1969) by J.T. Appleby

The Tudors (1966) by C. Morris

The Union of the Two Noble and Illustrious Families of Lancaster and York (ed. H. Ellis, 1809) by Edward Hall

The Usurpation of Richard III (ed. C.A.J. Armstrong, 1936) by Dominic Mancini

The Verney Letters, 2 Vols (1930) by Lady Verney

The Visitations of Kent 1574 (1923) Harleian Society

The War of the Windsors – A Century of Unconstitutional Monarchy (2002) by Lynn Picknett, Clive Prince, Stephen Prior & Robert Brydon

The Wars of the Roses (1965) by J.R. Lander

The Wars of the Roses (1973) by H. Cole

The Wentworth Papers (1705–1739)

The Windsor Tapestry by Conington Mack

The Wisest Fool in Christendom (1958) by W. McElwee

The Wives of Henry VIII (1905) by M.A.S. Hume

The Woman He Loved (1974) by R.G. Martin

The Year of the Conqueror (1966) by A. Lloyd

The Young Elizabeth (1971) by A. Plowden

The Youthful Queen Victoria (1952) by D. Creston

The Youth of Henry VIII (1913) by F.A. Mumby

This Sceptred Isle – The Dynasties (2002) by Christopher Lee

This Sun of York: A Biography of Edward IV (1973) by M. Clive

Three Consort Queens (1971) by G. Wakeford

Three Edwards (1958) by T.B. Costain

Tongue's Visitation of the Northern Counties of about 1530

Tudor Dynastic Problems (1973), Mortimer Levine

Tudor England (1950) by S.T. Bindoff

Two Tudor Books of Arms (1904), by J. Foster

Two Tudor Portraits (1960) by Hester W. Chapman

Vicky (Collins and Harvill, 1971) by D. Bennett

Victoria and Albert (1977) by J. Richardson

Victoria and her Daughters (1971) by N. Epton

Victoria County History – Hampshire, Vol 3, pp 228–9

Victoria R.I. (1964) by Elizabeth Longford

Victoria's Dark Secrets by Ed Sams

Warwick the Kingmaker (1957) by P.M. Kendall

Westminster Abbey: Official Guide (1966)

Who's Who in History, Vol. 1, 55 B.C. to 1485 (1960) by W.O. Hassall

Who's Who in History, Vol. 2, 1485-1603 (1964) by C.R.N. Routh

Wicked Uncles in Love (1972) by M. Marples

William I (1973) by Maurice Ashley

William I and the Norman Conquest (1965) by F. Barlow

William III (Longman, 1966) by S.B. Baxter

William IV (1971) by Philip Ziegler

William and Mary (1973) by H. & B.Van Der Zee

William and Mary (1974) by J. Miller

William's Mary (1972) by E. Hamilton

William of Orange (2 vols., 1966) by N. Robb

Windsor Castle in the History of the Nation (1974) by A.L. Rowse

Wits, Wenchers and Wantons (London, 1986) by E. J. Burford

List of Illustrations

We acknowledge with grateful thanks the permission to reproduce these various
illustrations from the owners and institutions concerned, as listed below.

Gallery, London
26 James II. National Portrait Gallery, London.
27 Henrietta, *née* FitzJames, Lady Waldegrave (1667-1730) Paul Mellon Collection (Earl Waldegrave)
28 James FitzJames, Duke of Berwick (1670-1734) The Scottish National Portrait Gallery (Earl of Rosebery)
29 Katherine Darnley, Duchess of Buckingham (1681-1742) - Enoch Seeman – National Portrait Gallery, London
30 Prince Charles Edward Stuart
31 Charlotte Stuart, Duchess of Albany (1753-89) National Portrait Gallery, London.
32 Arms of the Duchess of Albany.
33 George I. National Portrait Gallery, London.
34 Arms of George I.
35 Petronelle, Countess of Chesterfield (1693-1778) Schulenburg Collection.
36 George II. National Portrait Gallery, London.
37 Frederick, Prince of Wales. Royal Collection © 2006 Her Majesty Queen Elizabeth II.
38 George IV. Courtauld Institute.
39 William IV. National Portrait Gallery, London.
40 George Augustus Frederick Fitzclarence, Earl of Munster. National Portrait Gallery, London.
41 Arms of the Earl of Munster.
42 Sophia, Baroness De L'Isle & Dudley, *née* FitzClarence. National Portrait Gallery, London.
43 Henry Edward FitzClarence.
44 Lady Mary Fox, *née* FitzClarence (1798-1864) Courtauld Institute.
45 Lieutenant-General Lord Frederick FitzClarence (1799–1854). National Portrait Gallery, London
46 Rear Admiral Lord Adolphus FitzClarence (1802-56)
47 Reverend Lord Augustus Fitzclarence (1805-94)
48 Henry (Carey) Baron Hudson (1525/6-1606-7) Courtauld Institute.
49 Catherine, *née* Carey, Lady Knollys (b.ca 1424) National Portrait Gallery, London)
50 Mary Walter, Valence House Museum, London Borough of Barking & Dagenham..
51 Count Blomberg or The Rev. Frederick William Blomberg (1761–1847) © Christie's Images Ltd 1983.
52 Edward IV. National Portrait Gallery, London.
53 The Royal Arms.
54 The Hon. Maynard Greville (1898–1960) National Portrait Gallery, London.
55 The arms of the Hon. Maynard Greville.
56 Sonia Cubit, (née Keppel), (1900–86) National Portrait Gallery, London.
57 The Arms of the Earls of Albermarle.
58 Prince Albert Victor Christian Edward, KG, Duke of Clarence & Avondale National Portrait Gallery, London.
59 Edward VIII. National Portrait Gallery, London.
60 (William) Anthony, 2nd Viscount Furness (1929–95). Sovereign Military Order of Malta
61 Timothy Ward Seely (*b*.1935) © The Spotlight.

Index of Royal Bastards

The History Press

D-Day The First 72 Hours
WILLIAM F. BUCKINGHAM
'A compelling narrative' *The Observer*
A *BBC History Magazine* Book of the Year 2004
£9.99   0 7524 2842 X

The London Monster
Terror on the Streets in 1790
JAN BONDESON
'Gripping' *The Guardian*
'Excellent... monster-mania brought a reign of
terror to the ill-lit streets of the capital'
The Independent
£9.99   0 7524 3327 X

London
A Historical Companion
KENNETH PANTON
'A readable and reliable work of reference that
deserves a place on every Londoner's bookshelf'
Stephen Inwood
£20   0 7524 3434 9

M: MI5's First Spymaster
ANDREW COOK
'Serious spook history' *Andrew Roberts*
'Groundbreaking' *The Sunday Telegraph*
'Brilliantly researched' *Dame Stella Rimington*
£9.99   978 07524 3949 9

Agincourt
A New History
ANNE CURRY
'A highly distinguished and convincing account'
Christopher Hibbert
'A *tour de force*' *Alison Weir*
'*The* book on the battle' *Richard Holmes*
A *BBC History Magazine* Book of the Year 2005
£12.99   0 7524 3813 1

Battle of the Atlantic
MARC MILNER
'The most comprehensive short survey of the
U-boat battles' *Sir John Keegan*
'Some events are fortunate in their historian, none
more so than the Battle of the Atlantic. Marc
Milner is *the* historian of the Atlantic campaign... a
compelling narrative' *Andrew Lambert*
£12.99   0 7524 3332 6

The English Resistance
The Underground War Against the Normans
PETER REX
'An invaluable rehabilitation of an ignored
resistance movement' *The Sunday Times*
'Peter Rex's scholarship is remarkable'
The Sunday Express
£12.99   0 7524 3733 X

Elizabeth Wydeville: England's Slandered Queen
ARLENE OKERLUND
'A penetrating, thorough and wholly convincing
vindication of this unlucky queen'
Sarah Gristwood
'A gripping tale of lust, loss and tragedy'
Alison Weir
A *BBC History Magazine* Book of the Year 2005
£9.99   978 07524 3807 8

The History Press

Quacks Fakers and Charlatans in Medicine
ROY PORTER

'A delightful book' *The Daily Telegraph*
'Hugely entertaining' *BBC History Magazine*

£12.99   0 7524 2590 0

The Tudors
RICHARD REX

'Up-to-date, readable and reliable. The best introduction to England's most important dynasty' *David Starkey*
'Vivid, entertaining... quite simply the best short introduction' *Eamon Duffy*
'Told with enviable narrative skill... a delight for any reader' *THES*

£9.99   0 7524 3333 4

The Kings & Queens of England
MARK ORMROD

'Of the numerous books on the kings and queens of England, this is the best'
Alison Weir

£9.99   0 7524 2598 6

The Covent Garden Ladies
Pimp General Jack & the Extraordinary Story of Harris's List
HALLIE RUBENHOLD

'Sex toys, porn... forget Ann Summers, Miss Love was at it 250 years ago' *The Times*
'Compelling' *The Independent on Sunday*
'Marvellous' *Leonie Frieda*
'Filthy' *The Guardian*

£9.99   0 7524 3739 9

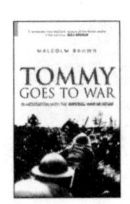

Okinawa 1945
GEORGE FEIFER

'A great book... Feifer's account of the three sides and their experiences far surpasses most books about war'
Stephen Ambrose

£17.99   0 7524 3324 5

Tommy Goes To War
MALCOLM BROWN

'A remarkably vivid and frank account of the British soldier in the trenches'
Max Arthur
'The fury, fear, mud, blood, boredom and bravery that made up life on the Western Front are vividly presented and illustrated'
The Sunday Telegraph

£12.99   0 7524 2980 4

Ace of Spies The True Story of Sidney Reilly
ANDREW COOK

'The most definitive biography of the spying ace yet written... both a compelling narrative and a myth-shattering *tour de force*'
Simon Sebag Montefiore
'The absolute last word on the subject' **Nigel West**
'Makes poor 007 look like a bit of a wuss'
The Mail on Sunday

£12.99   0 7524 2959 0

Sex Crimes
From Renaissance to Enlightenment
W.M. NAPHY

'Wonderfully scandalous' *Diarmaid MacCulloch*
'A model of pin-sharp scholarship' *The Guardian*

£10.99   0 7524 2977 9

If you are interested in purchasing other books published by The History Press, or in case you have difficulty finding any History Press books in your local bookshop, you can also place orders directly through our website

www.thehistorypress.co.uk